The Best American
Spiritual Writing 2005

The Best American Spiritual Writing 2005

EDITED BY *Philip Zaleski*

INTRODUCTION BY *Barry Lopez*

HOUGHTON MIFFLIN COMPANY

BOSTON • NEW YORK   2005

ISSN: 1555-7820
ISBN-13: 978-0-618-58642-4   ISBN-10: 0-618-58642-3
ISBN-13: 978-0-618-58643-1 (pbk.)   ISBN-10: 0-618-58643-1 (pbk.)

Printed in the United States of America

MP 10 9 8 7 6 5 4 3 2 1

"The Gift of the Call" by Christopher Bamford. First published in *Parabola*, Fall 2004. Copyright © 2004 by Christopher Bamford. Reprinted by permission of the author.

"The *Acusmata* of Pythagoras" by Brian Blanchfield. First published in *Jubilat* 8. Copyright © 2004 by Brian Blanchfield. Reprinted by permission of the author.

"Replies to the Immediate" by Scott Cairns. First published in *Western Humanities Review*, Fall 2004. Copyright © 2004 by Scott Cairns. Reprinted by permission of the author.

"Kaddish" by Richard Chess. First published in *Image*, Spring/Summer 2004. Copyright © 2004 by Richard Chess. Reprinted by permission of the author.

"Advent Stanzas" by Robert Cording. First published in *The Southern Review*, Spring 2004. Copyright © 2004 by Robert Cording. Reprinted by permission of the author.

"Best of Intentions" by Harvey Cox. First published in *The Christian Century*, November 30, 2004. Copyright © 2004 by Harvey Cox. Reprinted by permission of Houghton Mifflin Company.

"The Emergent Mystique" by Andy Crouch. First published in *Christianity Today*, November 2004. Copyright © 2004 by Andy Crouch. Reprinted by permission of the author.

"Joyas Voladoras" by Brian Doyle. First published in *The American Scholar*, Autumn 2004. Copyright © 2005 by Paraclete Press. Reprinted by permission of Paraclete Press.

"The French Guy" by David James Duncan. First published in *Portland*, Autumn 2004. Copyright © 2004 by David James Duncan. Reprinted by permission of the author.

Contents

Foreword

MY CHILDREN EXCEL at amusing themselves. They can transform stick and string into bow and arrow in the twinkling of an eye and fathom the intricacies of a new computer system without a glance at the owner's manual. There is one arena, though, in which their mastery over realms both classical and modern gives way to a humble admission of inadequacy. Each of my offspring comes to my wife or me at regular intervals to announce, "I need a new book to read."

Fortunately, Carol and I read voraciously and have no trouble suggesting good works for our kids to enjoy. We lean toward the classics, preferring works that have survived the ruthless winnowing of at least a few generations of readers. A children's book that has lasted fifty years has magic in it that will never cease to enchant. This is not always true of adult books; it may take a century for grownups to admit that a book famed for stylistic experiment or boldness of plot is really a bore. Children sniff out literary frauds more swiftly, for they read not to impress or to kill time or to fall asleep but for the sheer joy of reading. As our offspring have matured, so have our literary recommendations grown more challenging: from the talking animals of Beatrix Potter to those of George Orwell; from *Calvin and Hobbes* to Calvin and Hobbes. This last example is admittedly hypothetical, but as it happens, our oldest son is acquiring a taste for philosophy and theology, and these sixteenth- and seventeenth-century masters may soon appear on his crowded shelves.

Lately I've been thinking hard about what works to suggest to my children from the vast literary realm that we call spiritual writing. This question has serious ramifications, for ideas are food and one becomes, to a greater extent than many realize, what one reads. The process of identifying, ingesting, and digesting spiritual classics isn't important only for growing children. It matters or should matter to everyone. Read Plato, Blake, and Basho and you encounter not only three different worldviews but three different ways of assembling words — dialectic, poetry, and autobiography — to advance the creation of beauty, the transmission of truth, and the acquisition of virtue. As these multiple aims suggest, spiritual writing has serious work to do in the world. It can save lives; it can rescue the damned. It can shake us out of our cowardice, our pettiness, our self-absorption; it can cut away the cataracts imposed by modern civilization and disclose the wisdom of the ancients and the promise of the future.

These are admirable goals, and they offer good reasons to pick up a spiritual text. The truth is, however, that few of us read for self-improvement, nor am I sure that we should. There are surer paths to becoming a better person, such as rolling up one's sleeves to serve the poor or dropping to one's knees in prayer. There is but one entirely compelling reason to open a book, and here, as in so many other areas, children point the way. We do best to read for the sheer joy of reading. But what happens, exactly, when we find ourselves seized by this particular pleasure? C. S. Lewis, in *An Experiment in Criticism* (1961), identifies the event as an "enlargement of our being." Through reading we learn "to see with other eyes, to imagine with other imaginations, to feel with other hearts." This liberation is so exhilarating that we may derive enormous satisfaction from reading about ideas that we think untrue, actions that we find reprehensible, worlds that we know will never and perhaps ought never to exist. "Literary experience," Lewis tells us, "heals the wound, without undermining the privilege, of individuality . . . Reading great literature I become a thousand men and yet remain myself." Lewis likens this event to love, for in each "we escape from our self into one another." Reading and love need no justification, for in their intimacy, their gentleness, their transporting power and transfiguring effect, both carry hints, subtle but riveting, of a higher realm. Who knows but that in paradise, where every act is perfected, reading itself may be a mode of love?

The pleasures of literary travel depend, however, upon how well I read: attentively or distractedly, eagerly or reluctantly. This matter of attention is vitally important. Lewis reminds us of Matthew Arnold's dictum that our job as readers is not to judge a book but simply "to see the object as in itself it really is." The correct way to approach a text is with open arms; to embrace, if only for a time, the author's view of things, to engage his or her work not with suspicion (the default position of so much modern criticism) but with trust. We should read as a friend; and in the light of this friendship we will gain both enjoyment and a dash of wisdom. This approach, I would add, is a specifically spiritual exercise, a training in sympathetic understanding, a strengthening of one's ability to meet whatever comes one's way.

Well, then, I asked myself, bearing in mind Lewis's dicta and the other considerations I have mentioned, what spiritual books do I most want my children — and my great-great-grandchildren — to read? I came up with the following list. It contains twenty-five works that I have read and in many cases reread with enormous pleasure, and that I would recommend without reservation not only to my own flesh and blood but to all who enjoy this annual collection and all who love the genre of spiritual writing. It goes without saying that the list makes no pretense to being authoritative; it would take very little effort to construct a second, third, or fourth catalogue of works that rank as great spiritual or religious classics. Nor is it meant to be a gathering of the twenty-five best spiritual books: that venture would be not only presumptuous but preposterous, for to assemble it would require far more reading than anyone could accomplish in a lifetime. I claim for my selection only the merit that any expression of love accrues: these are twenty-five books that I hold close to my heart. Of necessity they reflect my personal tastes, and another editor might well pull a different set of titles out of his or her hat. I'm convinced, however, that all who compile a comparable list will find much on which to agree: that the classics of spiritual writing combine insight and beauty; that they speak to people of every faith; that they retain their value because they deal with eternal rather than ephemeral matters.

In the lineup below you will find autobiographies, allegories, memoirs, hymns, fictions, poems, philosophy, mystical and contemplative texts, and more. These writings spring from every corner of the globe and span more than thirty-five hundred years. The only kind of book that has been excluded is scripture; open the floodgates to holy writ and the list would consist of nothing but sacred texts. It is worth noting that six of the selections, nearly twenty-five percent of the whole, date from the twentieth century. This may reveal chronological provincialism on the part of the compiler, but it also testifies, I believe, to the intense vitality of the genre in recent decades.

The list is arranged alphabetically by author; the first four books are anonymous, either because the author deliberately effaced himself or because his identity was forgotten long ago. I would not venture to rank any of these works by importance or influence, other than to suggest that while many of them have given rise to great literary lineages, Saint Augustine's *Confessions* can probably be identified as the source from which the mainstream of modern spiritual literature — autobiographical, introspective, devotional — flows.

Twenty-five Great Works of Spiritual Writing

Anonymous, The Bhagavad-Gita
Anonymous, *The Cloud of Unknowing*
Anonymous, The Epic of Gilgamesh
Anonymous, *The Way of a Pilgrim*
Saint Augustine, *The Confessions*
Matsuo Basho, *The Narrow Road to the Deep North*
Black Elk, *Black Elk Speaks*
William Blake, *The Marriage of Heaven and Hell*
Martin Buber, *Tales of the Hasidim*
John Bunyan, *The Pilgrim's Progress*
Alexander Carmichael, *Carmina Gadelica*
Dante Alighieri, *The Divine Comedy*
John Donne, *Holy Sonnets*
T. S. Eliot, *Four Quartets*
Homer, *The Odyssey*
Søren Kierkegaard, *Either/Or*
C. S. Lewis, The Space Trilogy
John Henry Newman, *Apologia Pro Vita Sua*
Saint Nikodimos of the Holy Mountain (ed.), *The Philokalia*

Blaise Pascal, *Pensées*
Plato, *The Symposium*
Jalal Al Din Maulana Rumi, *The Mathnawi*
Saint Therése of Lisieux, *The Story of a Soul*
Thomas Traherne, *Centuries of Meditations*
Simone Weil, *Waiting for God*

May these works give you as much pleasure as they have given me.

As always, submissions are encouraged for subsequent volumes of this series. Please send manuscripts (with a self-addressed, stamped envelope) to Philip Zaleski, 138 Elm Street, Smith College, Northampton, MA 01063. The best way for a periodical to submit material is to add the *Best American Spiritual Writing* series, at the above address, to its subscription list.

I would like to thank all who contributed to this year's volume — Barry Lopez; Anton Mueller, Erica Avery, and everyone at Houghton Mifflin; Kim Witherspoon, David Forrer, and all at Inkwell Associates; and, as always, my beloved Carol, John, and Andy. We are truly lost without friends and family.

PHILIP ZALESKI

Introduction

ONE BENIGN, SUMMER MORNING I departed a small tent camp, pitched on the back of a valley glacier, and headed with a few friends for an embayment a couple of miles away in the La Gorce Mountains, in the interior of Antarctica. We were curious about the place, an unnamed natural amphitheater we'd examined through binoculars some weeks earlier. A curving wall rose sharply from the valley floor on three sides, towering over a dark expanse of frost-shattered porphyry and other igneous and sedimentary rock that had fallen, over dozens of millennia, from the walls and serrated ridge above, or been pushed up from the glacial ice below this rock barren.

It was a clear day of unusually still air. By now, at the end of a forty-five-day field season, the six of us were so accustomed to the steady cold I can't recall a specific temperature. It must have been around 0°F. The few people who have actually traveled in the interior of Antarctica have all done so recently and their journeys have been carefully recorded by the U.S. Geological Survey; so it's possible to say, with a high degree of certainty, that no one had ever been where we were headed. The La Gorce Range, with its many unnamed peaks, shoulders its way through the continent's permanent ice cover about 225 miles north of the South Pole. The vast, dead-slow river of ice, flowing off the polar plateau, around this range, and toward the edge of the continent, buries the lower seven thousand feet of these mountains. The upper several thousand feet are bare, wind-blasted rock and steep snowpack.

Eying our destination from camp and scrutinizing the topographic map, we guessed that the only problems we might face in our traverse would be a crevasse field, which we could skirt, and the steep pitch of an ice wall where Klein Glacier, on which we were camped, curved around the base of Kessens Peak, the valley's southeast portal. Like a river streaming around a boulder, an ice sheet moving around the corner of a mountain range leaves a cavity on the downstream side of any obstruction. It was this side slope of the passing glacier that we would have to descend to reach the mouth, about four miles across, of this deep amphitheater.

The pitch of the ice wall raised a few eyebrows but was not perilous to navigate. We descended, crossed the ice apron to the foot of the valley, and parked our snow machines at the threshold of the felsenmere, the dozen or so square miles of rock blown clear of snow by perennially strong winds (which happened not to be blowing on this day).

My tent mate, John Schutt, the expedition leader, had the same unannounced idea I did. The two of us hiked in a few hundred yards over the angular boulders and rocks, looking for a relatively flat patch in the rubble that had been soaking up solar radiation for weeks. Using a couple of sun-warmed boulders as backrests, we settled in to peruse what many would characterize as a scene of desolation.

To the northwest of us, on the right, was 10,823-foot Mount Paine, the other portal to the valley. From there a sharp ridge, an arête, swung toward us and curved around behind us to terminate on our left, at Kessens Peak, 8,645 feet. Directly before us, about a mile distant, the ice wall of Klein Glacier rose up some hundreds of feet, a rigid tsunami of translucent grays and brilliant whites cutting across a pale blue sky, a great expanse lighter than azure, darker than pearly blue, and without a cloud.

The silence around us was so deep it induced an aura of anticipation. The present, the time in which John and I were gazing west, grew taut, like a manufactured object tightened. And then it broke, in the manner of mercury dispersing. Each of us felt he was being given what he had deliberately sought here — an unbounded moment when immaculate light filled an immense space, a moment devoid of history, empty of language, without meaning.

I have experienced this emotion before, the sense of a sudden immersion in the profound mystery of life, a mystery that seems to originate in arrangements of time and space that precede the advent of biology. It is a sensation known to many people, often characterized as an awareness of unity with the divine, or as a release from the routine coordinates of life, as a greatly expanded sense of the present, or as a religious experience without the symbols of religion.

In reflecting on previous occasions when I have sensed this collapse of measured time, and been aware of a pervasive, almost tangible hush in a specific geographic place — once in the self-contained desert ranges of western Namibia, another time in the far reach of a spinifex grassland bordering a dry riverbed in Australia's Northern Territory, once at the Cliffs of Moher in western Ireland — I realized that certain elements were common to them all. I was always with a few friends; the physical place opened toward a generous horizon; the weather was clement; the atmosphere was silent; and light played a strong role, intensifying the clarity of the air. This has led me to believe, contrary to popular western folklore, that these apparently private experiences are actually social, that they have more in keeping with everyday life than with a grail quest. Further, since these experiences always release in me a floodtide of hope, I've come to associate the vistas — sharply lit land opening toward a horizon, a vast silence under benign skies — with that emotion.

That particular day in the La Gorce Mountains with my friend John, though, I saw something in addition, something I'd never noticed before, possibly because no human mark of any sort showed here, or because this landscape wasn't catalogued anywhere among the events we call history, or possibly because of the sheer immensity in which we were so comparatively infinitesimal in a nightless summer — I experienced space and time as one. I saw the flow of the glacier before me, the shifting of my chilly fingers in my mitts, and the disintegration, rock by rock, of the cirque wall behind me as the same event.

Months later, when the memory of the sensation did not recede, I began to wonder at the nature of the glue that might hold time and space together. To put it another way, what allowed a sense of space, a feeling for the volume of geography around myself, and a sense of time, a sensitivity to the different lengths of interval by which we notice change, to penetrate each other?

It could be reverence, I thought.

*

In a lyrical, beautifully human book called *Reverence: Renewing a Forgotten Virtue,* the classicist and philosopher Paul Woodruff describes the cardinal virtues — courage, reverence, wisdom, justice — as those that are recognized, admired, and upheld by all peoples, regardless of their other cultural beliefs. They go beyond religion, and no particular human tradition can claim that these virtues originated with them.

Reverence, writes Woodruff, "begins in a deep understanding of human limitations." He describes it as a capacity for certain feelings, most obviously awe and respect, which "prompt us to behave well." He stresses, further, that the ability to feel these emotions must be practiced if an attitude of reverence is to become part of one's character. A reverent attitude toward the world, he writes, is what we recognize in ourselves when we feel awe "at the immensity of the reality that does not conform to human wishes," and when respect for the ineluctable mystery of the world wells up in us. Finally, he points out that through all of human history, different peoples have celebrated and reinforced the virtue of reverence, individually and communally, in ceremony.

It occurred to me, after reading Woodruff's book, that the emotional elevation I felt that day in the La Gorce Mountains, and which I had experienced in other locales — a mix of awe and respect in the face of certain physical surroundings, a sense that in that moment the physical (outer) and emotional (inner) worlds were part of the same bolt of cloth, and that I was embedded in this setting, not a mere observer — grew out of a capacity for such feelings that I had intentionally practiced (although I'd always understood this as a consciously willed effort to be vulnerable to the world, in order to be intimate with it). I had anticipated that sitting in that rock-strewn amphitheater, emotionally susceptible to it, might give rise, in other words, to the sensation Woodruff calls "joyful reverence." I could not assume, though, that cultivating such a capacity would make the sensation inevitable.

Perhaps the most amazing aspect of any revitalizing experience like this is that no matter what we've done, such doors regularly swing open before us. A gift. You cannot expect, after months or even years of emotional barrenness and anxiety, to be elevated out of the ordinary merely because your desire is keen and constant. The elevation can't be earned. It's true, as Woodruff writes, that the capacity for such feelings must be cultivated — the gift always has to be acted upon — if these feelings are to go deep and sustain us; but the opportunity to enhance a sense of reverence — or of justice, for that matter — is sometimes upon us, overwhelmingly, when we least expect it.

To feel, suddenly and intensely, reverent toward the world can seem like a reprieve. It releases a person, at least for a few moments, I think, from the modern burden most of us feel over our complicity in the world's waywardness: injustice, religious contempt, ethical cowardice, rampant intellectualizing — the conditions against which the cardinal virtues are arrayed. As such, the unanticipated moment of elevation feels like an absolution.

It seems to me that this experience with the numinous, of release into a world that stands outside human comprehension, is what lies at the heart of "spiritual writing." The intent in the genre is to locate, make apparent, and celebrate the wellsprings of the cardinal virtues — justice, courage, wisdom, reverence. The term itself, of course, is problematic. For many, the notion of spiritual values is too closely identified with specific religious dogma. And experiences with the numinous are too easily associated by some with deism or theism. Or pantheism. Gods and religion, however, need play no role in the experience, cultivation, and exercise of virtue (which is why philosophers stipulate that the cardinal virtues are recognized by everyone, regardless of their doctrines).

Writing about the recognition and pursuit of virtuous life is one dimension, as I have come to see it, of a very old ceremonial history, one that celebrates mankind's affinity for, its longing after, a frame of mind sensitive to issues of reverence, wisdom, justice, and courage. Somehow, in experiencing these feelings, we experience the profundity of our own existence. It is a specific kind of human awareness that leads to just forms of governance, to good politics, to equity at all levels of a social order.

What caused me to sense a seamlessness of space and time with John that day in the La Gorce Mountains, I believe, was that the intensity of reverence I felt could not be distinguished in those moments from what I imagined the conditions for justice to be. There were no lines of separation.

I opened this essay with a description of events in a place nearly impossible for most people to travel to, implying, perhaps, that encounters like this which lead to a renewed awareness of the profun-

dity of human existence are most often wilderness experiences. I
don't mean to convey this. I recall emerging once from the
paleolithic cave at Altamira on a cool, fall day in northern Spain.
Suddenly I saw spread below me, as if for the first time, the bucolic
landscape that runs inland from the Bay of Biscay, near the village
of Santillana del Mar. I felt immense tenderness toward it. Two-
story farmhouses, compact and tidy, stood randomly on several
square miles of land, the fields divided by low stone walls and wind-
breaks of tall Lombardy poplars. Grain had been harvested; sheep
were penned; late-summer vegetables grew in straight rows in large
kitchen gardens; a Guernsey cow straddled the sill of a barn door; a
man was towing a manure spreader with a small red tractor. Having
just stepped from the cave, having stared in wonder for the past
hour at a Cro-Magnon record of life, the interpretations of that life
still glistening on the damp walls, as if they had been created only
that morning, I lost completely the sense of a time between these
painters and the man on the tractor. I was so overcome by the elimination of this familiar distance, I had to lean into a retaining wall
on the bluff above the valley to keep from reeling on the path.

That night I sat in a hotel room in Santander and wrote to a
friend in rural Kentucky, a well-read man with a great capacity for
reverence, about what I had seen. It seemed crucial to share the
sensation while it was still fresh with someone who would understand my observations about how ruthlessly insistent the modern
metronome of time can be about Progress.

One June morning, looking up a side street in Montmartre, I was
transfixed by how the reflection of early light gleaming on wet
paver stones and the sound of rainwater burbling around a scrap of
wood in the gutter included a woman emerging from a bakery with
a large clutch of bread loaves in the fold of her apron. Another
time, I felt myself "living outside the moment" as I gazed at Old Ha-
vana from the Malecón, the city's Gulfward edge, at the crumbling
pastel façades of rowhouses, and heard long runs of birdsong over
lulls in the traffic. And I would want to include in these "out of
place and time" experiences, which reawakened a sense of reverence for humanity, the moments of eerie luminosity and the collapse of language and analysis I felt the first time I saw a Vermeer,
Girl Interrupted at Her Music, at the Frick Collection in New York. I
remember having the same sensation when I turned a corner in

the Vatican Museums a couple of years later, a seventeen-year-old boy, and came upon Agesander, Athenodorus, and Polydorus of Rhodes' *Laocoön*. Most recently, I felt infused with a sense of regard for all life after I entered a Quaker meetinghouse in Houston, Texas, where a ceiling designed by the space-and-light artist James Turrell opens to accentuate the skyspace above the building. I watched for an hour hues shifting in a cloudless sky, while the sun set and three or four times blackbirds crossed over.

The essential ingredient in these experiences is humanity, not wilderness. If I were better at inducing a state of vulnerability in myself in cities, I believe I would experience there the same intensity of life-purpose I did in the La Gorce Mountains.

It is a commonplace observation that, like other cultures, we too yearn after justice, that we want civic life to hinge on mutual respect, and that we hope to cultivate in ourselves a capacity for virtue. What we truly wish for, I think, is not the impossible ideal of a life of just relations, of consistently wise decisions, courageous action against the afflictions that dog us, and respect for what lies beyond our ken, but simply the conditions that make such things possible. We seek out books, art, performances, and political groups that make the life we believe is possible plausible.

Spiritual writing, and some of what is called nature writing, are literary attempts, it seems to me, to explore and to keep alive the plausibility of virtuous life. Modernity, with its caustic contempt for virtue, its investment in the importance of individual life over social life, and its choice of cynicism and detachment as a safe way to approach the unknown, insists, of course, that real literature lies somewhere else. The attempt to write about spiritual matters, this argument goes — or to read about them — is work for the naive writer, the misguided reader.

What we must ask of spiritual writing, I think, is that it be of some practical value in a culture as ethically conflicted as ours. To overcome the charge, sometimes warranted, that it's a pious genre, spiritual writing has to point, as a literature, toward better systems of governance, toward more equitable economies, and toward the protection of diversity. From a certain perspective, it already does; but for too many it remains writing about "God," a sectarian subject. Few, if any, critics would see it as a part of the phenomenon described in other countries as postcolonial writing, or as a literature of social justice. In this, spiritual writing suffers the same fate as another sort of more obviously postcolonial writing, nature writing.

In several decades of international travel, I know I've missed a lot; but one thing that has not escaped me in visiting with indigenous people around the world is that these communities root their way of life — their social organization, their politics, their civics — in a seamlessly integrated perception of the world. This view consistently draws together spiritual awareness and biological knowledge to frame systems of governance. It is impossible, in other words, for many traditional people to imagine a social order not founded in ecological awareness and spiritual experience. The western doctrine of Progress, in contrast, stipulates that spiritual awareness and ecological knowledge are, ultimately, impediments to the smooth operation of any system of governance. The modern rise of spiritual writing and nature writing, in my view, is partly a response to this situation, by literary writers steeped in anthropology, comparative religion, the physical sciences, history, geography, and philosophy. It's a reaction to a system of governance that seems to mistrust reverence, and to be organized around a sense of justice that does not extend beyond an immediate ethnic culture and which also pits humanity against organizations.

What lies beneath the varied subject matter of any good piece of spiritual writing today, I would argue, is an awareness that if Western culture — to stay within the realm of self-criticism — does not successfully imagine a way to incorporate ecological awareness (i.e., find the courage to confront major biological problems facing *Homo sapiens,* including global warming, diminished supplies of perennial fresh water, and a falloff in species diversity) and spirituality (Woodruff's "capacities" for virtue) into its system of governance, it will go the way of Rome and the Khans, but with catastrophic consequences for everyone.

It's worth recalling, as Woodruff does in his book, that within our foundling mythology is an often overshadowed but crucially important episode. After Prometheus gives us fire and, with that, technology, Zeus offers us reverence and justice. Without them, in Zeus's view, no society, no matter how technologically adept, can stave off a disastrous end. Spiritual writing, to have a critical place in the forefront of American literature, must be about reinfusing our social order with ecological (i.e., communal) awareness and reinforcing behavior that responds to the call of Woodruff's cardinal virtues.

A few months ago I traveled to a place I had wanted to see for many years, the relatively unpopulated basin-and-range country of southeastern Nevada. I came in from the east at dawn, across the Delamar Mountains and into the Pahranagat Valley. With the sun behind me in an unclouded sky and the air empty of dust, the landscape before me — the sage and rabbit-brush flats, bounded by ocherous scarps in the Mount Irish Range to the north and the Pahranagat Range to the south — looked like an etching plate, illuminated at a low angle by intense yellow light. Sharp contrast and crisp definition, wherever the eye attached itself.

I crossed Hancock Summit and descended into the northern end of the Tikaboo Valley. To the south and east, behind me, were the Nellis Air Force Bombing and Gunnery Range and the Nevada Test Site. Ahead, the land was tightly covered with low, tawny brush, all growing to the same height. No tree rose anywhere in the basin. No fence ran through it, no pylons carried high-tension wires into the distance, no microwave towers gleamed on the ridges. Cattle were nowhere drifting through. The lone human mark was the narrow, blacktop scribe of road that would take me to the far side of the valley. It ran empty and straight as a runway for sixteen miles.

I pulled off the road somewhere in the Tikaboo when a low movement above the brush caught my eye — a golden eagle, hunting. I watched it through binoculars, studying it and the several ravens coursing its wake. The valley was beautiful. It was charged with early daylight, set apart from the sky by the long sweep of its lines, the sky itself a pale canopy over the valley's pointillist patterns. The glide, turn, and flapping rise of the eagle gave the scene a single stroke of animation and tension, in the way of shibui, the Japanese design principle that urges a gardener to leave two or three bright, fall-colored leaves behind on an otherwise immaculate surface of raked lawn.

The valley could have held herds of pronghorn antelope, but that morning it did not. It could have held herds of wild horses, but it did not, that I saw. I could have seen ten golden eagles hunting (as I would the next day); but here there was just the one and, a bit later, a second. I could have experienced, in that vastness and silence, in the plein-air bowl of that basin, with the cleave of early morning light incisive against that earth, a kind of ecstasy. But I did not. Perhaps because I was traveling alone. Perhaps because I was distracted by thoughts of home, and so not completely there.

Or perhaps because, that morning, nothing at all was compelled to occur.

BARRY LOPEZ

The Best American
Spiritual Writing 2005

CHRISTOPHER BAMFORD

The Gift of the Call

FROM *Parabola*

THE CALL comes gradually, or so it seems. We must be called over and over before we hear its whisperings. Then we begin to notice. We begin to respond. Unconsciously, hesitantly, we start to listen. Incrementally, our response deepens. Finally, we realize that we ourselves are the call; that call and caller are one in life lived in obedience to the gift of the call. We come to recognize that we were called from the beginning, "from the foundation of the world," as Saint Paul says. Looking back, we cannot remember a "first" call.

"Behind what we call the 'first' always lies a hidden sequence of other 'first' experiences," Allen Grossman writes of the poet's vocation. It is as if our lives were a palimpsest of memories, each experience collapsing back through other experiences to the beginning of conscious life; and reaching still further back, as Grossman says, "to the beginning of the world; and then, at last, to the great receptacle of all there is, the figure of no beginning."

If the call is without beginning, it is also without end. Every call seems to lie at the intersection of past and future. From one direction, it echoes up through time and memory from our source and origin, defining who we are, alerting us to whom we shall become. From the other, it comes toward us as destiny, drawing us toward an ineffable goal. You might say that to live is itself to be called. Perhaps that is why one of the meanings of *anthropos*, or human being, is "to look up," as one looks up when one hears one's name called. But how do you know your name? I think of the superfine rain masquerading as mist on certain northern islands. At first you cannot tell whether it is raining or not, but after walking awhile, say until midday, you come to your senses to find yourself soaked, and you realize you have been wet forever.

Often the call sounds first in childhood through nature and the senses, when the world is new, shining with the glory and the freshness of a dream, and the corn is orient and immortal wheat. First memories are frequently of light and color, or darkness and light, shadows, moving on the wall, or of pastel silks swaying in the breeze. The world seems luminous, though whether lit from within or without we cannot tell. Experience is unified. There is no need to question. Yet, if I remember it rightly, there is already a sense of a numinous other, though the ineffability is only intuited, not yet known. Beauty lies at the edge of consciousness, in the warm, dark, mothering embrace of a world in which we are one with all there is. Only later, when we have fallen into separateness, does beauty begin to draw us consciously from our isolation into the light. Then we begin to question and to hear the "something more," that luminous excess in nature that never quite arrives but whispers of greater good than we can imagine.

The call of beauty is always intimate, one on one. She is our mother; she raises us to our feet, so that we may see her face to face. As we learn to move, we express our delight by running, jumping, climbing. She gives us language and thought, whose first form is imagination, so that we may praise her in our hearts and proclaim what we have found.

Not for nothing is the garden called a figure of the soul. The soul herself is a garden, and it is in a garden that we first learn her ways. I, for one, found her there. My childhood garden was the kindergarten of the call, beauty's school. I loved her safe, enclosed spaces, filled with worlds and beings, each with its own alluring qualities. Dreaming my way in, I created houses, forts, caves, and tunnels — secret, hidden places in which to imagine magical encounters and make up stories, spontaneous prayers connecting me to the one whose breathing pulsed in its dark, embracing warmth. It was a complete universe, a whole. Each season called in its own way. Spring with its greening power of growth; summer with its expansive sense of immortality; autumn with its golden dying; winter with its solitude, darkness, and interiority. The garden is the first home. There is no horizon, and the call does not come from anywhere, it simply is.

The horizon too is a gift. I remember my first experience of it, standing on a beach, looking out at the vast expanse of ocean disappearing into the sky. When I looked up I thought I saw a second ocean, or perhaps the two were one, fire or water, I couldn't tell. At my feet certainly was sand, but it too seemed to extend indefinitely as far as the eye could see. Standing at the center, I picked up a handful. Countless tiny grains glistened and sparkled up at me. Everything seemed poised on the cusp between familiar and unfamiliar, near and far, visible and invisible. Awe and an indescribable feeling of friendship flowed together in my heart. The world shone with an inner light. Later, the locus of that light shifted, so that I no longer saw it, though I still knew it was there.

Older, I would go into the hills behind our house, passing through a dark copse of oak and pine to reach the gentle curve of the open moors, dense with heather and marked by scattered gorse and stumpy, solitary trees. The wind soughed like a being's breath, caressing my cheek, now gently, now gusting. One evening I met a human figure, who told me many things. The next day I returned and met him again. On the third day he was gone, and I cannot tell if he was ever there.

I tasted freedom and learned that beauty, in its heart-opening, never-quite-arriving (or always eluding) presence, communicated an undeniable, irresistible conviction of goodness and truth. I knew that the world was my home and that it was a blessed, sacred, holy place. The air, as Keats says, was my robe of state, the open sky sat upon my senses like a sapphire crown, the earth was my throne and the sea a mighty minstrel playing before it. Tiny rustling streams, silvery in the afternoon light, called me to their serpentine course. With clouds as my companions, I followed, and soon came upon some miniature waterfall, beside which I would lie down, eyeball to eyeball with the cascading drops.

We begin in dreams. Then we wake up. The world shrinks to the size of our own little selves. We become egotistic. The isolated, skin-bound, brain-bound, self-feeling being that has been growing within us since we recognized ourselves and proclaimed "Me!" takes over. Anomalies appear in the interstices of wonder. Gradually the paradigm changes, the call is muffled, the world becomes other. Like a sodden piece of paper that dries out, leaving only a ring, beauty, herald of the divine, seems to vanish, leaving behind only a memory, like a watermark in the soul. Where once as children we knew, growing into adolescence we struggle to hold to the memory of what we once experienced, but what we have left lives only as an inner conviction, vulnerable to the vagaries of doubt and despair. The possibility of faith is born in the growing darkness.

At first people are like angels, bathed in light and goodness. We move without separation, as if all beings participated in a unique identity, a communion of perfect understanding. Somewhere, neither within us nor without us, we still hear the echo of the single name we all share. Echoing in the depths, it calls us to the common task of playfully, joyfully cocreating the world. We are busy with it. We understand the mutuality of being, of our interdependence. The world is a marvelous piece of music, and like an angelic choir we busy ourselves with performing the heavenly composition, knowing that everyone is playing the same score.

Then comes the fall, which, like the call itself, appears gradually yet in fact, paradoxically, has always been there. Often it seems as if some single traumatic instance cuts the golden string by which we are woven into a higher tapestry. But if we pay attention and push beyond the "remembered" trauma, we find we can no more locate a "first" fall than we can a "first" call. It seems that we are not only always called but also always fallen, "from the foundation of the world." We know this because though each of us experiences the fall subjectively, we also know that we are not alone in our pain. We are hurt, but as we turn our attention from our own pain, we recognize that the world is in pain, and that fallenness is a universal condition. Individually, we may feel violated or betrayed in different ways, but whatever the circumstances of our falling, we recognize the bitter teaching that the world is riven by violence and deception and that we are all complicit in it.

Fall and call belong together. As the web of deception and death appears and the golden world fades, the memory of that world, which seemed once so safe and whole, continues to call. Nature remains beautiful. Though we no longer see its invisible source, we still intuit it at the edge of our perception. Fallen angels, we are still angels. The wonder and reverence that surrounded us, haloing parents and playmates alike, does not disappear. Transformed into curiosity, it becomes interest. People call us. They draw us. A glance, a smile, a touch, are now redolent of the mystery the greater world once held. The wound of our fallenness becomes a school of empathy. We learn sympathy and compassion. The faces of others, their physiognomy, centered in the eyes, open us inwardly. From the eyes above all, "mirrors of the soul," we learn to acknowledge the depths of our own interiority. This is a time when two phrases, made trite by overuse, become like mantras: "Nothing human is alien to me"; "There but by the grace of God go I." Art, literature, and music become messengers, intermediaries of the call. The unity, though fallen, is still a unity. Meaning still occasionally pierces the clouds of fragmentation, drawing us on. The call, which seemed perhaps to echo from the past, now sounds from the future.

"Religion," if not a given religion but one we make, is surely part of it. Equally surely, if given, we are also called to make it, for to respond to the call is to make it one's own. The way it comes is, of course, personal and subjective, depending upon imponderables, such as where we are born and to whom.

For me, there was always the sense of the divine ground, in whom "we live and move and have our being," and the corollary of this, that divinity "loved us first" and participates in our joys and sorrows. The unity, experienced in first love of beauty, seemed now to foreshadow the unity we could achieve by realizing God's identity with creation through the work of conscious human love and suffering. Thus, distorted though it may have been by its inflation and adolescent egotism, I understood somehow that what I suffered was not my own, nor in any sense for myself. Christ crucified seemed to me the image of the world. Only later would I realize that crucifixion without resurrection was meaningless, and that the way, like the call itself, was only a means. For the moment, I realized only the suffering, the pervasiveness of the fall.

My father had been on the first convoy of soldiers into Auschwitz. Haunted by what he had witnessed, he bore and transmitted the mark of Cain. He felt compelled to return again and again to what he had learned: that human folly and inhumanity knew no bounds. I came to understand the "century of night" that stretched from before Sarajevo through the Holocaust to Hiroshima and beyond: perpetual wars, mass death, dehumanization, environmental destruction, social and psychological fragmentation, meaning reduced to domination and manipulation, sheer matter made autonomous, and power given free reign.

The call to *metanoia,* transformation, and repentance comes to us in different ways. Yet we must all at some moment "hit bottom" and vow to change our lives. The "ego" crashes and the I AM, a light greater than the ego, breaks through the isolation and separation we have created. If the fall into ego lies on one side of the call, the vow to selflessness lies on the other. Such a vow is not made once but must be renewed with every breath.

Called to a different way of knowing and being, we begin to read as if for the first time. We do not read for information but to know ourselves and be changed. We want to know where we have come from, where we are, and where we are going. We want to know what it is to know and whether and how we can change. We seek testimonies of those who have done so. We seek evidence that we can make our own. We read philosophy, psychology, history, mythology. We read the great texts of the world's esoteric and wisdom traditions. But such untutored reading, no matter how passionate and committed, is not sufficient. We must learn to read differently. We must learn to think differently, to be differently. There is no mystery about this. We are given the world we think. For the world to change, our thinking must become different, selfless, endlessly responsive, ethical. We must learn not to consume a text but to allow it to call us. We must learn to listen, to receive and respond. Meaning becomes a gift that we allow to live within us and return to the giver with our whole being.

We are called to a new interiority, a new solitude, and a new kind of community. We discover that books and written words are only signs, as the body is the sign of the soul. We learn to read meditatively, to rise from the letter to the spirit. Perhaps we learn to do so from Guigo the Carthusian, who laid down the steps of "sacred reading," or from some other teacher, or perhaps the texts themselves teach us. We read the words before us slowly, reflectively, sentence by sentence, to understand exactly what is meant. As if called by name, we read with a heart filled with empathy and love, straining to hear what is really being said and demanded of us. With each reading the meaning sinks deeper into our body, as we discover level upon level of meaning and apply it to our lives. We ponder, associate, seeking insight wherever we can find it. We rest in awe at the richness we have been given. Entering a meditative state, we sit with our attention completely focused, as if the speaker understood us perfectly and the words were calling us and only us directly. Then we stop thinking, surrendered to the invisible author with open heart. Finally we let go of everything and, enveloped in a vast body of silence and inner peace, rest in emptiness, in pure, listening receptivity. A greater universe of consciousness, worlds within worlds, opens before us, filled with beings and their relationships, constituting a lineage and community in which we are called to participate.

We discover that despite its suffering and despair, earthly existence has a meaning. Working through history, there are traditions of those who have sought to enhance it. These traditions now call us one by one, individually, for we are no longer called simply by birth and geography. As we are called, we realize the reality of the invisible worlds. For we are called home, and home is not an exclusively earthly place but more like what Saint Paul calls "a cloud of witnesses." In Christianity, this is called the "community of saints," a body that encompasses the living as well as the so-called dead. In Buddhism it is called the *sangha,* the community of practitioners; in Islam, the *ummah,* or body of believers. Each communion has its own way of speaking of the precious gift of human birth and to what it calls us. Whichever path we take, once we take it, life becomes a pearl of great price, the receiving of which is the giving of ourselves to it.

Answering the call, one becomes a seeker. In my own case, following the call to live otherwise, I sought a different approach. Seeking to awaken from the nightmare of sleep, of egotism run amuck in the world, I studied alternative ways of knowing. I began time-tested practices of meditation, prayer, and attention. I steeped myself in esoteric theologies, cosmologies, and philosophies.

I explored many paths. One, the western Christian, finally called me. Inwardly, as my interest grew, I found I knew much more than I thought. It was as if gifts spontaneously accepted in earlier life were seeds planted in the soul, which, if watered in the right way at the right time, could germinate into gifts of another kind.

Grace taught me much, not the least of which was that the human state and the striving native to it are universal and that the call, though it takes different forms, is always one: to realize the unity of creation, the nonduality of reality, and thereby to transfigure the world. I learned too, especially in human relationships and above all in love, that if I become a question, if I shift from being an "I" to become a "who?," then experience begins the process of answering. It is a path from the monotony of the sameness of the ego to perpetually becoming "other," nonjudgmental, without boundaries, an open door. The way is unrestricted.

Having been called, one begins to call, and need only pay attention to the little prompting of one's heart and the apparently trivial events of the day to begin to receive the gift of a response. I called and Christ called me in return. He called first inwardly, then through scripture and tradition, until finally all of life was one great call.

Irresistibly, by choice, or by necessity of grief or gratitude, I was drawn into churches. In the often shabby, dusty darkness, prayer called on prayer. In the silence that wrapped the dark interior and muffled and made distant the voices and footsteps of others, a presence called. Mary stood in a small alcove at the back, her feet upon the moon, a star of crowns upon her head. Or she had her hands before her heart, palms touching, in an immaculate gesture of infinite compassion as in her appearance at Lourdes. Or she bore in her arms the infant Jesus, or in her lap, as in Michelangelo's *Pietà,* her crucified son. She gestured toward me in an aura of prayer, illumined by the tiny, flickering flames of innumerable votive candles.

It was her sweetness I recognized, kneeling at the prayer rail for the first time. It was not in the stone or the plaster, which were often quite ordinary. It was not physical at all, yet it was visible, like the invisible that surrounds and penetrates the edges of the beauty we see. She radiated waves of patience, selflessness, and a tender, loving humility. Suddenly I understood in a different way who Mary was and how she had given birth, not once but again and again, and still. I felt my heart melt at her approach. Her gentleness seemed to answer my question. I understood why I had to walk in her footsteps, become like her, and like her give birth and more. An answering silence descended and thickened. Somewhere in the distance the faint praise sounds of an organ could be heard.

To Mary's right, also in a small alcove, stood a statue of Jesus. His arms were raised slightly in a welcoming gesture, like an old friend not seen for many years. He seemed about to move toward me, but hesitated, as if waiting to be invited in. I experienced great closeness, but also distance. I realized that the distance was the lightning flash from my heart to his. His was open to me. Warmth and light streamed from it. He was risen, truly he was risen. What a paradox that this fallen world should be redeemed. Turning to the crucifix that hung above the altar, I understood why. Redemption, like creation, was continuous. Emmanuel meant what it said: "God with us." Jesus still hung on the cross, as he was still being born. He was still teaching, healing, suffering, dying, uniting with the earth, rising, and ascending. He would do so to the end of the world. Life was nothing but that. We were nothing but that, called for nothing but that, while remaining imperfect creatures to become perfect, to become cocreators, cosufferers, cohealers, coredeemers.

Somewhere, in the bowels of the church, I could hear mass beginning. A stranger, uncertain of the invitation, I joined a small group of worshippers, mostly older women, scattered in the pews. Without expectation, but inwardly quieted, willing to receive, I felt the readings flow through me like a cleansing stream. I felt a presence like an ocean of love. Now the priest was blessing the Eucharist. He held it up, saying, "Behold, the feast of the lamb, blessed are those who are called to his supper." The congregation responded: "Lord, I am not worthy to receive you, but only say the word and I shall be healed." Taking my place in line, I approached the host. Here was the whole perfection of the universe hidden in a tiny, white, almost tasteless wafer. If the creator of all, who was all, and united with the sufferings of all for their sake, could become so small as to enter into me, who was so thick with matter and dense with imperfection, then surely there was nothing that could not be penetrated, that was not already permeated.

We seek and we are found. We call and we are called. We give and we are given. We study, we form groups, we meditate. We pray. All this is good, but the heart of the matter lies elsewhere. There is only one universe, one search, one call, one love, one gift. Returning it in the form of the gift of ourselves, we recover not only what we have lost but the seed of the world yet to come. Then the way is clear and simple. Chosen from the foundation of the world, we are called "to the praise of the glory of his grace."

BRIAN BLANCHFIELD

The Acusmata *of Pythagoras*

FROM *Jubilat*

IT IS CUSTOMARY to think of Pythagorean teachings as two mutually exclusive disciplines: the scientistic philosophy based on math-
ematical principles and the religious mysticism whose dogma is
rooted partly in sympathetic magic. Since his death in c. 496 B.C.,
scholars and chroniclers interested in preserving Pythagoras's status as a pioneer of mathematics have sought to discredit his reputation as a charismatic and reform-minded mystic, a reputation spiritual seekers have burnished at various times since the third century
A.D. However, the fact is that Pythagoras himself insisted on the division as a principle of pedagogy.

Pythagoras of Samos moved to Croton in South Italy at age forty
(530 B.C.), made a great practical impact on the colony, and established a school that he divided into two parts. Students selected to
study directly with Pythagoras were called *mathematici* and lived
communally and learned elaborately the reasonings of Pythagorean philosophy, principally that all things are number or are ex-
pressible by number. Together they swore by the *tetraktys* (a dia-
grammatic arrangement of ten units in rows of one, two, three,
and four, in the shape of an equilateral triangle, which, however
turned, always exalts *monad* or the single unit, representative of a
primal unity) and through math learned the affinities among as-
tronomy, musical harmonics, and agriculture. The universal kin-
ship of things through number had great bearing on the social
realm as well. This was the sole purview (blindly) of the *acusmatici*,
the far larger class of unexceptional students, who, according to
fourth-century historians, received (some say, behind a veil) only

"summarized instructions" "without demonstrations or confer-
ences or arguments, . . . non-discussable, . . . which they promised
not to reveal, esteeming as most wise those who more than others
retained them."

Acusmata, known variously as maxims, injunctions, symbols, in-
terdictions, counsels, auditions, and precepts, literally translates to
"things heard." The cryptic advisories appear earliest in the testi-
monial biographies written by the Neoplatonists Iamblichus, Porphyry, and Diogenes Laertius, which cite as a primary source the
then six-hundred-year-old and now lost text "On the Pythagoreans"
in Aristotle, where these instructions covering diet, hospitality, hygiene, and sepulture were probably enumerated in print for the
first time. The present compilation may be the most comprehen-
sive in English, and mostly I have used the wording closest to consensus among the Neoplatonists; I have also given in a few in-
stances, as indication of the beguiling differences among accounts,
variants on an injunction.

Pythagoras left no writings of his own, and it was the rare disciple
who entrusted to a surviving son or daughter his commentaries for
secret safekeeping within the family. Therefore "inconsistencies" in
Pythagoreanism, writes W.K.C. Guthrie, "are no cause for despair
or for a hasty conclusion that the authorities are confused: they are
no less likely to be a faithful reflexion of historical fact." Obscurity
is key. Joined in inferiority, the auditors enroll, file in, and wait for
the veil to drop.

Touch not the balance above the beam.
   Do not pick up what has fallen from the table.
   Do not pluck the crown.
   Where blood has been shed, cover the place with stones.
   Do not sit on a bushel measure. [Also given as Sit not down on
the bushel; Do not sit on a choinix (gallon pail); Do not sit upon a
bushel basket; Do not sit on the corn ration.]
   On starting a journey, do not turn back.
   Enter not into a temple negligently, nor, in short, adore carelessly,
not even though you should stand at the very doors themselves.
   Sacrifice and adore unshod.
   Declining from the people's major highways, walk in unfre-
quented paths.

One must not dip one's hand into the lustral vessel, or wash in the public bath.

Abstain from the fish Melanurus, or the blacktail, for it belongs to the Earth deities.

Dig not fire with a sword.

Help a man to take up a burden but not to lay it down. [Also given as Working with others lifting, you may set down a load, but do not lift it up with them.]

When stretching forth your feet to have your sandals put on, first extend your right foot; but when about to use a foot bath, first extend your left foot.

Do not without light speak about Pythagoric affairs.

Efface the traces of a pot in the ashes.

Nourish a white cock, but sacrifice it not; for it is a suppliant and sacred to the sun and the moon and also announces hours.

Break not the teeth.

Counsel nothing but the best for him who is being counseled, for counsel is holy.

Wear not the image of a God in a ring.

Do not look at yourself in a mirror by candlelight.

One, two.

Concerning the gods, disbelieve nothing wonderful, and concerning the divine doctrines.

Be not seized with immoderate laughter.

Do not chase after your wife, for she is a holy suppliant, wherefore, indeed, we bring her from the Vestal hearth, and take her by the right hand.

It is best to sustain, and show wounds, if they are in the breast.

Lay not hold on every one with your right hand.

Speak not in the face of the sun.

Do not sleep at noon.

Put not meat in the chamber pot.

Rising from the bed, roll up the bedclothes and confound the imprint of the body.

Never sing without harp accompaniment.

Eat not the heart.

Nor the brain.

Receive not the fish Erythrynus.

Do not draw near to a woman for the sake of begetting children, if she has gold.

Abstain from beans. [Aristotle interpreted the rationale thus: A bean alone of almost all spermatic plants is perforated through the whole of it, and is not obstructed by any intervening joints; it resembles the gates of Hades.]

Transplant mallows in your garden but eat them not. [Also given as Grow the plant "moloche" but do not eat it.]

Wipe not out the place of the torch.

Make your libations to the gods at the ear of the cup.

Give way to a flock that goes by.

Avoid the weasel.

Refuse the weapons a woman offers you.

Kill not the serpent that chances to fall within your walls.

Feed not yourself with your left hand.

It is not right to eat generation, growth, beginning, or end, nor that from which the first development (hypothesis) comes. This includes loins, testicles, genitals, brain, head, and feet.

Abstain from flesh of animals that die of themselves.

Set down salt as a reminder of the just, for salt preserves all things, and is brought out of the purest thing, water.

Do not wipe the seat with a lamp.

Stick not iron into the footsteps of a man.

Sleep not on a grave.

Lay not the whole faggot on the fire.

Leap not from the chariot with your feet close together.

Threaten not the stars.

Write not in the snow.

Urine not being turned toward the sun.

Sail not on the ground.

Do not cherish birds with crooked talons.

Cleave not wood in the way.

Do not urinate or stand upon the parings of your nails or the cuttings of your hair.

Going away to a holy temple, kneel down, and the meanwhile neither think nor do anything pertaining to one's regular life.

One must not turn out of his way to a temple; one must not make God a side issue.

Avoid a sharp sword.

Wear not a narrow ring. [Also given as Do not wear a ring.]

Suffer no swallows around your house.

Spit upon your nail parings and hair trimmings.

When the winds blow, kneel down to Echo.
Eat not in the chariot.
Never break the bread.
Always turn a vinegar cruet away from yourself.
Quit not your post without your general's order.
Roast not what is boiled.
Abstain even from a cypress chest.
To the celestial gods sacrifice an odd number, but to the infernal, an even.
Turn round when you worship.
Touch the earth when it thunders.

SCOTT CAIRNS

Replies to the Immediate

FROM *Western Humanities Review*

No, he mumbled from the podium, the poems
are not my songs. A breeze
troubled the papers in his hands, and a shift
in the air also sent
a wave across those seated, tossing their hair,
their broad lapels, their scarves.
The programs in their hands also whispered. Nor,
the man continued, nor
are they my prayers. At that word, the air grew still,
and across his face passed both
a tremor and a calm. Song, he said, attains
to a condition the poem
dare not attend. And prayer? Who would frame a poem
when he had better find
his knees, in silence, having put his art away?

RICHARD CHESS

Kaddish

FROM *Image*

After Charles Reznikoff

27 Iyar 5763

29 May 2003

Upon Israel and
upon the rabbis and upon
the disciples and upon all
the disciples of the disciples and
upon all who study Torah in this place
and in every place, to them
and to you
peace;

upon Israel and upon all
who meet men and women
wired to explode
and who sit with professors
ministers, sheiks, and
the pious multitude in mosque
and chapel and at plenary sessions and
breakout meetings where
delegates from nations gather
to denounce, and on the street
among those who proclaim
Zionist = Nazi Zionism = Apartheid —
upon all who are proselytized or scorned
whose lives are interrupted
on a bus, in a pizzeria

during a sermon or a kiddush luncheon
or in the middle of an in-flight movie —
to them and to you
here in this land of boutiques
and a food bank, mountains
and a river, crosses and a ring of fire
and in every place
on earth and beyond
safety;

upon Israel and upon all who live
in a boardroom, on a conference
call, on the apron
of a pool and on poetry —
you descendants of
tenement and cotton mill
today dispersing your wealth like pollen
to seed a maternity wing
and to mature in the form
of a black man entering college
and a documentary
on Vilna
in this place and in every place
your influence is feared and celebrated
to you and to those
yet to achieve power
humility;

upon Israel
and upon their children and upon all the children
of their children, those who disappear
among good people of this earth
and those who thrive
in this place where the Sabbath
table is properly set
and in every place
to them and to you
life.

ROBERT CORDING

Advent Stanzas

FROM *Southern Review*

I.

Are we always creating you, as Rilke said,
Trying, on our best days,
To make possible your coming-into-existence?

Or are you merely a story told in the dark,
A child's drawing of barn and star?

Each year you are born again. It is no remedy

For what we go on doing to each other,
For history's blind repetitions of hate and reprisal.

Here I am again, huddled in hope. For what
Do I wait? — I know you only as something missing,
And loved beyond reason.

As a word in my mouth I cannot embody.

II.

On the snow-dusted field this morning — an etching
Of mouse tracks declares the frenzy of its hunger.

The plodding dawn sun rises to another day's
One warm hour. I'm walking to the iced-in local pond

Where my neighbors have sat through the night
Waiting for something to find their jigged lure.

The sky is paste white. Each bush and tree keeps
Its cold counsel. I'm walking head-on into a wind

That forces my breath back into my mouth.
Like rags of black cloth, crows drape a dead oak.

When I pass under them, their cries rip a seam
In the morning. Last week a lifelong friend told me,

There's no such thing as happiness. It's ten years
Since he found his son, then a nineteen-year-old

Of extraordinary grace and goodness, curled up
In his dormitory room, unable to rise, to free

Himself of a division that made him manic and
Depressed, and still his son struggles from day to day,

The one partial remedy a dismal haze of drugs.
My friend hopes these days for very little — a stretch of

Hours, a string of a few days when nothing in his son's life
Goes terribly wrong. This is the season of sad stories:

The crippling accident, the layoffs at the factory,
The family without a car, without a house, without money

For presents. The sadder the human drama, the greater
Our hope, or so the television news makes it seem

With its soap-opera stories of tragedy followed up
With ones of good will — images of Santas' pots filling up

At the malls, truckloads of presents collected for the shelters,
Or the family posed with their special-needs child

In front of a fully equipped van given by the local dealership.
This is the season to keep the less fortunate in sight,

To believe that generosity will be generously repaid.
We've strung colored lights on our houses and trees,

And lit candles in the windows to hold back the dark.
For what do we hope? — That our candles will lead you

To our needs? That your gift of light will light
These darkest nights of the year? That our belief

In our own righteousness will be vindicated?
The prophet Amos knew the burden of your coming.

The day of the Lord is darkness, he said, *darkness, not light,*
As if someone went into a house and rested a hand against a wall,

And was bitten by a snake. Amos knew the shame of
What we fail, over and over, to do, the always burning

Image of what might be. Saint Paul, too, saw
The whole creation groaning for redemption.

And will you *intercede with sighs too deep for words*
Because you love us in our weakness, because

You love always, suddenly and completely, what is
In front of you, whether it is a lake or leper.

Because you come again and again to destroy the God
We keep making in our own image. Will we learn

To pray: May our hearts be broken open. Will we learn
To prepare a space in which you might come forth,

In which, like a bolt of winter solstice light,
You might enter the opening in the stones, lighting

Our dark tumulus from beginning to end?

III.

All last night the tatter of sleet, ice descending,
Each tree sheathed in ice, and then, deeper
Into the night, the shattering cracks and fall
Of branches being pruned by gusts of wind.

It is the first morning after the longest night,
Dawn colorless, the sun still cloud-silvered.
Four crows break the early stillness, an apocalypse
Of raucous squawks. My miniature four horsemen

Take and eat whatever they can in the field
Outside my door: a deer's leg my dog has dragged
Home. Above them, the flinty sun has at last fired
A blue patch of sky, and suddenly each ice-transfigured

Tree shines. Each needle of pine, each branch
Of ash, throws off sparks of light. Once,
A rabbi saw a spark of goodness trapped inside
Each evil, the very source of life for that evil —

A contradiction not to be understood, but suffered,
The rabbi explained, though the one who prays
And studies Torah will be able to release that spark,
And evil, having lost its life-giving source, will cease.

When I finally open my door and walk out
Into the field, every inch of my skin seems touched
By light. So much light cannot be looked at:
My eyelids slam down like a blind.

All morning I drag limbs into a pile. By noon,
The trees and field have lost their shine. I douse
The pile of wood with gas, and set it aflame,
Watching sparks disappear in the sky.

IV.

This is the night we have given for your birth.

After the cherished hymns, the prayers, the story
Of the one who will become peacemaker,
Healer of the sick, the one who feeds
The hungry and raises the dead,

We light small candles and stand in the dark

Of the church, hoping for the peace
A child knows, hoping to forget career, mortgage,
Money, hoping even to turn quietly away

From the blind, reductive selves inside us.

We are a picture a child might draw
As we sing *Silent night, holy night.*
Yet, while each of us tries to inhabit the moment
That is passing, you seem to live in between
The words we fill with our longing.

The time has come
To admit I believe in the simple astonishment
Of a newborn.

And also to say plainly, as Pascal knew, that you will live
In agony even to the end of the world,

Your will failing to be done on earth
As it is in heaven.

Come, o come Emmanuel,

I am a ghost waiting to be made flesh by love
I am too imperfect to bear.

HARVEY COX

Best of Intentions

FROM *Christian Century*

IN MANY IMPORTANT RESPECTS the ethics of Judaism and Christianity are similar. Both emphasize the oneness of the human family and the responsibility we have for each other. Jesus continued and at times intensified the Old Testament prophets' defense of the poor and the powerless. But there is one matter on which the two traditions have diverged. Whereas Jewish thinking has emphasized actual deeds and their consequences, Christianity has often focused on intentions. Once, in the course of assuring his disciples that it was not so awful if they could not wash their hands before eating, Jesus said, "Out of the heart come evil intentions, murder, adultery, fornication, theft, false witness, slander. These are what defile a person, but to eat with unwashed hands does not defile" (Matt. 15:19, 20). He seems to be saying that the heart, not the hands, is the real source of a moral infraction.

The distinction is not absolute. Within the Jewish tradition, one of the Ten Commandments prohibits "coveting," which is an inner attitude; and Jesus condemned the pious people who ignored the beaten man on the road to Jericho. Whatever pity may have been in their hearts, they did not do what they should have done. But still, as the two traditions developed over the years, the distinction became a real one. For Christians this was evident several years ago when the Roman Catholic bishops of the United States condemned even the possession of nuclear weapons as a violation of the just war ethic. They argued that in order for these weapons to serve as a deterrent, a potential enemy had to be convinced that in certain circumstances we actually intended to use them. But such an intention, they argued, was already immoral. The underlying premise of their argument is that evil intentions spawn evil deeds, and it is better to nip the foul flower in the bud rather than wait for the wicked action to blossom.

In recent years, however, we have begun to see a certain convergence between these two ways of thinking about moral issues. Prodded by the need to reflect on actual policy options and their probable outcomes, Christian scholars have begun to probe more deeply into the possible consequences of actions, and not just what motivates them. Also, with the dramatic rediscovery of their mystical tradition, Jews have delved deeper into the inner self and its intricate labyrinth of impulses and desires.

I think this convergence is a healthy development. It is needed because once again our technology has outpaced our traditional modes of moral reasoning. There was a time when evil thoughts and evil deeds took place at close quarters. There was a time when you needed to wield a club or a spear to kill your neighbor. Now we can do untold harm to multitudes of people at a great distance, and without feeling personally involved. In her brilliant book *Evil in Modern Thought: An Alternative History of Philosophy,* Susan Neiman cites this impersonality as one of our gravest ethical dilemmas. It means, she argues, that we can no longer focus on evil intentions as a key to morality. We can now do great evil without intending to. What we need today is more awareness, a wider recognition of how the vast systems we are caught up in can do terrible things and how we can contribute to that evil without even being conscious of it.

This is a disturbing idea. It means that the traditional debate about deeds and intentions needs to be rethought. "I didn't really mean it" should no longer exonerate us so easily, nor should "I had no idea of what I was doing." In our century, to be unaware is to be less than moral.

This question came up with an unusual degree of forcefulness in my course on Jesus when we discussed his famous words from the cross: "Father, forgive them, for they know not what they do." I knew already that the students had strong feelings, if not always well-formulated ideas, on the topics we took up. But this discussion, more than any other we had, exposed the complexity of the moral world they live in.

It started innocently enough when I asked the students if they were surprised or puzzled that Jesus was ready to forgive those who were at that very moment torturing him to death. As usual, their responses varied. Some said they were not surprised. That, after all, was the kind of person he was. Others confessed that they simply could not understand it. They could not imagine themselves doing such a thing, so it made Jesus less credible as a moral guide by seeming to put him out of reach.

What puzzled all of them, however, was the phrase "for they know not what they do." How, they wanted to know, could they not be aware of what they were doing? Also, just who was included in the "them"? Was it mainly the soldiers who mocked and beat him, or did it include the passersby who taunted him, the officials who had passed sentence on him, the spineless disciples who had fled, the collaborator who had betrayed him for a bribe? Besides, what if they clearly had been aware of what they were doing, so that he could not have said, "They know not"; would he still have forgiven them? It was soon obvious that this single phrase from Jesus' lips was packed with layers of moral quandaries.

How, one student asked, could anyone engaged in something so blatantly cruel not be aware of what he was doing?

"Easy," another student answered. "We are rarely aware of the full implications of the things we do. There are always unforeseen consequences. Maybe that's what Jesus meant."

Another student pointed out that if by "them" Jesus was speaking of the Roman soldiers, we should remember that they were under orders. The Romans routinely used crucifixion as a form of punishment for people they adjudged dangerous to their rule. Maybe these soldiers had just gotten used to it, had become deaf to the moans of the victims. The text says they were relaxed enough to throw dice for Jesus' tunic as he twisted and pleaded for water. Certainly prison officials today seem able to inject lethal chemicals into the veins of prisoners or strap them into chairs to receive a 20,000-volt jolt of electricity when a judge tells them to do so. Maybe these soldiers thought they were just carrying out a routine order.

As for the Roman officials and their local collaborators, maybe they really believed Jesus was a genuine threat to civil order and had to be dealt with in the customary fashion. Maybe they thought that they were just doing their duty and did not feel the least uncomfortable. Still, most of the students were not satisfied. "How

could these people not know what they were doing?" they continued to ask.

Finally one young woman went back to a previous comment:
Maybe what Jesus wanted to say was that they were not aware of
the full extent of their actions, or of the long-range implications.
They were small cogs in a large machine. So in that sense they did
not really "know." A chemistry student agreed: How could any-
body ever be expected to accept responsibility for all the possible
implications of what he might do? His remark sparked some further discussion, especially among the science majors, of how difficult — maybe impossible — it is to foresee how scientific discov-
eries might eventually be used. This led to some reflection about
whether Alfred Nobel would have — or should have — given up
devising dynamite if he had known how often it would be used in
bombs. Another student, who had seen a production of the play
Copenhagen, deepened the argument by recalling the moral dilemma faced by Niels Bohr, Werner Heisenberg, and later Robert
Oppenheimer and others who were inventing the first atomic
bomb. Oppenheimer, for example, knew how destructive it was,
but knew (or thought) the Germans were trying to make one too,
so he went ahead with it. Later, however, he vigorously opposed de-
veloping the nuclear bomb.

The discussion was still raging on when I had to leave, and when
I came back an hour later most of the students were still at it, and
they had not come to any consensus. I was not surprised. This text
had propelled them into one of the most contentious moral issues
of our time. Because advances in technology, especially in weap-
onry, remove individuals from the results of their actions, they allow human beings to do enormous evil without feeling the least bit
involved. Pushing a red "fire" button at a target someone else has
charted thousands of miles away is different from stabbing someone with a javelin. There is a quantitative gap between the battle-ax
and the heat-seeking missile. Mass murder can become routine —
even "banal," as Hannah Arendt described it in the case of Adolf
Eichmann.

I learned a lot from the discussion of "they know not what they
do." Clearly the students were becoming more and more aware of
the bewildering complexity of many modern moral issues, but they
still desperately wanted to "do the right thing." We did not come to

any wholly satisfactory conclusion, but our probes into the questions of agency, awareness, and responsibility were valuable. They helped students to see that "the way it is done" is not always — maybe even rarely — the way it should be done. It stimulated them to imagine alternatives.

Also, the way the students struggled with the issues made me even more aware that — like most of us — they were human beings who really did want to act morally and responsibly. But most of them would always live and work in institutions in which someone else made the rules and set the standard operating procedures. For that reason, despite their best intentions, they would not always be clear about what it would mean to "do the right thing," and might not always be able to do it even when they were. It was for this reason, I reminded them, that we should not focus exclusively on the "know not" part of this famous phrase but should also remember that it begins with "Forgive them."

My suggestion, however, did not resolve the dilemma. "What do you mean by forgiveness?" they asked. When, they wondered, should we forgive people who do mean or awful things to us or to others? Can we expect people we have hurt to forgive us? What does forgiveness have to do with being sorry, remorseful, or penitent?

These are questions that sages have pondered for centuries, but it was fascinating to see how alive and immediate they were today for these young people, and I suspect for their elders as well. They are also unavoidable questions if one is studying the life of Jesus. The first words attributed to him in the oldest Gospel are "The time has arrived; the kingdom of God is upon you." The next sentence is "Repent, and believe the gospel" (Mark 1:14). There is every indication that those who heard these words of Jesus recognized what he was asking for, although not all were willing to comply. All Jews of the time, even those with a minimal exposure to their religious heritage, would have known that repentance involves three elements: genuine regret for one's misdeeds, sorrow and remorse for the injury they have caused others, and a deeply felt desire to avoid repeating the offense. Without these three ingredients, genuine forgiveness, either by God or by one's fellow human beings, was not in the picture.

*

All this would have been familiar to most of Rabbi Jesus' hearers. The new element was the urgent tone of his demand for repentance. The coming reign of God, for which the pious prayed, was beginning now, and the change of heart it required could not be postponed. As we have seen, Jesus' parables and sayings carry this same note of immediacy. *Today, now, this moment* is the time for repentance. The kingdom of God, albeit hidden and partial, is coming to birth in the midst of you.

For Jews today, God's demand for confession and penitence is enacted during the Days of Awe between Rosh Hashanah and Yom Kippur. In what is staged as a cosmic courtroom drama, the people gather and confess not only their own transgressions but also those of the whole people. At the last moment, just as the book of life is being closed, God's verdict is announced. Because God is ultimately compassionate, everyone is forgiven and afforded the opportunity to begin a new year with a clean slate.

During the nearly two thousand years since the earthly ministry of Jesus, the various Christian churches have also developed highly complex liturgies of repentance and forgiveness. But the core of the Christian understanding is crystallized in the ancient invitation to the commemoration of the Lord's Supper, which eventually found its way into the Book of Common Prayer. It reads as follows:

> Ye who do truly and earnestly repent you of your sins, and are in love and charity with your neighbors, and intend to lead a new life, following the commandments of God, and walking from henceforth in his holy ways: Draw near with faith, and take this holy Sacrament to your comfort; and make your humble confession to Almighty God, devoutly kneeling.

It would be hard to find a more compressed summary of the Christian understanding of repentance and forgiveness. First, this invitation assumes that human beings are free. They are endowed by God with the capacity for choice and are therefore responsible for their actions. True, in some of its forms, the Christian idea of original sin seems to qualify this key premise. Yet, recognizing the paradox involved, the overwhelming consensus of Christian theology is that however free will may be blemished or weakened within the actual conditions of history, human beings nonetheless do have the ability to choose. Otherwise, the call for repentance would be meaningless.

This is not a trivial observation. Jesus' summons to repentance to all who came within earshot — the pious and the reprobate, the weak and the strong, the powerful and the socially marginalized — undercuts any kind of religious, psychological, or sociocultural determinism. It constitutes a firm rejection of any notion of karma or kismet that would make God or destiny or behavior in a past life or childhood mistreatment responsible for one's actions. It suggests that although there can be mitigating circumstances, neither fate nor the psychological history of the person can be advanced as the sole reason for his or her conduct. Neither does it allow "It had to be done" or "Nothing can be done about it" as excuses. It endows even the most victimized and oppressed peoples with a continuing and genuine responsibility, if only to struggle against whatever deprives them of their personhood. My offenses are ultimately mine. The *cogito ergo sum* of the Christian view of repentance is: Since I can repent, I am responsible.

The words *truly and earnestly* also carry an important message. They remind us that there is such a thing as inauthentic repentance. In our secularized culture this spurious repentance often appears in the "public apology" that falls short of the real thing. The psychiatrist Aaron Lazarre has pointed out that our public discourse is rife with such bogus apologies. A frequent form is "I am really sorry that you feel that way" or words to that effect. The style of these utterances raises questions about whether they meet the standards of "truly and earnestly" preserved in the invitation to communion. Public apologies are often marked by the systematic elimination of personal reference and a reliance on the passive voice. The "I" somehow disappears. They rely on phrases such as "injuries . . . may have been done" or "mistakes were made." This erasure of the subject betrays a continuing reluctance to accept personal responsibility.

The phrase "are in love and charity with your neighbors" means that the truly penitent person has already taken the first step toward reintegrating him- or herself into the human community whose fabric has been torn by the betrayal of trust a transgression implies. Here the ancient Jewish emphasis on what was actually done continues to inform Christian practice. It is not enough just to intend to put things right. The word *are* is in the present tense. I must already be in love and charity with my neighbors, at least to some extent. Here reconciliation between a human being and his or her neighbors and reconciliation with God are indissolubly linked.

During the Days of Awe before Yom Kippur, Jews are reminded that God can forgive those sins we commit against him but that we must seek forgiveness from our human neighbors for the violations we enact against them. In the Christian view, this idea is modified to some extent. Since God is present in the neighbor, all sins, including those against the neighbor, are also sins against God. And since Christians usually retain the moral but not the ritual elements of Torah, it is hard to imagine a sin against God (in a Christian view) that is not also a sin against some neighbor.

The phrases "intend to lead a new life" and "walking from henceforth in his holy ways" suggest a determination on the part of the penitent person not to repeat the destructive conduct. But "intend" also allows for the weakness of human flesh. The invitation recognizes that we rarely live out even our most earnest intentions. Nonetheless, even though we fall short, we should still have those intentions. Further, the "new life" referred to is not one without moral guidelines. "Following the commandments of God" recalls not only the Ten Commandments but also the Golden Rule. In some forms of the communion service, the Ten Commandments are read just before the invitation is issued. This reinforces the notion that these biblical principles are intended to provide moral parameters for the "new life" the penitent person now intends to live.

Finally, and perhaps most important, is the invitation to participate in communion. It is, as it were, a readmission into the family of God, gathered around a table that in Christian belief symbolizes the whole of humanity. It is the gateway through which one is welcomed back into a fellowship whose trust and confidence one has broken. It is an avenue to the restoration of the multiple relationships without which human life would cease to be human.

This linking of repentance and forgiveness with restoration to community echoes Jesus' linking his call to repentance with his announcement that the kingdom of God — the healed and restored human community — is "at hand." The point is vital to the Christian view of repentance. Genuine repentance is an integral element in the coming of the reconciled world of justice and peace that God wills. Unlike Rousseau's famous observation that "man was born free, but is everywhere in chains," the Christian phrase would be "People were created to live together, but are everywhere divided and in enmity." The Christian liturgy of communion is a symbol of the ultimate goal of a restored human community.

In many Christian theologies, this *restoratio humanii* is believed to be no less than the purpose of the incarnation. Medieval paintings of the crucifixion often show the skull of Adam at the base of the cross. The idea is that a new humanity is now taking shape on the spot where the first human being met his tragic denouement. Jesus spent his earthly ministry breaking the social and cultural taboos that had excluded certain types of people (prostitutes, lepers, tax collectors) from table fellowship with respectable, pious people. For Jesus, this was an act of symbolic restoration. Inclusive table fellowship modeled an inclusive humanity. It prefigured the messianic feast foreseen by the prophets. The ultimate feast is unconditionally inclusive. As the Protestant theologian Karl Barth once remarked, the church should be "the provisional demonstration of God's intention for the whole human race."

It is important in both the Jewish and Christian traditions to avoid two extremes, which neither has always done successfully. The first extreme is to make penitence and forgiveness so easy they come to mean nothing. This overlooks the stubborn fact that repentance, forgiveness, and reconciliation all belong together, and that each requires real effort. Sometimes Catholics have misunderstood the sacrament of confession as a license to repeat their misdeeds, since one can always confess again. Likewise, Protestants have misread the idea of justification by grace as permission to do as they please, since it is God's business to forgive. This amounts to what the Protestant theologian Dietrich Bonhoeffer once called "cheap grace."

The other extreme is to make forgiveness so terribly demanding that, as in the mind of Stavrogin, the poignant hero of Dostoevsky's novel *Demons,* it becomes unreachable. If anything, I think our forebears, both Christian and Jewish, may frequently have made forgiveness too demanding. But I also fear that the "user-friendly" style of much contemporary religion may be sliding toward cheap grace.

In any case, although our extended dialogue as we pondered Jesus' words may not have solved this old dilemma, I hope it left the students with the conviction that the kingdom of God that Jesus announced was not for people who never did anything wrong. It was for "sinners," for those who — mostly — tried their best to do the right thing, often failed, but accepted the forgiveness of God and of others, forgave others and themselves, and started over.

ANDY CROUCH

The Emergent Mystique

FROM *Christianity Today*

ONE SPRING SUNDAY MORNING, I was on my way to visit Mars Hill Bible Church, one of the largest and youngest churches in the country, with 10,000 meeting weekly for worship in a converted mall outside Grand Rapids, Michigan. As I took the freeway exit, unsure of the exact directions, I noticed a bumper sticker on the car in front of me. LOVE WINS, it said, in distressed white type on a black background. In the rear window was a decal with an intricate pattern — half art deco, half Goth tattoo — that incorporated a cross and a fish.

Neither the bumper sticker nor the tattoo decal alone would have induced me to set aside my hastily scribbled directions and simply follow the car straight to the Mars Hill parking lot. But I knew I'd found my mark when I saw the passenger lower the sun visor, look into the makeup mirror, and meticulously adjust his hair.

Gentlemen, start your hair dryers — not since the Jesus Movement of the early 1970s has a Christian phenomenon been so closely entangled with the self-conscious cutting edge of U.S. culture. Frequently urban, disproportionately young, overwhelmingly white, and very new — few have been in existence for more than five years — a growing number of churches are joining the ranks of the "emerging church."

Like all labels, this one conceals as much as it reveals. But the phrase "emerging church" captures several important features of a new generation of churches. They are works in progress, often startlingly improvisational in their approach to everything from worship to leadership to preaching to prayer. Like their own members, they live in the half-future tense of the young, oriented toward their promise rather than their past. But if their own focus is on what they are "emerging" toward, perhaps most surprising are the places they are emerging from.

Weak Is the New Strong

Mars Hill's teaching pastor, Rob Bell, hair tousled and reddish brown, hops onstage in the center of what must have been the mall's anchor store. The huge space has been redecorated in utilitarian gray; a wooden cross reaches from floor to ceiling. Communion elements — the broken crackers and grape juice that are standard issue at Bible churches of every generation — are set at its base.

Bell is almost certainly the only pastor to have begun a mega-church-planting career with a sermon series from the Book of Leviticus. Today Bell's text — the story of Jesus rebuking Peter for drawing his sword in the Garden of Gethsemane — is more conventional. Bell has the comic timing, the charisma, and the confidence you'd expect from someone who speaks to thousands every week. And he has a gift for the preacher's memorable phrase. "Swords appear strong," Bell says, "but they're actually quite weak. Jesus appears weak, but he's actually quite strong." Inviting his congregation to embrace weakness, referring to Paul's words about his own infirmity in 2 Corinthians, Bell takes up a refrain: "Weak is the new strong."

It's a pithy way of describing Jesus' upside-down kingdom, and it's a striking way of introducing a communion service at the foot of a large cross. But "Weak is the new strong" is also an allusion to fashion-industry dictates like "Gray is the new black." Bell is both echoing and subverting a fashion-driven culture of cool. You could say that he puts the *hip* in *discipleship*.

Clearly cultural relevance was part of the reason for planting a church whose worship team requires a bass player who can play "in the style of Jimmy Eat World and Coldplay." No generation has ever been more alert to such nuances than the media-fed children of the 1980s and '90s, who can sense uncoolness at a thousand paces. As Rob Bell's wife, Kristen, tells CT in a joint interview after the service, "It's a cultural jump for our friends to come to church. It's a cultural jump for us, and we grew up in the church."

But it quickly becomes clear that these Wheaton College sweet-hearts have more on their minds than just cultural adaptation. "This is not just the same old message with new methods," Rob says. "We're rediscovering Christianity as an Eastern religion, as a way of life. Legal metaphors for faith don't deliver a way of life. We grew up in churches where people knew the nine verses why we don't speak in tongues, but had never experienced the overwhelming presence of God."

In fact, as the Bells describe it, after launching Mars Hill in 1999, they found themselves increasingly uncomfortable with church. "Life in the church had become so small," Kristen says. "It had worked for me for a long time. Then it stopped working." The Bells started questioning their assumptions about the Bible itself — "discovering the Bible as a human product," as Rob puts it, rather than the product of divine fiat. "The Bible is still in the center for us," Rob says, "but it's a different kind of center. We want to embrace mystery, rather than conquer it."

"I grew up thinking that we've figured out the Bible," Kristen says, "that we knew what it means. Now I have no idea what most of it means. And yet I feel like life is big again — like life used to be black and white, and now it's in color."

The more I talk with the Bells, the more aware I am that they are telling me a conversion narrative — not a story of salvation in the strict sense, but of having been delivered from a small life into a big life. The Bells, who flourished at evangelical institutions from Wheaton to Fuller Theological Seminary to Grand Rapids's Calvary Church before starting Mars Hill, were by their own account happy and successful young evangelicals. Yet that very world, as the Bells tell it, became constricting — in Kristen's phrase, "black and white."

An earlier generation of evangelicals, forged in battles with twentieth-century liberalism, prided themselves on avoiding theological shades of gray, but their children see black, white, and gray as all equally unlifelike. They are looking for a faith that is colorful enough for their culturally savvy friends, deep enough for mystery, big enough for their own doubts. To get there, they are willing to abandon some long-defended battle lines.

"Weak is the new strong," it turns out, is not just Rob Bell's knowing reference to the world of fashion, nor just his clever reframing of Paul's message of Christlike life. It's a roadmap for a new way of doing church, even a big church.

And how did the Bells find their way out of the black-and-white world where they had been so successful and so dissatisfied? "Our lifeboat," Kristen says, "was *A New Kind of Christian.*"

A Story of Two Friends

Brian McLaren is not particularly young — he was born in 1956 — and he doesn't have cool hair, if only because he has very little hair at all. With his blue-jeans-and-Birkenstocks dress code and a middle-age paunch, he looks like a suburban, nondenominational pastor who came of age playing the guitar for youth ministry meetings in the 1970s.

Which is exactly what he is. Yet he is also the de facto spiritual leader for the emerging church, thanks to his indefatigable speaking and writing schedule that produced, among his many books, 2001's *A New Kind of Christian.*

A New Kind of Christian became influential not just because of its content but also its form. McLaren cast the book as a story of two friends, a disillusioned evangelical pastor named Dan Poole and an enigmatic high school science teacher nicknamed Neo. On the brink of despair with his own ministry, Dan is led by Neo — who turns out to be a lapsed pastor himself — through a series of set pieces that introduce the initially skeptical Dan to a "postmodern" approach to Christianity.

The modern period of history, as Neo tells it, is coming to an end. We are entering "postmodernity," an as-yet ill-defined borderland in which central modern values like objectivity, analysis, and control will become less compelling. They are superseded by postmodern values like mystery and wonder. The controversial implication is that forms of Christianity that have thrived in modernity — including Dan's evangelicalism — are unlikely to survive the transition.

McLaren managed to connect abstruse concepts of intellectual and social history to a visceral sense of disillusionment among evangelical pastors. Dan's dissatisfaction with ministry, in McLaren's telling, was not primarily a faith problem, a psychological problem, or a sociological problem. It was a philosophical problem

— the result of a way of thinking that was no longer adequate. Pastors who would have had a hard time seeing the relevance of postmodernism could suddenly envision it as the key to finding, as the book's jacket put it, "spiritual renewal for those who thought they had given up on church."

The book generated an outpouring of intensely personal response. To this day McLaren continues to receive grateful e-mails from readers. The book also confirmed the intuitions of many who sensed that major changes were under way in the culture. By offering a fundamentally hopeful, rather than despairing or defensive, reading of those changes, McLaren staked out an attractive position for young people like Rob and Kristen Bell.

But *A New Kind of Christian* has also attracted plenty of critics. The most persistent question they raise is whether "modern" and "postmodern" can be divided so cleanly. Wheaton College philosopher Mark Talbot points out that skepticism about values like objectivity, analysis, and control was already present in Enlightenment figures like David Hume. Meanwhile, Talbot says, "the great irony is that by giving us these sharp categories of 'modern' and 'postmodern' ways of thinking, McLaren is doing the very sort of categorization he describes, and implicitly condemns, as modern."

The point Talbot and others make is not just a matter of quibbling over definitions. If a self-avowed postmodern Christian can't differentiate himself from the moderns he is critiquing, perhaps the divide between modernity and postmodernity is less like the San Andreas Fault and more like a crack in the sidewalk. And if there is no massive change under way in the culture, why make a case for a massive change in the church?

Envisioning a Postmodern Church

The real significance of *A New Kind of Christian*, though, may be not its answers but its openness to questions that are clearly widespread.

Even now McLaren resists calling Emergent, the emerging church network that he and several other church planters and pastors lead, a "movement," with that word's connotations of a clear leadership and agenda.

"Right now Emergent is a conversation, not a movement," he

says. "We don't have a program. We don't have a model. I think we
must begin as a conversation, then grow as a friendship, and see if a
movement comes of it."

Yet recently McLaren has started to sketch the outlines of his vision of a postmodern church. He sketches a big circle labeled
"self," a smaller circle next to it labeled "church," and a tiny circle
off to the side labeled "world."

"This has been evangelicalism's model," he says. "Fundamentally
it's about getting yourself 'saved' — in old-style evangelicalism —
or improving your life in the new style. Either way, the Christian life
is really about you and your needs. Once your needs are met, then
we think about how you can serve the church. And then, if there's
anything left over, we ask how the church might serve the world."

He starts drawing again. "But what if it went the other way? This
big circle is the world — the world God loved so much that he sent
his Son. Inside that circle is another one, the church, God's people
chosen to demonstrate his love to the world. And inside that is a
small circle, which is your self. It's not about the church meeting
your needs, it's about you joining the mission of God's people to
meet the world's needs."

With his circle diagrams, McLaren is popularizing the work of
the late British missionary Lesslie Newbigin, who returned from a
lifetime in India to spend his last years reflecting on the need for a
new theology of mission. "According to Newbigin, the greatest
heresy in monotheism is a misunderstanding of the doctrine of
election," McLaren says. "Election is not about who gets to go to
heaven; election is about who God chooses to be part of his crisis-
response team to bring healing to the world."

McLaren doesn't just want to turn the doctrine of election up-
side down (or, as Newbigin argued, right side up) — he has questions about other cherished words in the evangelical vocabulary.

"I don't think we've got the gospel right yet. What does it mean
to be 'saved'? When I read the Bible, I don't see it meaning, 'I'm
going to heaven after I die.' Before modern evangelicalism nobody
accepted Jesus Christ as their personal Savior, or walked down an
aisle, or said the sinner's prayer."

It's not that McLaren is interested in joining the liberal side of
modern Protestantism. "I don't think the liberals have it right. But
I don't think we have it right either. None of us has arrived at orthodoxy."

Comments like these make many evangelicals nervous. It doesn't help that postmodernism, in the popular imagination, often amounts to pure skepticism about getting anything "right" at all. How can a worldview built on critiquing — or in the postmodern argot, deconstructing — concepts like orthodoxy and salvation be faithful to the gospel? What makes the emerging church's dissatisfaction with traditional Christianity any different from that of liberal Protestantism, which embraced the culture's values only to wither as the culture changed a generation later?

Yet there are real differences between emerging-church leaders like McLaren and those who led the charge for liberal Christianity. Liberalism flourished in a time of Christian cultural dominance, and was championed by leaders eager to keep pace with modern culture. McLaren and his companions tend to be children of notably conservative churches — in McLaren's case, the Plymouth Brethren — who have never enjoyed, nor aspired to, cultural power. They are also evangelists who care passionately about reaching the unchurched.

McLaren describes his dissatisfaction when he first became a pastor: "My gifts were in evangelism, but I was spending all my time with Christians. Then I encountered Rick Warren and his conviction that the church could be evangelistic. We decided to take 10 months to regroup. Then we reconstituted the church with about 80 Christians — and in a year or so, another hundred previously unchurched people joined us."

If critics overlook the evangelistic energy of the emerging church, they also often lump together two very different kinds of postmodern thought. The most notorious postmodern thinkers have been the "deconstructionists" — French intellectuals like Jacques Derrida and Michel Foucault who seek to show that the cherished ideals of Western society (and Christian faith) are fatally compromised by internal contradictions.

But another stream, less well-known outside universities and seminaries, has taken dissatisfaction with modernity in a more constructive direction. It is these thinkers — the late philosopher Michael Polanyi and Notre Dame professor Alasdair MacIntyre, along with theologians like Newbigin — who are gaining the attention of the emerging church's more theologically inclined leaders.

From Newbigin, McLaren has drawn the idea of the church as "missional" — oriented toward the needs of the world rather than oriented toward its own preservation. From Polanyi and MacIntyre, he concludes that the emerging church must be "monastic" — centered on training disciples who practice, rather than just believe, the faith.

He cites Dallas Willard and Richard Foster, with their emphasis on spiritual disciplines, as key mentors for the emerging church. None of these thinkers has any inclination to throw out the baby of truth with the bathwater of modernity.

Indeed, these constructive postmodernists have been read and appreciated in many evangelical seminaries for years — but their ideas have been more often appreciated than applied. McLaren's innovation was to ask what it would mean to actually live out their ideas in a local church. Like Rob and Kristen Bell, he is passionate about the Good News. He just wonders if there is more to that Good News than evangelicals have yet imagined.

Cultural Collision

At the Emergent Convention in Nashville in April, it becomes clear that McLaren's insistence that "Emergent is not a movement" is not false modesty.

In the cavernous hall of the Nashville Convention Center, jerky loops of handheld video — an urban streetscape, an artist at work, a cross-country ski trail — play continuously on three separate screens throughout each general session. On one side of the room, the ancient and currently fashionable tradition of a prayer labyrinth has been revived, with the addition of bicycles.

At the opening session, Youth Specialties president Mark Oestreicher (hair: two-tone wavy locks) urges attendees to come and go at will, cheerfully undermining the credibility of the proceedings: "A lot of what conference speakers say is not really true — they take 20 years of reality and turn it into 90 minutes of unreality."

Thus prepared, the 800 conference-goers do indeed wander in and out through the videos, poetry, worship music, and plenary speakers, chatting on their cell phones in aimless motion. Like so much of American mass media culture, the overall effect is undeniably cool, but also seemingly designed to aggravate — if not generate — attention deficit disorder.

At the Emergent Convention, emerging theology and emerging culture don't so much coexist as collide, thanks to the somewhat uneasy partnership between Emergent and Youth Specialties. During one particularly experimental worship session, featuring a well-known British DJ (hair: spiked) whose pulsating techno music (complete lyrics: "It's just you and God") builds to a climax that would have played well in pagan Corinth, I find Brian McLaren outside the convention hall.

"I hate it," he says ruefully of the worship music. Another Emergent leader tells a seminar, "The general sessions are a betrayal of everything Emergent stands for."

The truth is that the convention makes it difficult to tell what Emergent does stand for. Even the invited guests seem bewildered. Plenary speaker Robert Webber, whose book *The Younger Evangelicals* celebrates the emerging church, is clearly taken aback by what he sees: "They claim to be rejecting the last 30 years of evangelicalism — and they're repeating the last 30 years of evangelicalism."

Twentysomething writer Lauren Winner, dismayed by the video loops playing incessantly behind her during her address, tells me, "I feel so alienated from my generation."

Hair Today, Gone Tomorrow?

Any movement — or conversation — that can inspire such ambivalence, even among its friends, has an uncertain future. Nor is it easy to quantify the emerging church's present.

McLaren guesses that "only a few dozen" churches across the country are fully committed to the theological journey he sketched in *A New Kind of Christian.* Even Rob Bell did not start that journey until after founding Mars Hill Bible Church. The number of churches whose pastors have cool hair is, of course, much larger — but hardly qualifies as a single movement any more than the number of churches whose pastors wear ties. For the moment, as the Emergent Convention demonstrates, the confusion of style and substance makes for strange bedfellows.

Meanwhile, McLaren's fellow travelers — whether they are dozens or, as Emergent book sales would suggest, tens of thousands — are not the only Christians responding to the challenges of postmodern culture. Manhattan's Redeemer Presbyterian Church attracts several thousand culturally savvy young people with unapologetically Reformed preaching and worship, and churches inspired by Redeemer are thriving in several cities on both coasts.

Catholic journalist Colleen Carroll Campbell has documented the rise of "the new faithful," a growing group of young Americans, often drawn from the same locations and vocations as the emerging church, who are embracing orthodoxy without McLaren's qualifiers.

Implicitly responding to Emergent's disaffection with modern evangelicalism, in March the National Association of Evangelicals attracted more than 200 "young evangelicals" to the inaugural meeting of a network led by Carolyn Haggard, the niece of NAE president Ted Haggard. The 23-year-old Wellesley College graduate says, "The Bible has been relevant for 2,000 years, and popular culture isn't really going to change that. Saying that we're cooler than the generation before, we're more savvy, and we're obviously more intellectual than the generation before — that's not something we'd be at all interested in promoting."

So Emergent has no lock on the next generation. In this respect it may prove no different from the previous Christian movement characterized by male hair, the Jesus Movement. It coexisted, often uneasily, with more cautious expressions of church, was animated by a combination of beautiful ideals and foolish ideas, and ultimately merged into an evangelical mainstream that had adapted to its presence.

But the Jesus Movement, largely composed of converts, was generally unconcerned with theology. Emergent, whose leaders are evangelicalism's own sons and daughters, may yet contribute something more profound than one more fleeting form of cultural relevance.

At least that's what Rob Bell hopes. "People don't get it," he told me. "They think it's about style. But the real question is: What is the gospel?"

That question, of course, is not new. It was asked by, among others, a devout young German monk named Martin Luther who found church increasingly dissatisfying. His answer, rooted in Scripture, changed the direction of Christian history at a moment of epochal cultural change.

Is it possible that a compelling new answer could emerge from McLaren's "conversation"? If so, Bell may have a head start, with props to the apostle Paul.

"Weak is the new strong." The emerging church, and evangelicalism, could do a lot worse.

BRIAN DOYLE

Joyas Voladoras

FROM *American Scholar*

CONSIDER THE HUMMINGBIRD for a long moment. A hummingbird's heart beats ten times a second. A hummingbird's heart is the size of a pencil point. A hummingbird's heart is most of the hummingbird. *Joyas voladoras*, flying jewels, the first white explorers in the Americas called them, and the white men had never seen such creatures, for hummingbirds came into the world only in the Americas, only here, nowhere else in the universe, more than three hundred species of them whirring and zooming and nectaring in hummer time zones nine times removed from ours, their hearts hammering faster than we could clearly hear were our elephantine ears pressed to their infinitesimal chests.

Each one visits a thousand flowers a day. They can dive at sixty miles an hour. They can fly backwards. They can fly more than five hundred miles without pausing to rest. But when they rest, they come close to death: on frigid nights, or when they are starving, they retreat into torpor, their metabolic rate slowing to a fifteenth of their normal sleep rate, their hearts sludging nearly to a halt, barely beating, and if they are not soon warmed, if they do not soon find that which is sweet, their hearts grow cold, and they cease to be. Consider for a moment those hummingbirds who did not open their eyes again today, this very day, in the Americas: bearded helmetcrests and booted racket-tails, violet-tailed sylphs and violet-capped woodnymphs, crimson topazes and purple-crowned fairies, red-tailed comets and amethyst woodstars, rainbow-bearded thornbills and glittering-bellied emeralds, velvet-purple coronets and golden-bellied star-frontlets, fiery-tailed awlbills and Andean hill-stars, spatuletails and pufflegs, each the most amazing thing you have never seen, each thunderous wild heart the size of sand, each mad heart silent, a brilliant music stilled.

Hummingbirds, like all flying birds but more so, have incredible enormous immense ferocious metabolisms. To drive those metabolisms they have race-car hearts that eat oxygen at an eye-popping rate. Their hearts are built of thinner, leaner fibers than ours. Their arteries are stiffer and more taut. They have more mitochondria in their heart muscles. Anything to gulp more oxygen. Their hearts are stripped to the skin for the war against gravity and inertia, the mad search for food, the insane idea of flight. The price of their ambition is a life closer to death; they suffer heart attacks and aneurysms and ruptures more than any other living creature. It's expensive to fly. You burn out. You fry the machine. You melt the engine. Every creature on earth has approximately two billion heartbeats to spend in a lifetime. You can spend them slowly, like a tortoise, and live to be two hundred years old, or you can spend them fast, like a hummingbird, and live to be two years old.

The biggest heart in the world is inside the blue whale. It weighs more than seven tons. It's as big as a room. It *is* a room, with four chambers. A child could walk around in it, head high, bending only to step through the valves. The valves are as big as the swinging doors in a saloon. This house of a heart drives a creature a hundred feet long. When this creature is born, it is twenty feet long and weighs four tons. It is waaaaay bigger than your car. It drinks a hundred gallons of milk from its mama every day and gains two hundred pounds a day and when it is seven or eight years old it endures an unimaginable puberty and then it essentially disappears from human ken, for next to nothing is known of the mating habits, travel patterns, diet, social life, language, social structure, diseases, spirituality, wars, stories, despairs, and arts of the blue whale. There are perhaps ten thousand blue whales in the world, living in every ocean on earth, and of the largest mammal who ever lived we know nearly nothing. But we know this: the animals with the largest heart in the world generally travel in pairs, and their penetrating moaning cries, their piercing yearning tongue, can be heard underwater for miles and miles.

*

Mammals and birds have hearts with four chambers. Reptiles and turtles have hearts with three chambers. Fish have hearts with two chambers. Insects and mollusks have hearts with one chamber. Worms have hearts with one chamber, although they may have as many as eleven one-chambered hearts. Unicellular bacteria have no hearts at all; but even they have fluid eternally in motion, washing from one side of the cell to the other, swirling and whirling. No living being is without interior liquid motion. We all churn inside.

So much held in a heart in a life. So much held in a heart in a day, an hour, a moment. We are utterly open with no one, in the end — not mother and father, not wife or husband, not lover, not child, not friend. We open windows to each, but we live alone in the house of the heart. Perhaps we must. Perhaps we could not bear to be so naked, for fear of a constantly harrowed heart. When young we think there will come one person who will savor and sustain us always; when we are older we know this is the dream of a child, that all hearts finally are bruised and scarred, scored and torn, repaired by time and will, patched by force of character, yet fragile and rickety forevermore, no matter how ferocious the defense and how many bricks you bring to the wall. You can brick up your heart as stout and tight and hard and cold and impregnable as you possibly can and down it comes in an instant, felled by a woman's second glance, a child's apple breath, the shatter of glass in the road, the words *I have something to tell you,* a cat with a broken spine dragging itself into the forest to die, the brush of your mother's papery ancient hand in the thicket of your hair, the memory of your father's voice early in the morning echoing from the kitchen where he is making pancakes for his children.

DAVID JAMES DUNCAN

The French Guy

FROM *Portland*

I WAS RECENTLY ASKED by Earth Ministries of Seattle to speak on the feast day of Saint Francis, October 4. In preparing that talk, I thought it appropriate to say a few words about what sort of man Francis "really was." In trying to capture the Assisian on paper, however, I met with near-complete literary failure.

My failure began with research and notes. I noted, for example, that he was not named Francis. He was named John by his parents, Peter and Pica Bernadone of Assisi, but Peter spent so much time on the road, enriching his already rich self, that he was off trading in France when his son was born, causing mischievous neighbors to nick his son's name to Francesco, which basically means "the French guy."

I researched the saint on-line and found some distressingly cuddly Web sites that called Francis stuff like "the Father of the Ecology Movement." I couldn't see this at all. Francis, for all his love of nature, was consumed not by any kind of ecology but by burning love for Jesus Christ. Francis was not an activist or a contemplative per se, but an active contemplative who could conduct his outer life at full speed without his inner life being overwhelmed or lost. And he was a nonintellectual and a terrible literalist, to wit:

Because Jesus said *Give everything to the poor and follow me,* Francis gave away his home, patents, dignity, lute, hat with the cool feather, and clothes and stood naked as a baby in the public square;

And because Genesis said that God made and blessed all creatures, plants, landforms, and elements, Francis loved them all, including wolves, lizards, snakes, blizzards, volcanoes, rain and lightning storms, and every creepy crawly biting stinging insect, plant, or human on earth, especially those that attacked, and so in his view blessed, the person of Francis himself;

And because the Son of Man had no place to lay his head, Francis refused to own property of any kind, including even sandals to negotiate the stone terrain of Umbria, and so spent his life bare- and bloody-footed, which is to say "blessed" by all those stones.

What most of us might consider our imaginative or prayer or inner lives, Francis considered his vivid, immediate, physical life. The visible body of his boon companion, Jesus, for instance, left this world some twelve hundred years before Francis was even born, reducing lesser men and women to a relationship consisting chiefly of prayer, hymns, or the recitation of old Bible stories. Francis, however, not only prayed and sang to and told stories about Jesus, he talked with and danced for and bowed and babbled to him constantly, like nothing we've seen except the street-mad and bag ladies, really, thanking Christ for every blow received at the hands of thugs, every insult from skeptics and mockers, every pang of hunger, every turn of the weather, especially turns for the worse, every scrap of begged food.

But even old Francis had a body. And in and of this body was a comfort-loving animal, like our own. And there were times in his long marriage to Poverty when his animal body hadn't eaten for days, or even weeks, and was literally starving, so that when Francis and his brothers finally begged a little food, and perhaps cooked it, it smelled so marvelous that, upon bowing over it, even in Christ's presence, poor Francis's eyes would crave the food not only because it was the gift of Christ but because *dang* it smelled *good!* and he was stark raving starvin'! Any "ecologist" I know would thank the earth for its bounty in such a circumstance, and devour the food with utmost happiness. But when this kind of feeling rose in the Assisian saint, his heart stopped him on a dime, *errt!*, stood him up, and sent him to the nearest stove or campfire, where he'd grab a fistful of ashes, return to his lovely food, and sling on the ashes.

Why o why? Perhaps because food topped with ashes is darned hard for mind and body to desire. And desirelessness, said the excommunicated saint Meister Eckhart, is the virgin that eternally gives birth to the Christ. Having preserved this virginity and this birth, Francis lit into his meal with gooey, gray-mouthed relish.

I felt awe for a while on all this. But as Francis's Christ-loving deeds multiplied and the desperation of deed deepened, it occurred to me, in the animal comfort of my study, my clothing, my socks and my shoes, that to give a man as average as me a chance to speak of a man as sublimely love-crazed as Francis is to give that average man a chance to sound like a high-flown platitudinous ninny. Francis's love for his Lord was so ecstatic, creative, physical, and contagious that even though there are things I believe I would die for, I feel, in comparison to this man, that I have hardly begun to love at all. As far as I can see, Francis had no "average" or "everyday" sense of things: for him every creature was a miracle, every moment a gift, every breath a prayer in God's Presence, and if we were sitting with him tonight disbelieving in his miracles, gifts, and Presence completely, he'd go on believing in them so much more powerfully than we bums know how to disbelieve that we would have to run from the room to escape the great gravitational pull of his love.

Feeling all this as I reviewed my meager Feast Day paragraphs, I suddenly felt so lamely literary, so papery, inky, and abstract, that I did something strange: with all the love for the French guy I could muster, I abandoned my computer and office, marched to the kitchen, grabbed a teaspoon, took it in the living room, opened the woodstove, dug out a heaping teaspoonful of ashes, and — hoping to learn at least the flavor, if not the feeling, that Francis once knew well — shoved them in my mouth.

Guess what? I got two more paragraphs out of it.

Paragraph one: The taste wasn't as shocking as I'd feared — at first. Woodstove ashes taste the same way they smell — at first. But the mouth encloses this taste so completely, and your taste buds and salivary glands then greet it so confusedly, that the encounter intensifies, soon taking you places well beyond anything you could detect from the smell. Ashes taste, after you've worked them around in your mouth awhile, like a message from somewhere far beyond this life. The literary part in me wants to say something like "Ashes taste like the most incinerated piece of sixth-circle infernal bowge-meat Dante ever imagined!" But ashes taste like something beyond the literary part of me. A lot of my dear friends and family are ashes today. I began to taste them in the ashes — yet the taste did not sadden me. If I were to put a single word on the flavor in

my mouth, I would say it was that of finality, which has something in
common with eternity — and what eternity is to time, infinity is
to space; and as the great Indian gospel, the Upanishads, long
ago put it, *There is no joy in the finite. There is joy only in the Infinite.*
This joy source, I believe, is why Francis threw ashes on every animal pleasure: he was not a killjoy: he was joy's greatest lover, choosing, each time he threw ashes on the wondrous flavors of food, a
life of no joy but Infinite soul-joy. This equation is way beyond me.
Yet next thing you know I felt joy rising in me, not despite but because of the spoonful of finality/dead friends/eternity/infinity I
had shoved in my mouth.

Paragraph two: But woodstove ashes come in extremely dry, pow-
dery form. And the taste of joy was so surprising to me that though
I didn't quite gasp, I did draw a sharp breath of surprise — and so
inhaled a whole cloud of ash and commenced to cough my lungs
out. I spent the next few minutes at the kitchen sink, discovering
that it's surprisingly hard to wash the deep gray color of Finality
Flavor of *ashes* off your tongue and out of your gums. I also had a
stomachache for reasons I hope the chemists in the crowd will keep
to themselves.

That's the end of my two ashen paragraphs, and the end of my
attempt to fathom the fathomless Assisian in ink upon paper. But I
say this at least with Finality: There will never be an end to Francis's
and yours and my and every living earthling's relationship with
the beauty, finality, eternity, and infinity of regular, normal, there-
they-lie-under-everything ashes. Never. And I taste in this seemingly hard fact a grayish-tongued, paradoxical, yet undeniable hint
of joy.

JEAN BETHKE ELSHTAIN

"You Kill It, You Eat It," and Other Lessons from My Thrifty Childhood

FROM *In Character*

THOSE OF US who were raised by male and female veterans of the Great Depression and World War II walk around with our heads stuffed full of injunctions calling us to thrift. In my own case, these injunctions take the form of my mother's voice enjoining me in a variety of ways.

"Jean, you're cutting off too much of the carrot top. You're wasting too much carrot."

"But Mom," I rejoined, "we've got a garden full of carrots, and the part at the top doesn't taste as good as the rest."

"It's wasteful. Just do as I say. Waste not —"

"I know, 'want not.'" I would complete the nostrum, no doubt rather cheekily, as I can recall my mother's pursed lips and frosty glare following a number of such exchanges.

Habits of thrift extended to every single aspect of our daily lives. We gathered wild asparagus in season, clambering over irrigation ditches, mucking about in thorny underbrush, fighting off mosquitoes in order to break off the succulent asparagus stems. You needed to harvest the wild asparagus before it went to seed. But even after it had gone to seed you harvested it, knowing that the asparagus would be chewy and stringy as you ate it — but eat it we did. "Waste not, want not."

We gathered blueberries off wild blueberry bushes and picked up black walnuts beneath the tree at the home of our "Grandma and Grandpa in the Country." My maternal grandparents, Volga German immigrants, lived on a farm. I lived in a metropolis, Timnath, Colorado, of 185 human souls. Timnath is in the high plains country of northern Colorado. It is an arid climate with a few registered inches of rainfall in a normal year. So you gathered and grew everything you could and as efficiently as you could. The growing season was short, as the earth remained frozen well into spring, given the severity of the Colorado winters.

My sisters and I possessed two pairs of shoes — one for everyday and one for Sunday school. These shoes were worn until they wore out. All our clothes — there were three girls in the family at this point — were made by my mother from flour sacks. Flour used to be purchased in bulk and came packaged in colorful cotton sacks. Once the flour was used, the cotton fabric was washed and ironed and out of it was constructed simple dresses. My mother was an expert seamstress, so our flour-sack dresses often included bits of lace around the collar or other touches that distinguished our outfits. Girls in those days were pretty much obliged to wear dresses — certainly for school they were required. I remember my excitement when, at age ten, I came into possession of my first ever store-bought dress — it was green, with a Peter Pan collar and short, puckered sleeves. I paid for it with my own 4-H Club money that I'd earned from my vegetable garden.

What clothing wasn't handmade was usually hand-me-downs. I was spared a good bit of this as I was the oldest in the large crew of cousins on my mother's side of the family. My sisters, given the luck of the birth order, wore my hand-me-downs, or some from my cousins. And we in turn traded hand-me-downs with them. We were permitted shorts or slacks in the summer. In winter we wore leggings under our dresses and we covered our feet in rubber boots. It was a sin to get your shoes soaking wet, as that impaired their life expectancy.

Our dog, Laddie, fed off table scraps. The notion that you would buy separate food for a dog, no matter how beloved the animal, was out of the question. We just had to remember not to give him soft chicken bones, as they might stick in his craw and choke him. We got our milk from Grandma and Grandpa's farm. It wasn't pasteurized until pasteurization requirements of a legal sort set in. In the summertime, after tomato harvest, my mother, grandmother, Aunt

Mary, and Aunt Martha gathered — with their respective broods
— in the canning cellar, sunk into the ground at Grandma's house,
in order to put up homemade ketchup. I'd enter the cool of the
cellar, but before long, with the steam coming off the huge pot
in which the ketchup mixture stewed, little beads of perspira-
tion formed on my forehead and my bangs got damp. The aroma
was wonderful — tomato with a strong hint of nutmeg and clove,
added to spice up the mixture. This homemade ketchup wasn't as
thick as store-bought, but it was delicate and had a wonderful taste.

Grandma's cellar was also the site of sausage making. Cleaned
and sterile pig gut was placed on a sausage-making device and the
mixture of ground pork, beef, or chicken — all spiced up — was
fed into the gut. Then the long strands were sliced into individual
sausage segments and the gut tied off. My mouth waters to this day
when I think of the liver sausage and German red sausage that
emerged from these day-long efforts. Liver sausage with some of
Grandma's famous rye bread, hot out of the oven and smeared
with her homemade butter, was about as close to heaven as one
could get in a culinary sense. (Although Grandma's butter balls,
floating in golden chicken soup, and her black walnut cookies
made with real butter, of course, gave the sausage and rye bread a
run for their money.)

We only resorted to the grocery store for what was called "essen-
tials": flour, sugar, lard, toilet paper, and Kleenex. You ate vegetables in season. This meant there was about a nine-month hiatus in
between green salads, as you couldn't store lettuce in the root cellar. In my own family's case, this meant a corner of the basement —
which also featured the coal furnace — that was piled high with
dirt. Buried in this dirt, which remained cool but didn't freeze in
the winter, were potatoes, carrots, turnips, and other root vegetables. These, in addition to whatever my mother had canned over
the summer, when it was in season — including string beans, cabbage turned into sauerkraut, and sour dill pickles — provided our
vegetable supply.

Before home freezers were available, sometime well after World
War II, the meat supply was whatever you could keep in the one
frozen food locker in town. This was a huge communal place
where, for a rental fee, you stored freezable perishables — fish and
meat. The fish were trout, blue gill, and sometimes perch. Carp

were plentiful, but they were "bottom feeders," and even for the thrifty were not considered fit to eat. Into the locker went butchered chickens — you butchered them when they had become fryers, though some were permitted to reach the roaster or stewing stage. Grandpa fed the animals until they were butchered and then we bought them from him. The meat was stored in the locker, and my mother or my sisters and I would run down to pick up a package the night before it was destined for dinner.

We saved every bit and piece of string — a practice I challenged repeatedly, as I didn't get the point of it. But each piece of string got wound into the huge string ball my mother kept. We saved every rubber band that came our way. We saved jars and lids. We saved paper bags. One way or another, almost everything was used. When my two brothers came along and the youngest turned out to be a kid who liked to shoot and spear things, my mother announced the rule: "You kill it, you eat it." This included rattlesnakes and squirrels. The frozen-food locker that my parents eventually bought for the house was the stuff of a Stephen King nightmare. Just about every creature known to northern Colorado humankind could be found in a frozen state within it. And yes, even the rattlesnake was consumed. I was away from home by then, so I didn't face the test of whether or not to try the stuff. Like everything else, it allegedly tasted like chicken.

Now, what sorts of claims can be made from this kind of experience? One could simply expand on the descriptions I have already offered of a way of life now long gone and treat it as an exercise in literary memory, larded with nostalgia. Or one could recall with a moral purpose in mind, along these lines: Can the lessons of the normal thriftiness of a half-century ago offer useful and edifying tidbits for our understanding of thrift in the here and now? Can this be done without stretching the point — and without the moral one-upmanship that sometimes characterizes such discussions — that once we were good and now we've become slovenly or even decadent? How does this ideal of thrift embedded in the Colorado village of my childhood hold up in the harsh glare of the present? Is any of it recoupable or even desirable?

The *Oxford English Dictionary* (*OED*) offers as its first definition of *thrift* words that we do not think of ordinarily when thrift comes to mind, namely thriving, prospering, prosperity, and success. That's the first definition. The second lists means of thriving — industry, labor, profitable occupation. Way down on the list, at number three, is the definition that dominates our own cultural consciousness: economical management, economy, sparing use or careful expenditure of means, frugality, saving. Euphemistically, the *OED* continues, parsimony or niggardliness. One might think of an excess of thrift, or niggardliness, as the deformation of what is assuredly a virtue, analogous to the manner in which Aristotle articulated legitimate regimes, like monarchy, and then alerted us to their deformed manifestation, viz., tyranny.

So thrift is both prosperity and that sparing use and economical management which is conducive to prospering. Many would cavil at this as a statement of fact, of course, going on to insist that there are loads of folks who work from dawn to dusk but never prosper. We will not linger over that question, because it is an entirely separate one, involving debates about justice and equity that lie off to the side of our primary concern: What was thrift?

Often thrift is linked historically and culturally to the Protestant Reformation. Max Weber sealed this connection with his enormously influential book *The Protestant Reformation and the Rise of Capitalism*. The book has been much debated by historians, but Weber's connection stuck in the popular mind. Protestantism, with its code of hard work and self-denial — by contrast to late medieval Catholicism, with all those saints' days, massive numbers of days off, and other practices that permitted people to slack off — was and is associated with those qualities that created modern economies, both economic in the strict sense and *moral*.

There is a particular moral economy attached to any understanding of an economy. The Protestant moral economy uplifted and underscored thrift in the meaning the *OED* lists third, namely, a form of good stewardship and of husbanding one's resources, and made that understanding dominant. It required postponing satisfactions, avoiding self-indulgence and romanticism, engaging in salutary forms of self-denial. There is no doubt that such virtues could degenerate into vice — the vice of niggardliness, of a cramped and cribbed, soul-killing spirit. One could never permit oneself a moment in which to slack off, to take it easy, to make oneself pretty (if one were a girl or woman), to drink a bit and to dance, to go to the movies. Or, more accurately, you couldn't do these things without incurring a heavy load of guilt.

I think about this often, given my mother's internalization of the hard-working code of the German-speaking Protestant peasant. There is so much to admire in this that it is painful to think of the excesses of self-denial it also invited. Certainly the virtue of thrift held the Volga German immigrants of my childhood in good stead. They worked from dawn to dusk, they saved, they spent nothing on themselves. The entire family, including very young children, labored long and hard. One of the first surviving photographs of my mother is of a little blond girl on her knees next to her mother, my grandmother, who is, at that moment, standing with a hoe in hand, as they thin sugar beets in a dry, rocky, sun-burnt field in the glare of a northern Colorado sun. She is no older than two.

The downside was this: my mother could scarcely permit herself a moment off. Not to be working was to be slovenly. Whenever she caught me reading a book during the day, she would say, "Jean, get to work." Or "Jean, don't you have anything better to do?" I didn't, of course, but reading a book was not "work" in my mother's definition. It didn't contribute in ways that were palpable to the household economy, and it seemed very, very close to sliding over the edge into that indulgence that was anathema to the moral economy. This habit of thrift served immigrants, like my maternal grandparents and all their children, well. They were able to own their own farms, and by the time the family got to grandchildren, like myself, the expectation was that you would not only complete high school but go on to college. This held for girls and boys alike.

World War II wasn't such a wrench to my mother as it no doubt was to the average middle-class householder, because the savings, the Victory Gardens, the doing without, the rations, were already deeply encoded as her preferred way of life. World War II was just more of the same. The virtue of thrift was a constituent and necessary feature of both worldly success and moral achievement. The proof was in the pudding. Had the person backslid into self-indulgence, perhaps drink and laziness? If so, it would show. He (or she) would lose a farm, or shame himself before the neighbors, or drive his car into a tree. The children of such persons would be screwed up and not know right from wrong.

And eternal life was definitely in jeopardy, unless the person "saw the light" and came around. You do not understand the sort of thrift I am talking about if you try to sever it from religious faith. Thrift was an ethic that flowed from religious conviction. Religious beliefs, in turn, legitimated and secured the virtue itself. These religious beliefs were tethered to certain theological understandings, although I suspect that the vast majority who embraced the beliefs didn't probe too deeply into the theological underpinnings. Specifically, thrift, withholding, certain forms of denial, were linked to crucifixion. God's son made incarnate came to earth, practiced a form of self-denial (for he certainly had the power to take himself down off the cross), all in order to redeem humankind from its sins. The second person of the Trinity figured most importantly in the theology of the thrifty.

If this was thrift, and in our very recent history, what happened to it?

Thrift got a bad name in the 1960s. It was no doubt under pressure well before that, given the unprecedented domestic prosperity of the immediate postwar decade, with pent-up consumer demand gobbling up everything the mighty engine of the U.S. economy, transformed from military to domestic use, could produce. People who never had things could now acquire them: home freezers, electric stoves, big refrigerators, vacuum cleaners, automatic washing machines, and even clothes dryers — allegedly labor-saving devices.

Then came television, and it exploded so remarkably that a decade after its introduction as a consumer item, the TV set was a fixture in the overwhelming majority of American homes. People went to the movies in droves, with one third of the American population going to the movies every single week in the 1950s.

This was also the decade that saw a flight from the farms and villages and into the cities. Fort Collins, Colorado, the nearest "big town" to the village of Timnath, was a bustling town of ten to fifteen thousand when I was growing up. Its population began to explode in the 1950s: twenty-five thousand; then, suddenly, forty-five thousand. (Now it is in the neighborhood of one hundred thousand in the greater Fort Collins area.)

It was hard for the thrifty to grow accustomed to this new wave of buying in the '50s. The way they had done things, always, and continued to do them was to ask, "What do we really need?" And they never bought on credit. You did not get the new stove until you could pay for it outright. Such habits gave way under the relentless assault of advertising. In fact, buying on credit was extolled using the language of thrift: you were helping the economy overall, and you could do otherwise immediately needful and useful things for your family with the cash available that would not otherwise be done unless you purchased items on credit. This was pretty intricate, but somehow it worked for many. Also, traditional religious belief, with its emphasis on the cross and its historic hold on the minds of Protestant Christians, underscored good husbandry and thrift, although the disconnect between this message and the wider culture grew wider and wider as the '50s came to a close.

By the 1960s, even the 1950s pretense of upholding thrift started to break down. Americans were told that it was stupid to deny themselves anything. Thrift was linked to unhealthy self-denial and repression. Herbert Marcuse preached the doctrine of letting it all hang out — doing what you want; the pleasure principle should triumph, not dour Sigmund Freud's "reality principle," which insisted on a tough-minded realism about the world and one's role in it. Nature got romanticized as something we should get closer to, and those who wrested a living from nature — like all those hard-working Volga German immigrants — were represented as harsh exploiters of nature, somehow damaging the earth by using it rather than standing in worshipful repose before it.

Much of this was unintelligible drivel to the immigrant and immediate postimmigrant generation, like my parents and grandparents. I recall my grandfather's — and my mother's — ire when countercultural hippies began to effect the casual rural look by wearing long overalls with their bib tops and metal suspender snaps as they smoked dope and gyrated in serpentine configurations. (These were invariably the images seen on television.) My grandfather knew he was being mocked, and he didn't like it. Those farm overalls represented hard, long days in the harsh sun and remorseless winters. They represented crawling out of bed at 2 A.M. when the water had come in and you needed to switch the rows being irrigated.

The mocking of old habits of thrift, then, took a popular cultural and a more philosophic form. The philosophic form was to insist that thrift made people mean, sexually repressed, and probably conservative. This was the Marcusian hypothesis of "surplus repression." The popular form I have already noted — living for the moment, getting high, hanging out, hanging loose, not getting hung up. Curiously enough, the hippie culture promoted its own form of anticonsumerism, but this didn't flow from a moral economy of thrift. Rather, it derived from a vague animus against "capitalism" and "the system." Acquiring got a bad odor, but consuming triumphed. You could take anything into your body but you should wear shabby or secondhand clothes, fashion your own, swap with others, and so on. The moral economy underlying such cultural habits was that of a particular form of self-indulgence.

There was also, in this era, lots of loose talk about the "greening" of America as part of the back-to-nature movement. Yet again the departure from the older notion of a human relationship to nature tied to the moral economy of thrift could scarcely be more striking. Nature was romanticized frequently as somehow offering an ethic that humans should get closer to. Environmentalism began to enter the popular mind and political discourse but in a variety of often conflicting ways. There were utilitarian approaches: we must conserve or we are all doomed. There were romantic, anti-Christian, pagan sources: nature vs. the machine, what is real vs. what is artificial. Deep ecology asserted an identity between human beings and nature that had somehow been violated along the way as we had become alienated from nature rather than remaining at one with it. None of these environmentalisms — although some of the tasks called for, like recycling, mimed what the thrifty had done a generation or two earlier — relied on the virtue of thrift, however.

The earlier notion of thrift was underscored, as I have argued, by a Protestant moral economy. The new notion of recycling played to utilitarian self-interest and cultural guilt (we are consuming more than our fair share of resources), and got heavily politicized as one feature of a generally left-wing political outlook. To some of us, tying right or left politics to whether or not one recycled cans and newspapers never made a lot of sense, but there it was. My point here is that whatever one finds salutary or unconvincing or even reprehensible about the new environmentalisms, they are not the same as the classic, culturally realized virtue of thrift. The new "thrift" was not a constitutive virtue but the way all *bien pensant* folks did things. One could recycle and pat oneself on the back.

And what happened to Protestant Christianity all this time? At the risk of considerable oversimplification, it got political and went to protest marches. Christians were still called to responsibility, but that took external forms — civil rights, Vietnam, other forms of "oppression" and "exploitation." (I use quotes because of the loose way in which such potent terms often were applied.) The inner moral formation of persons to certain habits, save a kind of "perpetual, flaming rage" at injustice — in philosopher Charles Taylor's locution — dissipated. Confirmation school classes got softer — less theology, more sociology.

Even the extraordinary rise of evangelicalism did little to abate this trend. Of course, many evangelicals are political in quite different ways from those manifested in traditional Protestantism. Contemporary evangelicalism tends to be a religion of the Holy Spirit. The emphasis is on the third person of the Trinity, on being seized personally by God and shown the light. But that light doesn't seem to have anything to do with habits of thrift in the old moral-economy sense. One is still enjoined not to store up riches on this earth, but I don't know of any solid evidence that evangelical young people are less consumer-oriented than young people in general.

The theology underlying thriftiness is gone, and the wider culture eschews it in any case. Evangelical youngsters surely have their hands full trying to stave off the premature and hyped-up sexualization they find all around them, I suspect, and adding thrift to their list of dos and don'ts — unless one counts postponement of sexual gratification a form of thrift — is, or would be, too much to expect.

Americans work longer and harder than any population of people anywhere on the globe, so far as our best sociological data tells us. Indeed, we work like dervishes but in a way disconnected from earlier habits of character. The Protestant part of the work ethic has been severed from the ethic itself. The good at which the work ethic aims nowadays is precisely in the direction of certain forms of self-indulgence, or what would have counted as such to the generations of the thrifty: a bigger house, a fancier car, a longer vacation, designer clothes, tutors for the kids so they get into an elite college, etc.

I am struck daily by all the McMansions going up in and around our neighborhood of modest, good-sized houses in Nashville, Tennessee. Some of these gigantic abodes have gone up on our street, looming in ungainly ways over the modest-sized lots. A person looks at one of these massive structures and wonders if the family has, maybe, eight kids. But no, there is the usual — one point five or two kids. Maybe a dog.

So what is this about? In his 1899 work, *The Theory of the Leisure Class,* Thorstein Veblen spoke of conspicuous consumption, of displaying one's prosperity before one's neighbors. The big house is a status symbol — never mind the fact that most of the rooms will be beautifully decorated but go unused. Never mind that the hard-pressed resources we are supposed to be concerned about are stretched to provide water and energy to these homes. What is on display is not thrift but aggressive wealth. Narcissism, not thrift, is in the air these days.

Can thrift be recovered? Will the thrifty rise again? Probably not — at least not in the classic form I have described. We are too far removed from that way of life. But I do believe we might, as a knowing and explicit cultural project, retrieve some notion of what counts as "enough" — an ideal and virtue long ago lost when thrift went the way of the wringer washing machine. It doesn't seem to be beyond us as a culture to revivify an ideal of knowing how to stop, of resisting cultural and peer pressures as a good, old-fashioned act of American dissent.

But the thorny matter of what shall generate and sustain a new thriftiness remains. If the old thrift was rooted in religion, specifically Protestant Christianity, where will the motor of the new thrift arise? We cannot count on religion, as it too has given way before the ethic of consumption. Save, perhaps, and interestingly enough in light of the history of thrift, within Catholicism. It is within Catholic social teaching that one finds currently the strongest case being made on behalf of what is reasonably called thrift as a theologically grounded virtue. But it will take a lot more than that for flour-sack dresses to come back in style.

MARGARET ERHART

An Entomologist's Dilemma

FROM *Turning Wheel*

EVERY DAY this Buddhist kills something. Many things. And not just thoughts. Creatures. Sentient living beings. Butterflies. Robberflies. Beetles, wasps, bees, spiders, anything soft-shelled or hard that moves, flies, creeps, scuttles, or runs for its life. If I can catch it, I do, in order to kill it. In order to record what lives here, and in what numbers, and what it's eating, and what's eating it. In the interest of science, I carry a special jar for killing — a killing jar, it's called. (When it comes to language, I feel the least I can do is not equivocate.) The jar contains ethyl acetate. Cleaning fluid. I put the hard-bodied insects in the jar and usually I watch them struggle and die. I'd rather not watch them. But it seems the wrong time for that particular preference. Watching them causes me sadness and regret, yet this is a death I have brought them. Chosen to bring them. It seems vital (exactly that word) to witness the consequences of my actions. Catching them also causes me sadness, to arrest motion and then life. The soft-bodied bugs like spiders, or the aquatics like water striders or back-swimmers, I put in a small vial of ethyl alcohol. The butterflies, skippers, and moths go in little glassine envelopes after I've caught them in a net. I catch them and squeeze the thorax, which is the center section of their three-part bodies. I squeeze gently but firmly with the nails of my thumb and forefinger. For the butterflies and small moths this isn't difficult. I feel something in there break (I imagine a tiny rib breaking, though of course butterflies have no such thing), and then the creature is dead, I've killed it. Sometimes nothing happens in me, and sometimes something does. Something always happens in me when I kill skippers, which, like butterflies, have clubbed antennae, but their bodies are large and mothlike. Most of us would just call them butterflies and never know the difference. Except when it comes to killing them. They are hard to kill, hard to squeeze. They have tough bodies, and there is seldom the pop of that imaginary breaking rib. Instead they wiggle their antennae and legs long after I've put them in the envelope. Even when I squeeze them again, they still wiggle. I've taken to placing the envelope inside the killing jar for a few minutes, and even then they are sometimes still moving when I pull them out. Movement I assume to equal life. But does it? The philosophical questions don't interest me while I'm in the middle of killing something. I feel a need to enter right into the killing, yet at the same time I long to keep it separate from me. The use of equipment, the refinement of the method of death, the moving away from causing death with one's own hands — all of this is part of the desire to separate. Just as the remarkable and beautiful face of a butterfly is not called "face," because we want what we kill to be separate from us, not to share this intimate and human feature. The first time I took a long look at a bug's face was four years ago, downstream from Lava Falls on the Colorado River. A tiger beetle. The man who brought it to me (alive) wore thick glasses that enlarged his eyes. The faces tell mind-boggling evolutionary stories, as do the wings, the colors, the mouth parts, the barbed stickiness of the legs. Dragonflies, incredible predators that they are (and hard to catch — they seldom succumb to my predation), have mouths, in their nymph stage, that under a microscope look like earth-moving machinery. The jaw unhinges to accommodate large prey objects. Eat what you can, catch what you can, live while you can. Dragonflies are, for me, the most difficult to kill. More difficult than the most beautiful butterfly. Though I notice in the bug-hunting world the same emotional law as in the bird-and-mammal-hunting world: the larger it is, the harder it is to take its life. As if more size equals more life. Easier, then, to kill a child than an adult? Easier to kill a fetus than a child? In the bug world, the large insects and spiders are harder for me to kill, and the small, numerous drab ones are almost easy. Like shore flies and mosquitoes. Though not ants. I remember the first time I took a good look at an ant. The house that summer was overcome with ants. Some were eating our sugar — not an insoluble problem — but another hidden species was down in the darkness below our feet, chewing away at the house's foundation. So the exterminator came. He brought pamphlets showing how the poison would work its way into the colony and kill it. Pink arrows flowed toward the nest where cartoon ants lay on their backs, feet in the air. When he left I felt unsatisfied. I felt the way I do when I read a newspaper that's too conservative or too liberal. The facts were skewed. The sugar-eating ants were going to die along with the foundation-eaters, and this felt wrong to me. It made me angry. I decided to see what an ant was, before there weren't any left in the house to see. To my astonishment, when I picked one up and put it on a piece of paper and watched it move around, it looked like a tiny horse. It lifted a front leg. It reared back. It settled and put its head down and raised it and did the whole dance again. Tiny horses. I can no longer kill an ant. I've caught dragonflies in my hands when they were trapped inside trying to get out. Is this what makes them hard to kill? The contact? The touch relationship? Or is it their prehistoric nature, the sense of killing elders, killing wisdom, killing continuity? Butterflies are younger. They are a much younger life form. But I've been places where they landed on me (one *Vanessa cardui,* common name painted lady, stayed for more than twenty minutes on my right thigh as I walked up and down a water-filled culvert), and killing would have been impossible. And unnecessary, as the killing's purpose is to record what lives here. "Collecting" is killing for science, but when science lands on your thigh and you can identify it without question, you can record without killing. But "without question" is an ideal, especially for those who classify bugs. Taxonomists, as they are called, are said to believe only a specimen. A photograph, an eyewitness account, an educated guess — often these won't do. When it comes to bugs, the internal characteristics are where the distinctions are made between one subspecies and another. The shape of the reproductive organs is what you have to look at to see what you've actually got. And what do we gain from knowing that this and not that lives here? That this used to live here and no longer does? That that which was scarce is now abundant? The pulse of the environment, that's what bugs are. The patient is healthy, the patient is not. Look at the bugs. They shed light on evolution, genetics, social behavior, geography. They tell us how the land used to look, where old inland lakes used to lie. The killing I do has a purpose and logic to it that most of the time I can live with. But logic is one thing, connection another. My heart still sinks to watch life beat its wings against the glass of the killing jar and die. I hope it will always sink. I hope I will always take notice of these moments of transition, to know that the Great Matter is at hand. I am utterly uncertain that it is right to kill, even knowing why I kill and what these bodies are for and how difficult it is to hear what they have to tell us, exactly what species or subspecies they are, without the convenient stillness death provides. Connection lives outside of logic. Connection, compassion, is in its own way an outlaw activity. To engage in it is to take on relationship, and relationship to what we are about to kill is, as any hunter knows, confusing, strong, both power-ridden and helpless, regretful, gratifying, frightening, mind-opening, heartbreaking, and transformative.

HELEN GARNER

Sighs Too Deep for Words

On Being Bad at Reading the Bible

FROM *Portland*

IT WOULD BE ABSURD to pretend that I have "read the Bible." Ten years ago I sat down with three translations and toiled my way through it, taking months. It was an experience of weird, laborious intensity. But you can't just read the Bible once. All that this endeavor did, in the long run, was to give me a sketchy map of an enormous, madly complicated territory (a map which passing time has blurred and distorted), and to offer certain touchstones of beauty or mystery which I desperately hang on to when life leaks meaning, or which leap spontaneously to mind when I'm "surprised by joy."

Every two months the reading roster from church comes in the mail: a list set out in boxes with dates. A helpful person at the parish office has highlighted my name in pink or green. I never imagined that I would be one of the people who get up and "read the lesson." I used to think that the people who were allowed to do this had something I knew I didn't have: unshakable, worked-out faith. Well — there are people like that at our church. Or that's how they appear, from outside. One morning a woman whose husband, I'd heard, had died only a few days before got to her feet nevertheless to read her part. She held the book out flat in the air in front of her and almost shouted: "The Lord giveth and the Lord taketh away: blessed be the name of the Lord!" Her face was shining, but tears were streaming down it.

*

I have done a fair bit of reading in public; I can get up in most company and read without raising a sweat. But when I have to read the Bible at church, my knees shake and I can hear my voice go squeaky. It's because I have to struggle to get the meaning out of the words, and the meaning is often not clear to me. I like the way the three readings in each communion service — Old Testament, epistle, gospel — are linked thematically. I like sermons in which these linkages are embroidered or explicated. Sometimes I take notes in the margins of the pew sheet. Often I think, "When I get home, I will read these passages again and see what I can make of them." But by the time I get home the concerns of ordinary life have overwhelmed me again and I have forgotten my resolution. And anyway there is always this feeling of intellectual inadequacy: I don't know enough to read the Bible. The job of it is so colossal and complicated and endless; I am already too old; whatever response I come up with will have been shown by some scholar somewhere to be feeble and ignorant — or so my thoughts run.

In the early 1980s, when I wrote theater reviews, there were nights when I had to pinch myself to stay awake through turgid, self-important productions of the classics: my inner thighs were black and blue. But once, long before I realized I was interested in the godly business, I sat in a dark theater while an actor put his elbows on a wooden table with a book open on it and read — or spoke — the Gospel according to Saint Mark. I can't recall the expectations I had of this "performance": just another job, I suppose I thought, and I must have had the critic's notebook on my knee and the pencil in my hand. But Mark's Gospel was such a *story* — so fast and blunt and dramatic, skipping the annunciation, the birth of Jesus, starting with his baptism, rushing headlong to the cross — that by the end I was on the edge of my seat, thrilled and trembling.

When I read in the paper, a few years back, that Rupert Murdoch was buying the publisher Collins, whose biggest seller is the New English Bible, I got hot under the collar.

"Bibles should be handed round in typescript," I said crossly. "Every hotel should have one ragged copy, and if you need it, you call up the desk and they bring it to you on a tray."

"But what if more than one person calls for it?" said a passing skeptic.

"Well — then they invite all of the inquirers into a special room, where they can share it. And maybe talk about why they feel they need it. Have you got a Bible?"

"Yep. A bloke I know gave me one. It's a Gideon."

"You mean it's a stolen Bible? He stole a Gideon?"

"They want you to steal them. That's the whole point of 'em. Isn't it?"

I used to have an American friend who'd been a nun in a French order that started in the Sahara, the Little Sisters of Jesus of Charles de Foucault. She got leukemia, and for a variety of reasons, including the fact that whenever she left the nuns' house for a month or so her blood picture improved, she quit the order and went to live in a caravan on the banks of the Darling River. She came to Sydney one winter, when I lived in someone else's house and couldn't offer her a spare room; but somehow we managed. One morning the excitement of being in the city, plus too much coffee on top of her chemo pills, brought on an attack of enfeebling nausea. She stayed all that day under the quilt on my bed, lying silently behind me in the room, while I sat at my desk and worked. I suppose nuns have to learn how to absent themselves: I felt as if I were alone. Later, when we had set ourselves up for the night, with the French doors open onto the balcony — she with her aching bones in the bed, me with my menopausal ones on a foam strip on the floor — she read me Rilke's "Ninth Duino Elegy." She was such a pragmatic person, I was surprised — not only that she liked the Rilke, but that she read it with such ease: beautifully, with natural feeling for the syntax, so that it made sense as it left her lips.

Look, I am living. On what? Neither childhood nor future grows any smaller . . . Superabundant being wells up in my heart.

We lay there quietly. Then she said, "Read to me in French, Hel."

She passed me her Nouveau Testament: "It belonged to a Little Sister in Peru who died. And they gave her Bible to me because they thought I was going to die too." I opened it at random: *L'annonciation* in *L'evangile selon S. Luc.* ("Yes, read Luke," she said. "He's fairest to women.") *Le sixième mois, l'ange Gabriel fut envoyé par*

Dieu dans une ville de Galilee . . . Salut, comblée de grâce, le seigneur est avec toi . . .

Yes, she did die. Of course she died.

I once interviewed a young woman who had blasted her way out of the Moonies. She told me she had been so brainwashed in the sect that the mere sight of whatever the Moonies' holy book is, a single glance at the arrangement of the print on the page, at its typeface, was enough to flip her back into her state of mental servitude. Nevertheless, I venture to remark that sometimes just picking up a Bible is calming. At other times, though, I only need to see its spine on the shelf to feel sick. Sick with fatigue; with ignorance, and the sullen anger of the ignorant.

I saw at somebody's house a book I coveted: Brown's *Dictionary of the Bible*, an eighteenth-century publication that had come down to this man through his Scottish Calvinist family. I wanted the book because it was a sort of concordance, fanatically useful, with its thin paper and mad tiny print and passion for accuracy; but the thing that drove me crazy with desire to possess it was the first entry my eye fell on: "Grass: the well-known vegetable."

At an Anglican private school one was brought up on the King James version of the Bible. You cannot beat it for grandeur, rolling periods blah blah blah — all the things people want who are reading the Bible, as Auden narkily put it, "for its prose." But a lot of the time, with the King James, you don't actually know what it means.

One day, a long time ago, I picked up J. B. Phillips's 1950s translation of the New Testament. I flipped it open snobbily and came upon a passage in one of the gospels about the arrest of Jesus in the garden of Gethsemane. What I was used to, from schooldays, was along the lines of "they smote him" or "they laid hands on him"; these King James phrases had a dull familiarity that could no longer reach me. But Phillips's text was blunter; it said something like this: "Then they took him outside and beat him." For the first time the story touched the world as I know it. I grasped that he was beaten up, like a man in a police station or a lane behind a nightclub — that he was sent sprawling, that blood came out of his mouth, that his eyes closed under swellings. At that moment the story smashed through a carapace of numbness: it hurt me.

You can't really read the Bible without some sort of help. This is why I need to have at least two translations open at once: the King James, plus an edition that is cross-referenced and copiously annotated. (I like the New Jerusalem, the "Catholic" one.) Here are three versions of the same text, which I mention because once I asked Tim Winton about praying: I said, "I want to do it but I don't know how," and he referred me to Romans 8:26:

> (King James): "Likewise the Spirit also helpeth our infirmities: for we know not what we should pray for as we ought: but the Spirit itself maketh intercession for us with groanings which cannot be uttered."
>
> (New Jerusalem): "And as well as this, the Spirit too comes to help us in our weakness, for, when we do not know how to pray properly, then the Spirit personally makes our petitions for us in groans that cannot be put into words."
>
> (Revised Standard Version): "Likewise the Spirit helps us in our weakness; for we do not know how to pray as we ought, but the Spirit himself intercedes for us with sighs too deep for words."

The third. No contest. Because of the phrase *with sighs too deep for words*.

Cynthia Ozick in a recent *New Yorker* quotes Vladimir Nabokov on what he demanded from translations of poetry: "copious footnotes, footnotes reaching up like skyscrapers . . . I want such footnotes and the absolutely literal sense." That's what I want. Often, though, I can't face it — the studiousness of it. I'm just too tired and impatient and lazy. I have twenty-first-century reading habits: I want to rip along, following the path of narrative. In great stretches of the Bible it's a long way between meanwhiles. You need a different sort of reading style, and most of the time, at home by myself, I lack the discipline.

You can sit down, open the Bible at Genesis chapter one, or Matthew chapter one, or anywhere you like, and start to read. Or you can scan it like a magazine. People do this! I have done it. But the thing is so immense, so complex, so infuriating, that it forces you back on yourself. If you're in the wrong frame of mind — restless, demanding, looking for a quick fix — the book will fight you. It will push hideous violence in your face, or stun you with boredom, or go stiff with familiarity — then just as you're about to give up and put on a load of washing, it will casually tell you, in Exodus, that the God of Israel, when Moses saw him, was standing on "what looked like a sapphire pavement." Or, in Judges, that when Eglun the greedy king of Moab was stabbed, "the fat closed upon the blade." Or, in Bel and the Dragon, of the Apocrypha, that the angel of the Lord took the prophet Habakkuk "by the crown" (still holding the dinner he had just cooked in Judea) "and bare him by the hair of his head, and through the vehemency of his spirit set him in Babylon," right over the lion's den where Daniel had been flung and was lying hungry. Or, in Tobit, that "the boy left with the angel, and the dog followed behind." Or, in John, that Christ came into this world so that people "might have life, and that they might have it more abundantly."

Abundance! And an answer to what Kafka calls "a longing for something greater than all that is fearful."

During the months of first reading the Old Testament I saw *Lawrence of Arabia* again. Four hours of male codes, not a single woman character, and a vast absence of psychological insight. Those desert landscapes, though; the violent tribal life of war and travel . . . Around that time, sick in bed, reading Genesis, I came on this: "Jacob on the other hand was a quiet man, staying at home among the tents." The marvelous visual flash this gives, of what their dwelling was, of how they lived. All these wanderers! Jealous, envious, lustful, cruel — lying and cheating, just like us. And Abraham, when his wife dies, has to buy a piece of land to bury her in!

I shared a house in Melbourne, back in the eighties, with a friend who had recently, as he put it, been "saved." He was, at the time, one of the most maddening people I have ever known. When confronted by life's setbacks, he used to say in a way I heard as smug, "I've got a resource in these matters." I feared he was determined to convert me. He carried a small black New Testament in his shirt pocket wherever he went, and kept the big fat Bible beside him on the dining room table while we ate. I hated this. The book seemed to radiate an ominous, reproachful righteousness. I knew he would have liked to say grace, so as soon as I put the food on the table I picked up my fork and started to eat, to deny him the pleasure. Secretly I longed for grace — to hear it, say it, receive it — but I was too proud to admit to him that my heart was broken, that I was all smashed up inside. And I was damned if I would let him preach to me from his horrible black book.

In our loneliness, that year, he and I used to read aloud to each other. His mild suggestion, once, was the Acts of the Apostles. I stonewalled him, and insisted on Conrad or Henry James. Now I wish I hadn't been so dictatorial and defensive. Years later, when I was happier, I saw a movie with a scene where a couple lie in bed reading the Bible aloud together, for comfort. It filled me with silent longing.

Even now there are days, as I go about my business along certain streets, when my past cruelties, my foolishnesses, my harsh egotisms hang around me like a fog — or, rather, when they haunt me like a pack of cards which offer themselves to my consciousness one by one and with a clever appropriateness, as if a tormentor's mind were actively choosing and shuffling them, so that their juxtapositions are forever fresh, always bright and with a honed, unbearable edge. Because of this I understand and treasure the Bible's repeated imagery of water, of washing; and of the laying down or the handing over of burdens. I like the story of the woman at the well. First, she was a woman. She belonged to the wrong race. She had had five husbands and was living with a man she was not married to, but she was the one Jesus asked to draw water for him. She bandied words with him, but he told her about the other kind of water — the sort that never runs out — the water that he was offering.

A friend once said to me, and now I know what he meant, "Communion — I'd crawl over broken glass to get to it." It's quite simple. You examine yourself, formally, in calm and serious words, together with everyone else in the building; you acknowledge that you have, well, basically stuffed things up again; in the name of Christ you are formally forgiven; and then they say to you, formally, Come up here now, and we'll give you something to eat and drink.

*

Dorothy Sayers: "There is no act, no sermon, no parable in the whole Gospel that borrows its pungency from female perversity."

Well, that's a relief, anyway.

I told Tim Winton that the Holy Spirit was the only aspect of God that had any reality in my personal experience. He wrote to me: "How it works for me (which is all I can honestly go by) is that the stories work on me. That they seem true as stories, and that I believe them. Not just because I accept that their authors are reliable and their witnesses numerous and their repercussions beyond anything I know of in human history . . . but because they convince me emotionally, instinctively. As stories, as lives . . . They ring true to me . . . Probably a matter of imagination, for what else is belief mostly built on."

Martin Buber, according to the editor of his book *The Way of Response,* in dealing with "the immense Hasidic literature, . . . disregarded its intricate theology and concentrated on the folk tales and legends where the heart speaks." Buber himself, about someone reading the scriptures, wrote: "If he is really serious, he . . . can open up to this book and let its rays strike him where they will . . . He does not know which of its sayings and images will overwhelm him and mold him, from where the spirit will ferment and enter into him, to incorporate itself anew in his body. But he holds himself open. He does not believe anything a priori; he does not disbelieve anything a priori. He reads aloud the words written in the book in front of him; he hears the word he utters and it reaches him."

My second sister has a passionate hatred for the parable of the prodigal son. "It's so unfair! And such terrible child-rearing practice!" There's a novel in there somewhere . . . as there is in the Book of Tobit, from the Apocrypha. Ten years had passed between my reading of Tobit and my urging a Jewish friend to read it. He came back a week later pop-eyed: "Fabulous! And the way it ends with the destruction of Nineveh!"

It does?

I had recalled only a tight plot, a boy and a dog, a sad girl with a curse on her, an angel loftily explaining to people who've seen him eating that it was "appearance and no more," and a blessing the father gives to his daughter when she leaves his house: "Go in peace, my daughter. I hope to hear nothing but good of you, as long as I live." That's the blessing I've been longing for all my life, the one I have given up hope of getting from my own father. I need it. I have to have it. What's the destruction of Nineveh, compared with that tender and trusting farewell?

TODD GITLIN

A Skull in Varanasi, a Head in Baghdad

FROM *American Scholar*

VARANASI — the British name was Benares, based on a mispro-
nunciation — is not just any city of gods. Devout Hindus go there,
alongside the sacred Ganges, the better to extricate themselves
from the wheel of rebirth and climb the slippery ladder up and out
of the slog of existence. So this Indian city of one million, of teem-
ing crowds and temples, is renowned for its pilgrims, for immer-
sions, and for cremations.

We drove into town past banyan trees with their multiple trunks,
past men squatting in the fields, past women in saris of startling
brightness bearing water on their heads, past old men pushing
carts bearing huge sacks. The road thickened with animals (cows,
water buffalo, goats) and with trucks and buses carrying passengers
on their roofs, and, as we got closer to the city, with auto-rickshaws
and human-powered rickshaws — our driver scattering them all
with his imperious horn. As the road continued to clot with traffic,
we passed a long truck that had on its roof a long object wrapped in
bright blue, yellow, green, and red ribbons — a corpse, our guide
said, being borne to the burning ghat on the river. A solitary ele-
phant lumbered along. Well, that sort of thing was what we came
for. Why pass this way in the April heat, well to the wrong side of
100 degrees Fahrenheit, if not to be jarred out of the ordinary?

Close to the river, where the lanes thinned and the density grew,
a man squatted in the street in front of another man, choosing
from an array of files, drills, and miscellaneous metal objects. A

dentist practicing his profession, the guide said. Perhaps there was no connection to the natural toothbrushes women were selling: twigs from the useful *nam* tree. There was a profusion of shrines, one after another — sidewalk shrines, roadside shrines. A shiny red statue of a bull outside indicated that the shrine in question was Shiva's, and complicated Shiva, destroyer and lover, is Varanasi's distinct god, singled out from among the Hindus' thousands of gods.

Some pilgrims come to die by the Ganges, their corpses to be dipped in the holy waters, then to be burned. More come to behold.

The Ganges is narrow, the heat intense, the air fragrant, the mood expectant and festive. Brahmins set up their assemblage points, where a ceremony will be performed at sunset: chants, horns, bells, fireworks, flags bearing the word *Om.* Colored stripes are painted on the foreheads of the worshipful. Dozens of young men are selling paint-it-yourself kits and thrusting postcards into the faces of tourists. Cows graze, sit, amble — they're just there, part of the life of the city. Monkeys scamper along a roofline.

Along the bank of the Ganges one ghat abuts another — arrays of concrete steps running from the river up to shrines and palaces built by maharajahs and other worthies. Women in saris are bathing, as are men in loincloths and robes. Prayers, colors, aromas: a profusion of life.

We hire a boat and the boatman makes for the burning ghat — the ghat dedicated to the burning of corpses. Throughout the day and night, there's at least one cremation in progress. Each body is carried along the narrow lanes, past the shops where men squat and chat and women prepare meals, down to the riverbank, there to be immersed and splashed by the mourners, then left on the steps until its turn comes for burning.

Close to the river, three sandalwood fires are flaming atop the concrete. Steps away, by the water, an expanse of bundled wood lies in readiness. Sandalwood smoke cancels the smell of burning hair. No photos, please.

A few feet from us, men are playing cards.

The sun is fading as a priest, using a long bar, smashes at the skull of the dead man to liberate his soul from its temporary prison. It doesn't break easily, the human skull. A woman's pelvis, a man's chest — these are slow to crumble too, and so, if need be, the remains will be buried across the river when the pyre is cleared for the next corpse.

Nearby, a man talks on a mobile phone. Tourists sip soft drinks. Boys scamper around the ghats, selling cremation photos, officially banned. A goat wanders by. Mourners pay no attention. As our boatman rows us away, I count four corpses lying on the concrete steps, waiting their turns.

What did I feel? Wonder. Awe. Exhilaration. Feelings that perhaps should not be examined too closely. Better to buy a little dish with a candle, light it and make a wish, set it afloat on the river.

Bells. *Om.* Say farewell to the sun. The burning goes on.

Not so much has changed in Varanasi, perhaps, since Mark Twain was here 107 years ago, the not-so-innocent abroad, writing thousands of words about sights that struck him as peculiar and, often enough, disgusting. Here he is on the burning ghat (from *Following the Equator*):

> Meantime the corpse is burning, also several others. It is a dismal business. The stokers did not sit down in idleness, but moved briskly about, punching up the fires with long poles, and now and then adding fuel. Sometimes they hoisted the half of a skeleton into the air, then slammed it down and beat it with the pole, breaking it up so that it would burn better. They hoisted skulls up in the same way and banged and battered them. The sight was hard to bear; it would have been harder if the mourners had stayed to witness it. I had but a moderate desire to see a cremation, so it was soon satisfied. For sanitary reasons it would be well if cremation were universal; but this form is revolting, and not to be recommended.

I agree with Twain that "India is a hard country to understand."

I am not religious in any God-attached sense that I can easily explain, let alone defend, but I have long been attracted to the Hindu idea of Brahman: the creative principle that is everywhere, without boundaries, the All, or the Absolute, if you like, a seamless existence where separateness dissolves into a dimension beyond other dimensions — something like the Buddhist no-thing-ness, or maybe not. It is this all-over universal being (F.S.C. Northrop called it the "undifferentiated aesthetic continuum") that many a western pilgrim has sought, often ludicrously, in the East, chasing from ashram to ashram in search of a guru and a paint-by-numbers procedure to relieve him or her of the weight of distinct existence.

I'm not the ashram type; gurus incite my rebelliousness. But the thought of liberating the self from what Auden called "the prison of his days" is an inspiration, and I certainly grasp why for millennia human beings have been tantalized by the fervor to believe that by gathering in the right places and performing the right genuflections and uttering the right sounds and straining from the profane to the intermediate world they call sacred, they could extricate themselves from the bog of the everyday and set themselves on the way toward some firmer, realer, more lasting realm. So the smack of the priest's stick against the recalcitrant skull was a sort of awakening — like the rap of the Zen master's stick on the head of the unenlightened novice, saying, *Wake up, you dumb cluck, to the illusoriness of your ego's illusions! Like it or not, you're at large in the universe, and your consciousness belongs there whether you feel at home or not!* So much for illusions of omnipotence, or omniscience, or omni-endurance. So much for grandeur and arrogance. So much for the white man's burdens.

So, since leaving India, I have continued to think about the burning ghat and the smashing of the skulls. That great leveler: smack! So much for a fine pate reduced to fine ash, or a not-so-fine pate, or any pate at all. So much for the spirit, so much for the brain, so much for the rejoicing nose and tongue, discerning eyes, so much for so much. Pompous as it may sound, the memory of the ghat helps me muse on the weakness of the Cartesian idea of a mind that's been pried, analytically, out of the body; on the damages of monotheism, the peculiar (though in its way wonderful) idea that there is a center to all that happens; and on the benefits of the all-embracing poly- or trans-theism of the Hindus.

No doubt there is a great deal about these beliefs I don't begin to get. But these are the mind's pastimes of an amateur, a curious dilettante.

As it happens, the day I got home, May 8, was the day the decapitated body of the young American Nicholas Berg was discovered

78 TODO GITLIN

in Baghdad. A few days later, a videotape of his beheading surfaced, one of those loathsome artifacts of our time, teasing with its vile promise of horror: the masked kidnappers, the suddenly unsheathed knife, the stop-tape, stop-heart moment when the brutes — no, let's not blame it on animals, let's call them evil men — slaughter an American to demonstrate that they are instillers of terror and destroyers of worlds . . .

And where are the fancy ideas about Western vanity now, the arrogance of persons and the limits of individualism?

Be careful how fast you dispose of the individual self and its pretensions, boy. If the self is no longer inviolable, evil will violate it. And who will there be to judge that this is wrong?

I remain a child of the West, and a grateful one — and even if I weren't grateful, this would be who I am. Inside my skull, which is inside my body, which right now resides inside New York City and formerly traveled to the city of Varanasi in India, on the same earth, inside the same universe, there lives the sole self that I know and that has all the curiosity and limits, all the curiosity about limits, that I have. This small self is the gift, and burden, I have, and am. It is the self who goes out into the world to see how the others live. It is the same self who calls murder murder.

When the Candle Is Blown Out

FROM *Shambhala Sun*

Te-shan asked the old tea-cake woman, "Who is your teacher? Where did you learn this?"

She pointed to a monastery a half-mile away.

Te-shan visited Lung-t'an and questioned him far into the night. Finally, when it was very late, Lung-t'an said, "Why don't you go and rest now?"

Te-shan thanked him and opened the door. "It's dark outside. I can't see."

Lung-t'an lit a candle for him, but just as Te-shan turned and reached out to take it, Lung-t'an blew it out.

At that moment Te-shan had a great enlightenment. Full of gratitude, he bowed deeply to Lung-t'an.

The next day Lung-t'an praised Te-shan to the assembly of monks. Te-shan brought his books and commentaries in front of the building and lit them on fire, saying, "These notes are nothing, like placing a hair in vast space."

Then, bowing again to his teacher, he left.

On a Thursday night I flew into Minneapolis and saw Katagiri Roshi's body laid out in the zendo, dead eighteen hours from a cancer he fought for over a year. It was incomprehensible that I would never see my beloved teacher again.

My father was the only one I knew who had sneered at death's bleak face as he fought in the righteous war that marked his life. Of everyone I knew, he alone did not seem afraid of the great darkness. "Nat, you're here and then you're not. Don't worry about it. It's not a big deal," he told me as he placed a pile of army photos on my lap. "The Japanese, you have to give it to 'em. They could really fight. Tough, good soldiers." Then he held up a black-and-white. "Here's your handsome daddy overseas."

Roshi also fought as a young man in World War II. He told a story about not wanting to kill and shooting in the air above enemy heads. I told that to my father. "What a lot of malarkey," my father sneered. "You don't believe that, do you? You're in battle, you fight."

My father met my teacher only once, about a year after I had married. We had just bought the lower half of a duplex on a leafy tree-lined one-way street six blocks from Zen Center in Minneapolis. I was in my early thirties, and my parents drove out for a week in July. They were still young, in their early sixties.

In the middle of one afternoon when no one was around, we slipped off our shoes and stepped onto the high-shined wooden floor of the zendo. My parents peered at bare white walls, black cushions, and a simple wooden altar with a statue and some flowers.

I heard the door in the hall open. "I bet that's Roshi."

My father's eyes grew wide. His face swung to the large screened window, and for a moment I thought he was going to crash through in a grand escape. Pearls of sweat formed on his upper lip.

Roshi turned the corner. They stood across the room from each other. The meeting was brief. They never shook hands. My father was subdued, withdrawn, and Roshi too wasn't his usual animated self.

I remember thinking, *My father has become shy in front of a Zen master — finally someone tamed him.*

I got it all wrong. He didn't give a shit about that. He had just encountered the enemy face to face. After Roshi exited, he hissed, "I fought them, and now you're studying with them."

"If this were your last moment on earth" — Roshi cut the silence with these words late one night — "how would you sit?" We were waiting for the bell to ring. It was the end of a week-long retreat. Our knees and backs ached. The candle flame hissed; the smell of incense from Eiheiji monastery (the Japanese training center for Soto Zen), shipped in cartons to Minnesota, soaked our clothes.

You've got to be kidding. Just ring the damn bell was the only thought that raced through my head.

On other occasions when he asked similar questions, my mind froze. Me, die? Not possible.

Death was something aesthetic, artistic; it had to do with the grand words *forever, eternity, emptiness.* I never had known anyone who had died before. It was merely a practice point: everything is impermanent. Sure, sure. But really it was inconceivable that my body would not be my body. I was lean, young, and everything worked. I had a name, an identity: Natalie Goldberg.

What a shock it was for me to see my great teacher's stiff body. This was for real? The man I had studied with for twelve years was gone? Stars, moon, hope stopped. Ocean waves and ants froze. Even rocks would not grow. This truth I could not bear.

I was guided by three great teachings I received from him:

Continue under All Circumstances.
Don't Be Tossed Away — Don't Let Anything Stop You.
Make Positive Effort for the Good.

The last one Roshi told me when I was divorcing and couldn't get out of bed.

"If nothing else, get up and brush your teeth." He paused. "I can never get up when the alarm goes off. Nevertheless," he nodded, "I get up."

Once in the early days I was perplexed about trees. I asked at the end of a lecture, "Roshi, do the elms suffer?"

He answered.

"What? Could you tell me again? Do they really suffer?" I couldn't take it in.

He shot back his reply.

It pinged off my forehead and did not penetrate. I was caught in thinking mind, too busy trying to understand everything.

But my confusion had drive. I raised my hand a third time. "Roshi, just once more. I don't get it. I mean do trees really suffer."

He looked straight at me. "Shut up."

That went in.

The amazing thing was I did not take it personally. He was directly commanding my monkey mind to stop. I'd already been studying with him for a while. Those two words were a relief. Dead end. Quit. I rested back into my sitting position and felt my breath go in and out at my nose. The thought about trees that evening stopped grabbing me by the throat.

With him extraneous things were cut away. My life force stepped forward. After a sleepy childhood I was seen and understood. Glory! Glory! I had found a great teacher in the deep north of this country. Maybe that had been the purpose of my short marriage: to bring me here. Both Roshi and I did not belong in Minnesota, yet we had found each other.

I positioned Roshi in the deep gash I had in my heart. He took the place of loneliness and desolation, and with him as a bolster I felt whole. But the deal was he had to stay alive, continue existing, for this configuration to work.

The third year after his death was the worst in my life. Our process had been cut short. In a healthy teacher-student relationship, the teacher calls out of the student a large vision of what is possible. I finally dared to feel the great true dream I had inside. I projected it onto this person who was my teacher. This projection was part of spiritual development. It allowed me to discover the largeness of my own psyche, but it wasn't based on some illusion. Roshi possessed many of these projected qualities, but each student was individual. When I asked other practitioners what impressed them about Katagiri Roshi, the reported qualities were different for each person. One woman in Santa Cruz admired his unerring self-confidence. She stood up and imitated his physical stance. She said that even when no one understood his English and we weren't sure of the Buddhist concepts he discussed, he bowed in front of the altar and walked out after his lecture as though all time and the universe were backing him.

I'd never even taken note of that. What I loved was his enthusiasm, his ability to be in the moment and not judge and categorize me. He had a great sense of humor. I admired his dedication to practice and to all beings and his willingness to tell me the truth, with no effort to sweeten it.

Eventually, as the teacher-student relationship matures, the student manifests these qualities herself and learns to stand on her own two feet. The projections are reclaimed. What we saw in him is also inside us. We close the gap between who we think the teacher is and who we think we are not. We become whole.

Roshi died before this process was finished. I felt like a green fruit. I still needed the sun, the rain, the nutrients of the tree. Instead, the great oak withered; I dangled for a while and then fell to the ground, very undernourished.

How many of us get to live out the full maturation process? Our modern lives are built on speed. We move fast, never settle. Most of us grab what we can, a little from here, then there. For twelve years I had one source. I should have been satisfied. He gave me everything. I knew that when I saw his dead body, but how to live it inside myself?

This projection process also can get more complicated if we haven't individuated from our original parents. Then we present to the teacher those undeveloped parts too. Here the teacher needs to be savvy, alert, and committed in order to avoid taking advantage of vulnerable students. I have read about Zen ancestors who practiced with their teachers for forty years in a single monastery, and I understand why. There would be no half-baked characters in those ancient lineages.

But, oddly enough, Te-shan had only that one meeting with Lung-t'an, and he woke up. Of course, he was a serious scholar of the dharma for a long time. Who is to say scholarly pursuits — studying books intently and writing commentary — don't prepare the mind as well as sweeping bamboo-lined walkways, sitting long hours, or preparing monastery meals?

Zen training is physical. But what isn't physical while we have a body on this earth? Sitting bent over books, our eyes following a line of print, is physical too. So that when Te-shan had that single evening in Lung-t'an's room, he was already very ripe. Lung-t'an merely had to push him off the tree, and Te-shan was prepared to fall into the tremendous empty dark with no clinging.

Te-shan was shown true darkness when Lung-t'an blew out the light; he held at last a dharma candle to guide his way, but he still had a lot of maturation ahead of him. Don't forget the next morning he made that grandiose gesture of burning his books in front of the assembly of monks. He was still acting out, choosing this and leaving that. He was not yet able to honor his whole journey, to respect everything that brought him to this moment. Te-shan still envisioned things in dualistic terms: now only direct insight mattered; books needed to be destroyed. He didn't see that all those years of study had created a foundation that supported his awakening with Lung-t'an. Originally he traveled from the north with his sutras on his back to enlighten the southern barbarians. Here he was doing a complete reversal, torching his past and revering his present experience. Someday he would embrace the north and the south, unify all of China in his heart, and attain a peaceful mind. But he was not there yet. We see him engaged in drama, presenting a flaming pageant in front of the other monks.

His life has not yet settled and become calm.

After he left Lung-t'an, he wandered for a long time, looking to be tested and sharpened. He already had left his place in northern China to wander among what he thought were the southern barbarians. He might be the precursor to our fractured American way of searching for peace.

How can anyone survive if the way is so splintered? What we learn is it's all whole, been whole all along. It is our perception that is broken and that creates a shattered world. But each of us has to discover this in our own lives. That is what is so hard.

"I wish you'd gotten to meet him," I'd tell writing students.

"We are," they'd say, meaning they did through knowing me.

I scoffed. "You don't know what you're talking about."

At a party in San Francisco, Ed Brown, a longtime Zen practitioner and author of many books, pulled me over. "Nat, I have another story about Katagiri for you to steal."

I laughed. I'd asked his permission and acknowledged him with the last one I used. I put my arm around him. "Sure, Ed, give it to me. I'd love to steal from you again."

He began, "I'd been practicing for twenty years when the thought suddenly came to me, 'Ed, maybe you can just hear what your heart is saying. You can be quiet and pay attention to yourself.' It was a big moment of relief for me. Tears filled my eyes."

He showed me with his fingers how they fell down his cheeks. "I'd tried so hard all my life. Made such effort, lived in a monastery since I was young. And now this. Could it be that simple?

"The next day I had an interview with Katagiri. I asked him, 'Do you think it's okay to just listen to yourself?'

"He looked down, then he looked up. 'Ed, I tried very hard to practice Dogen's Zen. After twenty years I realized there was no Dogen's Zen.'"

Dogen was a strict patriarch from thirteenth-century Japan. We chanted his words each morning. He was a yardstick by which we measured ourselves.

I felt my legs buckle. I reached out for the back of a chair. Just us. No heaven Zen in some Asian sky out there.

I put my hand on Ed's shoulder. "Ed, I vow to once again misappropriate your story." He nodded, satisfied.

I was reminded again how simple, sincere, earnest Roshi was. I was happy, and then it ignited my anger. I was mad he died. I had found the perfect teacher.

I tried practicing other places. I did two fall practice periods at Green Gulch, part of the San Francisco Zen Center. While I was there, an old student told me about the early years at the Zen monastery in Carmel Valley.

Tassajara was in a narrow valley. The sun didn't reach it until late morning, rising over an eastern mountain, and it dropped early behind the slope of a western one. The practice was difficult, and the days and nights were frigid and damp. But American students of the late sixties were fervent about this path to liberate their lives. One particular winter retreat, which lasted for a hundred days, was being led by Katagiri, fresh from Japan.

One young zealous woman, a fierce practitioner, a bit Zen-crazed, was having a hard time. She was full of resistance when the four o'clock wake-up bell rang on the fifth day of *Rohatsu sesshin,* an intense week that honored Buddha's enlightenment and signaled almost the finish of the long retreat. Practice that day would again be from four-thirty in the morning until ten at night, with few breaks except for short walking meditations and an hour work period after lunch. It was her turn that morning to carry the *kyosaku,* that long narrow board administered in the zendo to sleepy students' shoulders. Her hands were frayed and her bare feet were ice on the cold wooden floor when she got there. She picked up the wake-up stick and passed quietly by the altar to do the ritual bow to Katagiri, the head teacher, who was facing into the room. The flame on the candle was strong. The incense wafted through the air. The practitioners were settled onto their cushions, facing out toward the wall.

A thought inflamed her just as she was about to bow in front of Katagiri: *It's easy for him. He's Asian. He's been doing this all his life. It's second nature. His body just folds into position.*

Though it is a rule of retreat that people do not look at each other, in order to limit social interaction and provide psychic space for going deeply within, at this moment she glanced up at Roshi.

She was stunned to see pearls of sweat forming on his upper lip. Only one reason he could have been perspiring in this frozen zendo: great effort. It wasn't any easier for him than anyone else. Was she ever wrong in her assumptions. She had gotten close enough to see what no one was supposed to see. All her rage and stereotyping crumbled.

My heart jumped. I imagined the small hard dark hairs above his lip — he did not shave for the whole week during *sesshins*. I recalled the shadow building on his cheeks and shaved head as the days went on, how he bowed with his hands pressed together in front of him, elbows out and shoulders erect. His small beautiful foot as he placed a step on the floor during walking meditation. Though retreats were austere, singular, solitary, there was also a rare intimacy that was shared in silence and practice together.

Just two weeks before the end of my second Green Gulch retreat, in December 1995, almost six years after Katagiri Roshi had died, in a stunning moment in the zendo that shot through me like a hot steel bolt, I realized that this regimented practice no longer fit me. The known world blanked out, and I was lost in the moving weight of a waterfall. For me, the structure was Katagiri Roshi. I learned it all from him. If I stepped out of it, I'd lose my great teacher. I knew how to wake at four o'clock in the morning, to sit still for forty-minute periods, to eat with three bowls in concentration, but it was over — other parts of me needed care. Structure had saved my life, given me a foundation, and now it was cracking. It was a big opening, but I wasn't up to it.

Roshi was the youngest of six children. His mother barely had time for him. He'd spoken fondly of the single hour that he once had with her when she took him shopping. No other brothers and sisters. Just the heaven of his mother all to himself.

My mother was mostly absent in my life, not because she was busy but because she was vacant. She woke in the morning, put on her girdle, straight wool skirt, and cashmere sweater, and then sat in a chair in her bedroom, staring out the window.

"Mom, I'm sick and want to stay home from school."

"That's fine."

The next day I wrote the absentee note for the teacher, and she signed without glancing at it. I was hungrier than I knew. I wanted someone to contact me, even if it was simply to say, "Natalie, you are not sick. That wouldn't be honest. As a matter of fact, you look lovely today." As a kid I needed a reflection of my existence, that I was indeed here on this earth. The attention I received from my father was invasive and uncomfortable. I hoped at least for my mother's affirmation, but there wasn't any.

Roshi was the one person who directly spoke to this hunger. When I went in for *dokusan* (an individual face-to-face interview with the teacher), we sat cross-legged on cushions, opposite each other. He wasn't distracted, "aggravated," or impatient. He was right there, which inspired me to meet him in that moment. I had friends, acquaintances I interacted with, and we sat facing each other across luncheon tables, but this was a man whose life's work was to arrive in the present. The effect was stunning. Life seemed to beam out of every cell in his body. His facial expressions were animated.

I could ask him a question, and he would respond from no stuck, formulated place. I think it was the constant awareness of emptiness: that although this cushion, this floor, this person in front of you, and you yourself are here, it isn't of permanent duration. Knowing this in his bones and muscles, not just as a philosophical idea, allowed him a spontaneity and honesty.

"Roshi, now that I am divorced, it is very lonely."

"Tell me. What do you do when you are alone in the house?"

I'd never thought of that. I became interested. "Well, I water the plants." I faltered, then continued, "I wash a few dishes, call a friend." The momentum built. "I sit on the couch for hours and stare at the bare branches out the window. I play over and over Paul Simon's new album about New Mexico — I miss it there."

His attention encouraged me. "Lately, I've been sitting at my dining room table and painting little pictures." I looked at him. Suddenly my solitary life had a texture.

"Is there anything wrong with loneliness?" he asked in a low voice.

I shook my head. All at once I saw it was a natural condition of life, like sadness, grief, even joy. When I was sitting with him, it didn't feel ominous or unbearable.

"Anyone who wants to go to the source is lonely. There are many people at Zen Center. Those who are practicing deeply are only with themselves."

"Are you lonely?" I entreated.

"Yes." He nodded. "But I don't let it toss me away. It's just loneliness."

"Do you ever get over it?"

"I take an ice-cold shower every morning. I never get used to it. It shocks me each time, but I've learned to stand up in it." He pointed at me. "Can you stand up in loneliness?"

He continued, "Being alone is the terminal abode. You can't go any deeper in your practice if you run from it."

He spoke to me evenly, honestly. My hunger was satiated — the ignored little girl still inside me and the adult seeker, both were nourished.

I understood that Roshi too had been neglected in his childhood.

Even though he had tremendous perseverance, he was human, with needs and desires. All of us want something — even the vastly wise like a good cookie with their tea and delight in good-quality tea. Maybe it was that very perseverance that broke him. He couldn't keep it up, and his human needs leaked out. "Continue under all circumstances," he barked out, so often that that dictum penetrated even my lazy mind and became a strong tool for my life. But as I grew older I understood its drawbacks: if you are crossing a street and a semi is coming, step aside. If you have hemorrhoids, don't push the sitting; take a hot bath. That one tactic — perseverance — can put you on a dead-end road, and then what do you do? Continue to march deep into a blind alley?

Touching Roshi's frailty finally brought him closer to me, unraveled my solid grief. At the end of January I had a painful backache that lasted all day. At midnight in my flannel pajamas I got up out of bed, went to the window, and looked out at the star-studded, clear, cold night sky with Taos Mountain in the distance.

"Where are you? Come back!" I demanded. "We have things to settle."

I let out a scream that cracked the dark, but one raw fact did not change: nothing made him return, and I was left to make sense of his life — and mine.

MARY GORDON

Appetite for the Absolute

FROM *Portland*

WHATEVER ELSE IT WAS, and it was many things, the flying of a plane, two planes, into the towers of the World Trade Center on September 11, 2001, was an act committed in the name of God.

And whatever else they are, the suicide bombers of Palestine are men and women acting in the name of God, a God who they believe will reward them for their deaths with the gift of paradise.

And whatever else these events create, and they create much, mostly products of darkness, they should awake terrible questions in those of us who harbor, however fleetingly, tentatively, ambivalently, a belief in God, a hope for the reality of God, for those of us who shape a life, however irregularly, however haphazardly, however frantically, around a center that is a yearning for the face of an eternal God.

So I write this only to raise questions, questions born of anguish and shame, of self-doubt, of fear.

I cannot write this without questioning whether I have chosen to repress or ignore or minimize the reality that the forces of religion have been linked, throughout history and up to the present moment, with the forces not only of repression but of relentless bloodletting.

I must ask myself if engaging in the kinds of speculation I am doing here, describing acts of terrorism as being motivated by an appetite for an absolute, might be enraging to someone who has lost someone precious. I understand how it would seem as if I thought of these acts not as if they were acts that shattered flesh, stopped breath, stole life, but as a series of ideas. What would be the good of this kind of questioning? Only another step in the thinking person's road to paralysis?

But I glimpse, if dimly, a glimmer of a hope that in a time where there are no good answers, or when answers arrived at too quickly might bring in their wake more death, perhaps standing still and questioning the incomprehensible may lead to a fuller understanding of what is to be done.

I live with the possibility that what I am saying is nonsense, and what needs to be done is best not considered, is the work of swift and brutal action taken to stop further death because the cold reality is that the Other wants only our deaths and this is all that we can focus on.

I do not know.

I only know that when people call the acts of suicide bombers incomprehensible, I cannot agree with them, because these kinds of extreme acts are entirely comprehensible to me.

I do not for a moment excuse them. I mean simply that I understand the flavor of desperation turned to exultation. I understand what it could be like to imagine that a living body is less important than a threat to the homage due to the Lord of All. And the source of my understanding is precisely the history and experience of my own religious life, and my having been steeped in the centuries-old tradition of Roman Catholicism.

Certainly I understand the inner life of a suicide bomber much better than I understand the inner life of, say, Donald Trump. That is to say, I understand the flavor of wanting to give up your life for an ideal that seems greater than yourself, that seems eternally valuable and true, even though it results in death, far better than I understand wanting more cars than you can drive, more houses than you have time to live in, more suits than you have places to wear them to, more pneumatic blondes than you can remember the names of. I can only imagine the life of Donald Trump as a kind of living death.

But what does it mean about me that I find Osama bin Laden easier to understand than Donald Trump?

However true this is, it may sound flip: bin Laden is responsible for the deaths of thousands and Donald Trump is not. I am simply saying that I find bin Laden's beliefs a grotesquely and murderously perverted version of beliefs I once held, and in some sense still do. Certainly the impulse toward self-sacrifice was imbibed by me, if not with mother's milk, then with my first communion wine.

What is the source of this impulse to sacrifice? Why do we imagine the divine glories in death? Although the Old Testament tells us that God does not require burnt offerings, the entire shape of Christianity is based on a death, the offering of a life for something larger than itself. The offering of the visible to the invisible, of the living body to what is beyond the body. *Greater love than this no man hath but that he lay down his life for his friend.* I grew up with those words drumming constantly in my brain; it made me feel that as long as I was alive, I hadn't done enough. As a child, I believed that I was meant to pray for what was called the grace of a martyr's death. I was meant to pray that if the Russian Communists held a gun to my head and demanded that I deny Christ, I would gratefully have my brains splattered all over the streets of Long Island.

The secular world provided fantasies for martyrdom as well. Mine were concerned with Hitler, dead before my birth. I used to fantasize about parachuting into the bunker, killing Hitler, gladly being shot by brownshirts for the sake of having saved Anne Frank.

I was terribly afraid of dying a martyr's death and yet fascinated by the martyrs, particularly the virgin martyrs of the early Christian days. It was the clarity of the statement of such a death that was appealing. A martyr, we were told, went straight to heaven. Leading an ordinary life, dying an ordinary death, brought no such guarantees. Each day I began with the ideal of perfection. On days when I went to daily mass, I would try to keep myself from distraction during the whole of the mass, to keep my back perfectly straight when I knelt, to fold my hands perfectly on the way back from communion. But I couldn't even get through one daily mass — however short, and a really efficient priest could do it in fifteen minutes — without some sort of failure of attention, some lapse of posture. During the Lent of my twelfth year, I decided I should practice the penance of saying the daily office while walking around with thorns in my shoes. But I couldn't get through even one prayer without walking on the sides of my feet, like Jerry Lewis, to try to avoid having my soles pierced by the thorns. I had to live with the reality of the gaps between my fantasies of my self and my practice. My practice was full of lapses. But a martyr's death had no lapses; it was clarity only, perfection insured. A kind of impermeable cover over the porous element of human life.

But why should we want such a cover? Why is the porosity of human life, its imperfectability, to some natures intolerable?

It cannot be denied that people who are attracted to a religious way of looking at the world are attracted as well to something that is beyond the human, beyond what could be called human self-interest, beyond what is thought to be the most essential instinct of all animals: the instinct for self-preservation; therefore, most importantly perhaps, beyond death. Beyond the failures of the body, of desires, of will. Beyond what most people would think of as this life. Even if one's religious perspective has no place in it for life after death, the impulse to worship is at least a hope that there is something other than what our senses can apprehend.

Does this otherness necessarily have in it the flavor of the absolute? And what do we mean by absolute? The dictionary defines it in this way: perfect in quality or nature; complete, not mixed; pure; not limited by restrictions or exceptions, unconditional, unqualified in extent or degree; total, unconstrained by constitutional or other provisions, not to be doubted or questioned; positive, something regarded as the ultimate basis of all thought and being, something regarded as independent of and unrelated to anything else. When I read this dictionary definition, I am struck by its enormous mysteriousness. Not that it is difficult to understand. The mystery stems from the fact that it is not difficult to understand, that it is entirely comprehensible.

Where did we get our idea of the absolute? Why is it that the complete, the unmixed, the unlimited by restrictions or exceptions, the unconditional, the unqualified in extent or degree is an accessible concept to most minds? For the unmixed, the unqualified, the unconstrained do not exist in nature. Nothing alive is only one thing: nothing alive is unconstrained or unqualified. Nothing observable is immune to change; even supposedly imperishable stone is susceptible to fire; stars, even planets burn up and die; all that is most dear to us is dear to us because of its variety. "Glory be to God for dappled things," says Gerard Manley Hopkins. The lover of absolute oneness is not the lover of the brindled cow that the poet treasures. Hopkins reminds us that the changeable, the movable, the mixed is our lot and that we, and they, in our mixedness, Praise Him.

Where, then, did we get this taste for what we have not known? What is the appeal of pure mathematics, of formal art, both of which suggest a series of forms or relationships that are immune from change, therefore from death? Is the only way that we can come to understand our hunger for the absolute to find analogies, similes, metaphors? Is our appetite for the absolute something like our appetite for beauty, for sex, for sleep — these states in which the *I* seems to disappear? How can it be that these experiences of losing the self are seen by us not as frightening but as desirable, perhaps the things we live for, or that we need to live by? "Our souls were made for God," Saint Augustine says, "and will not rest until they find their rest in thee." But what kind of creatures are we to find our satisfaction in that which we can have access to only by giving up our creaturely life?

It is very easy to mock or condemn the appetite for the absolute. To call it a fear of life, a love of death. I may be accused of stretching a point, and I do not for a moment blur the distinction between giving up one's own life and taking the lives of others, but I would like to speculate that Glenn Gould driving himself to illness unto death in an attempt to achieve a perfect Goldberg Variations, Mark Rothko killing himself over his failure to realize a perfect melding of color and form, and the murderers who killed in Allah's name taste the same flavors, hear the same tonalities, with wildly different results.

What artists and murderers have in common is an impulse, a yearning to give up the self in favor of something larger, a perfection only imagined, never achieved, never unachievable.

Consider Dostoyevsky's *The Brothers Karamazov*. The section of the novel that I will focus on here is a section that is often excerpted, read independently, the chapter of the novel called "The Grand Inquisitor." But it is important, I think, to put the section in its context. "The Grand Inquisitor" is a tale composed by Ivan Karamazov, the freethinking rationalist brother. It occurs during a conversation between Ivan and his brother Alyosha, the saintly young monk.

Ivan asserts his refusal to bend the knee to God because of the suffering of children. He cannot forgive, he will not worship a God who allows innocent children to suffer. He presents a catalogue of atrocities committed against children, and insists that these atrocities cannot be forgiven, even by the children themselves.

Alyosha counters that it is only Jesus who can forgive such heinous acts, because he too was an innocent whose blood was shed; only he chose the shedding of his own blood for the salvation of the world.

In response to the mention of Christ, Ivan recites what he calls his poem of the Grand Inquisitor. It is a tale set during the Spanish Inquisition. Jesus has come back to earth and is performing good works in the town of Seville, in the grips of the most ferocious of inquisitorial practices. He cures the sick, raises the dead. The Grand Inquisitor, in authority in the town, finds this unacceptable. He arrests Jesus and then accuses him, sitting across from him in a jail cell, of having loved human beings insufficiently by having burdened them with not the gift but the curse of freedom. Human beings, he declares, are not up to freedom, it only causes them unhappiness. Jesus' terrible error, the cause of centuries of human suffering, was in having refused the three temptations in the desert: to turn stone into bread, to throw himself down from the temple, and to lay claim to earthly kingdom. The Inquisitor accuses him of having rejected three things that human beings crave and need: miracle, mystery, authority.

The Grand Inquisitor tells Jesus that people want nothing more than to give up their freedom, that they will jump at the chance to do it. "For the mystery of man's being is not only in living, but in what one lives for," he tells Jesus. "Without a firm idea of what he lives for, man will not consent to live and will sooner destroy himself than remain on earth, even if there is bread all around him . . . Did you forget that peace and even death are dearer to man than free choice in the knowledge of good and evil? There is nothing more seductive for man than the freedom of his conscience, but there is nothing more tormenting either. And so, instead of a firm foundation for appeasing human conscience once and for all, you chose everything that was unusual, enigmatic, and indefinite, you chose everything that was beyond men's strength and thereby acted as if you did not love them at all.

"All that man seeks on earth: someone to bow down to, someone to take over his conscience . . ."

And the Grand Inquisitor tells Jesus that for the love of the people, he will put Jesus to death. All during the Inquisitor's accusations, Jesus has sat silent and still. Finally he gets up and kisses the Inquisitor on the lips. The Inquisitor allows him to leave but orders him to depart forever, and does not change his mind.

For Jesus promises a reward in absolute, not human, time. Is it possible, then, to be a Christian without an appetite for the absolute? In what sense would one be a Christian if she were unwilling to admit the pull of the impulse to worship? And could one properly use the word *worship* in relation to a being whose difference from oneself was only a matter of degree? If one bends the knee or bows the head, to what is one inclining? What kind of Christian is possible who does not admit of a relationship to a being entirely other, unmovable by death and time?

"Who is it you say I am?" Christ asked, and two thousand years later the question is fresh, crucial.

If we cannot excise the Jesus who tells us to pluck out the eye that offends, who seems to reject the exception, the vague, the flexible, we must also come to terms with another problematical Jesus, the paradoxical one, who wrote mysterious words in the sand to the woman taken in adultery and seemed to be advising Judas to forget about the poor in favor of ointment.

Is it not possible then that we can find in the often contradictory figure of Jesus, in the character (and I use the word deliberately) made known to us in the gospels, and the stories centered around this character (the story of the prodigal son, of the woman taken in adultery, the miracle of the loaves and fishes), the complexity that would save us from our impulses to tyranny and murder?

Is it possible that we might find in the gospels' comedy (the woman who won't take no for an answer and nudges Jesus into miracle, Zaccheus shy in the treetops, Peter the braggart panicking as he tries to walk on water like his Lord, Jesus the crabby son, annoyed that his mother wants him to turn water into wine) the leaven that will keep the mystery and authority that the Grand Inquisitor says we need from being always in the service of death?

Comedy and contradiction: it is this that makes the gospels possible as story; it is this that marks the central doctrine of Christianity: the incarnation. What could be more contradictory, more anti-ideal, than the notion of the word made flesh?

The incarnation insists on a theology of mixture. The word is made flesh. The flesh does not disappear; nor does it become word. Word becomes flesh. Flesh would seem to triumph, to absorb the abstract. Can we then be Christians without honoring the flesh?

But an absolutist feels he or she is freeing himself from the limitations of the flesh. Is the taste for the absolute an escape from what we really are?

I have no way of knowing what the source of the appetite is. We may very well find out in time that it is genetic, or chemical, the product of a gland's work — as some scientists say the religious impulse might be. But what would the world be if some future geneticist, rightly fearing the bloodletting that seems to be its handmaiden, excised the gene for the absolute from the pool, or if each baby upon birth was required to have the appropriate gland amputated? Even if the religion gland were removed, would atrocities committed in the name of the absolute disappear? Consider the atrocities committed in the name of a Nazi, Fascist, or Marxist absolute, no less atrocious for being irreligious. And consider this question as well: If life is to be lived only for what is pleasant but not dangerous, entertaining but not difficult, profitable but not extravagant, a world of self-protectiveness and self-regarding, a world in which the eye is always on the self's most immediate interests, where not too much is ever put at stake . . . if life is to be lived that way, what kind of life is it?

What do we live for if there is nothing we would die for?

Could it be that this is one of our tasks as Christians, to maintain our appetite for the absolute while realizing that it is not our primary realm while we are alive, that it is a realm we can honor, even hunger for, but should not seek to participate in regularly while we are living in our bodies? Rather, that we should look upon it fleetingly, as we do the sun, to hunger for it, to require it, as we do the sun's light, and then to cast our eyes down to the earth, the earth populated by creatures of flesh and blood? To vary our gazes, to move from Beethoven to the Beatles, from Shakespeare to Wilde, from Vermeer to Majolica, from the mountain to the garden — to refresh ourselves by what is clearly made by the human hand. Refreshed, reinforced by the comic and the mixed. In this, could we cast our lot with the Jesus who insists on the freedom of the will, on a gift freely given, whose response to his executioners is silence and a kiss?

What would happen if we staked our lives on belief in an absolute love rather than absolute power?

If we bent the knee to an idea of absolute forgiveness rather than absolute retribution?

Power and retribution are solid and bounded; love and forgiveness are amorphous and mysterious. But is it not these amorphous mysteries that render earth a place of life rather than death?

Miracle, mystery, and authority, the Grand Inquisitor asserts, are the three needs of human beings. Is it not our task, as people of faith, to search after and witness to true miracle, mystery, and authority, to discern the difference between these and trickery, mystification, and tyranny, with which they are so often confused?

We live in murderous times. Might it be the proper work of those of us who say we are people of faith to use the Light of the World to illumine the path that leads to the Lord who is the Lord of life?

Who lived, not that we should die, not that we should have perfection, or even only the promise of eternity, but that we should have, for the time that we are in our bodies, *life:* mixed, vexed, conditional, relational, tragic, comic. All that it is. Life.

PATRICIA HAMPL

Pilgrim

FROM *Granta*

I ASKED TO BE TAKEN TO A HOSPITAL. I was possibly dying, and thought I should say so. Our guide, roaming the hotel to round up his charges for the morning tour, looked down where I had flung myself on a low padded bench against a wall in the pretentious lobby, and laughed out loud. Hooted. Then he turned and walked away, down the desert-colored marble corridor that swam with gold light.

I had been stricken suddenly. The day before we had "done" Masada, stopping first to float in the creepy buoyancy of the Dead Sea. Then back on the bus, passing Qumran but not stopping to see the caves where, in 1947, Bedouin shepherd boys looking for a stray goat had found the Dead Sea Scrolls rolled up in ancient amphoras. I had walked without trouble to the top of the Masada citadel, surveyed Herod's realm in the high wind, and imagined the Roman armies advancing mercilessly across the open plain. Our guide described the mass suicide of the Jewish forces as they faced certain Roman victory. This is the landscape, I thought, that gave religion God "out of the whirlwind."

While we all stared out, stung with elegiac sentiments, our guide murmured — as if it were a minor footnote of no great matter — that "the historians" now dispute the suicide story. A legend, he told us airily, but a beautiful one, yes? Then, his usual gesture — a finger tapping his gold wristwatch on his upraised arm. We must get back down to the bus.

Later, at the hotel, drinks on the terrace as the setting sun turned the baked gold of East Jerusalem sweetly pink. Everything we looked at from the Hilton terrace on King David Street was an-

cient except for the hotel, built to mimic the old stone. And ourselves, sitting with our vodka tonics.

But now, without warning, this swoon just after breakfast. My
eyes ached all along the optic nerve, my body was no longer mine.
Waves of nausea hit me. I held the sides of the bench so I wouldn't
be pitched overboard, swept off in a stream of murky gold liquid
that was — I could still make the connection with part of my mind
— also the main floor lobby of the Jerusalem Hilton. I closed my
eyes and turned to the wall like an old peasant in a hut whose time
has come.

Our guide, who had told us he had fought in the Six-Day War
and who had a wry leathery face I had liked until our last ex-
change, returned. He touched my shoulder. He held out a can of
Sprite. "Drink this," he said. He made me sit up, which I thought
was extremely unwise.

Then he was gone, but other people, members of the "friendship
mission" I was part of, gathered around. They too urged the Sprite
on me, and then, apparently reassured, one by one they left for the
bus. Two women I had been avoiding during the trip, for complex
reasons I could no longer recall, stayed behind. They sat down
wonderfully close, one on either side of me, stationed like abut-
ments holding up my wobbly span. I drank the Sprite. They too insisted. I mentioned the hospital again — and heard with shame
that I was whimpering.

Oh no, no hospital, I was told with a pat, though neither one of
the women laughed, thank God, the way the veteran of the Six-Day
War had laughed.

These women I had not liked assured me that I wasn't dying.
They spoke with the same brisk certainty they had used several days
earlier when, over drinks on the Hilton terrace with its heart-stop-
ping views of the everlasting hills of the Old City, they had attested
stoutly to their atheism as to a matter of basic hygiene. Culture —
yes, they had said. But religion? A ruinous mixture of nonsense and
trouble. Evil, one had said.

Now, hips snug against my own, they displayed an unmistakable
lack of alarm about my situation, drifting away from my desperation to chat about the day's itinerary. We were going to Caesarea,
we would see the Roman aqueduct. A good lunch was promised. I
sipped the Sprite, peevishly thinking, *Nobody takes me seriously.*

I was dehydrated, one of the women was saying. It was not serious. It could be serious, but it wasn't. Not yet. Finish the Sprite. I tried to explain that I wasn't thirsty, that I couldn't be dehydrated. I indicated my water bottle. We all drank prodigious quantities of water. This is a desert, remember, we kept telling each other.

"Electrolytes," the heavier woman said. "Your electrolytes are out of whack. It happens in the desert." She was a museum curator but spoke as one accustomed to sandstorms, camels, and dry, blowing nights, though all of us were from Minnesota, where the license plates read LAND OF 10,000 LAKES.

She went somewhere and came back with another Sprite. She snapped open the can and handed it to me. As I raised it to drink, the sweet fizz of carbonation sprayed my face, and a collision of ecstasy and shame struck me as my mind and my body, lost lovers, found each other again in an instant. I saw in a saving flash that I had been wrong, that the war veteran tour guide and the two kindly atheists were right. I wasn't dying. Feeling the grainy champagne of Sprite spark through me, I was distinctly not dying.

Perhaps the shock of disorientation with its tincture of fear renewed my spirit on this guided trip through Israel and as far as Petra in Jordan. "What gives value to travel," Camus said, "is fear." Like most people, I prefer to think of myself as an independent traveler, not given to group tours. Yet I had gladly joined, when invited, this busload of American midwestern "community leaders and artists" (the two categories being understood as mutually exclusive). A junket to the ancient place, stage set of history and myth I had grown up calling, from years of Catholic schooling, the Holyland.

It was before the second — and still current — intifada, and I think all of us on our big bus felt safe — safe enough to have come in the first place. It was still possible to see "incidents" as separate, widely spaced, unlikely. We didn't talk about our safety. We discussed the politics of the region as if everything were either in the past (violent, impossible) or somewhere in the future (hopeful, though indistinct). None of us really knew anything about it.

We had toured around Israel and Jordan with stops at opposing camps for the past week. The Palestinian mayor of Bethlehem gave us sweet dense coffee in minute, intensely patterned cups passed from a brass tray in a second-floor office where a ceiling fan whirled slowly, as if in a scene from *Casablanca*. He seemed to think we were influential in some way, and he gave us more time than any of the Israeli officials did, speaking with great courtesy, without bitterness, appealing to our better selves as he described the situation.

Later we visited an American Israeli householder in his American-style suburban house, a bland air-conditioned split-level in a subdivision he insisted on calling a settlement. He handed around a huge container of Coke and plastic cups. Out the window we could see a fenced area where Palestinian families were camping in a kind of shantytown of tarps and sagging cardboard.

Camels and SUVs, the persimmon walls of Petra, the depressing vacancy of emotion I felt at the Church of the Holy Sepulcher, the groaning buffet tables of the Israeli hotels, the conservative Catholic op-ed page writer from Minneapolis who said loudly to the Holocaust survivor before we were taken to tour Yad Vashem, "I'm not going along if this is intended to make me feel guilty."

Group tourism, in other words. By the time I collapsed in the Hilton lobby, I had reached a stress point of crabbiness, a sense of being held hostage by our handlers, a feeling of being . . . well, a tourist. Worse, a functionary in the middle management of culture, greedy hands across the cultural divide. Why had I come? I was furious with myself for going on this freebie junket, my paw held out for experience, a gluttony like any other.

Tourism, that dishonored if massively indulged modern habit, bears its voyeuristic taint with a shrug. We all want to go . . . elsewhere. We all want to see . . . what's there. Much has been written in recent years about the toxic nature of "the gaze" — the man staring boldly at the woman, the vacationing rich gawking at the local-color poor, the unfair advantage of being the observer. Yet what does the world come to if *to look*, that once unabashed gesture, is understood to be an evil? Even Adam and Eve were allowed to gaze at the Tree and its fruit, after all. They were even instructed to enjoy it — an object to be regarded, if not touched or tasted. The world's first museum moment — if we'd just left it at that. But who does just leave it? We keep reaching, eating up the world.

That afternoon, after our handlers had returned us from our round of gawking in Caesarea, the gentle atheist who had given me back my life in a can of soda pop invited me to go with her while everyone else napped. She wanted to visit the souk in East Jerusalem. Perhaps to shake my sour antisocial feeling, perhaps because I was still wary of being alone, I went along, trotting beside her purposeful self like a good pet.

Her appetite for our trip was still lively, lacking my fussy annoyance, and the souk was an easy walk from the hotel. She had a camera, a fancy one she had been wielding the past week wherever we went. A person with an eye sharp for detail, her curiosity buoyant and benign. I could tag along with her, could maybe silence my inner grumble and rise again to the occasion of travel, the pure act of looking. In any case, I was still a little wobbly, and she was my angel.

There was the feeling of *entering* the souk, as if the narrow streets constituted a sort of crumbling ancestral house, the streets being in effect corridors leading to chambers that were somehow secretly attached, all belonging to one large, breathing self, an organism of architecture. Passageways along the open stalls gave way here and there to little coffee shops, each embedded like a fossil under a building's arch. The market radiated a satisfying paradox, as if permanence and flimsiness met in an eternal congruence that held everything mysteriously together.

It was deeply satisfying to walk along the passageways, taking in the ancient buildings where people still lived in dark, cool, cavelike apartments, the collapsible-looking market stalls on the ground floor spilling into the walkways, their corrugated roofs sloping, creating dusky interiors. Produce and wares were piled along the common hallways of the streets.

We allowed ourselves to get lost, reassured by the landscape of fruits and vegetables, the sharp sniff of coffee, the dust of sugar from the sweets on display, milled chickpeas, baskets of speckled beans, lacquered olives in stone vats. Narrow shops displayed bright woven fabrics — a heavily embroidered gown that seemed to contain all of Araby and flimsy silks lofting in the breeze like delicate soutanes. Clothes of the desert.

A double row of Palestinian men carried aloft a long dark shape on a pallet — a body on the way to burial: they turned between two buildings and were gone with their package held above their heads. We saw — I did, anyway — smiles gleaming behind the display tables, eyes sizing us up: no sale to these hotel dwellers. But mostly it was just the vegetables and us, the pleasure of passing along the brilliant stalls as if through a pure element without any meaning beyond the delight of color.

Then my companion came to a halt, seized by the display of a spice merchant. We were in the densest part of the souk, surrounded by stalls before us and behind us, the passageway turning to yet more mounds and baskets. But this was *the picture* for her. She asked me to hold her bag for a moment while she snapped it. "I just have to get all this color," she said. And it was wonderful — the deep saturated dye of turmeric, a hypnotic yellow having nothing to do with the sun, belonging entirely to the mineral earth, sumac crushed to powder like pulverized red wine, baskets of color so intense they were delicious already, just looking at them. She put her face close to the fragrant surface, drawing in scents.

I reached for her bag as she had instructed. As I bent down, I saw the face of the boy standing behind the table full of spices. He could not have been more than twelve. I felt my own face begin to move into its let's-be-friends tourist smile — *Your spices are beautiful.* My companion lifted the camera to her pale face, aimed down at the palette of color. The boy was shaking his head, saying something, frowning. He was becoming agitated. It took me a moment to understand he didn't want her to take the photograph. She saw nothing, her head down and focused on what she had framed.

It happened fast. Which is to say slowly, in the endless way of moments that will be inscribed in memory. The boy said something harsh, and finding no hope of getting the attention of the woman taking the picture, he turned to me. He said something again, hissed across the dazzling table of his wares. Then he spat. A sharp, targeted bullet of projectile fury. It hit me sharp in the eye, exactly where he intended, I think.

He did not turn away, did not look abashed. Calm descended. I knew with that uncanny knowing of real experience — *Ah, so this is why I came, for this.* Real travel wants to be dangerous, wants to smoke out the truth of the Other — providing, of course, you get out alive. I put my hand to my face, astonished, my fingers damp with his thick wrath.

BROOKS HAXTON

Gift

FROM *Atlantic Monthly*

> All our righteousnesses are as filthy rags;
> and we all do fade as a leaf
> — Isaiah 64:6

After my mother's father died,
she gave me his morocco Bible.
I took it from her hand, and saw
the gold was worn away, the binding
scuffed and ragged, split below the spine,
and inside, smudges where her father's
right hand gripped the bottom corner
page by page, an old man waiting, not quite
reading the words he had known by heart
for sixty years: our parents in the garden,
naked, free from shame; the bitterness of labor;
blood in the ground, still calling for God's
curse. His thumbprints faded after the flood,
to darken again where God bids Moses smite
the rock, and then again in Psalms, in Matthew
every page. And where Paul speaks of things
God hath prepared, things promised them who wait,
things not yet entered into the loving heart,
below the margin of the verse, the paper
is translucent with the oil and dark
still with the dirt of his right hand.

EDWARD HIRSCH

Self-Portrait

FROM *The New Yorker*

I lived between my heart and my head,
like a married couple who can't get along.

I lived between my left arm, which is swift
and sinister, and my right, which is righteous.

I lived between a laugh and a scowl,
and voted against myself, a two-party system.

My left leg dawdled or danced along,
my right cleaved to the straight and narrow.

My left shoulder was like a stripper on vacation,
my right stood upright as a Roman soldier.

Let's just say that my left side was the organ
donor and leave my private parts alone,

but as for my eyes, which are two shades
of brown, well, Dionysus meet Apollo.

Look at Eve raising her left eyebrow
while Adam puts his right foot down.

No one expected it to survive,
but divorce seemed out of the question.

I suppose my left hand and my right hand
will be clasped over my chest in the coffin

and I'll be reconciled at last,
I'll be whole again.

CHARLES JOHNSON

Dr. King's Refrigerator

FROM *StoryQuarterly*

IN SEPTEMBER, the year of Our Lord 1954, a gifted young minister from Atlanta named Martin Luther King Jr. accepted his first pastorate at the Dexter Avenue Baptist Church in Montgomery, Alabama. He was twenty-five-years old, and in the language of the academy he took his first job when he was ABD at Boston University's School of Theology — All But Dissertation — which is a common and necessary practice for scholars who have completed their coursework and have families to feed. If you are offered a job when still in graduate school, you snatch it, and if all goes well, you finish the thesis that first year of your employment when you are in the thick of things, trying mightily to prove — in Martin's case — to the staid, high-toned laity at Dexter that you really are worth the $4,800 salary they are paying you. He had, by the way, the highest-paying job of any minister in the city of Montgomery, and the expectations for his daily performance — as a pastor, husband, community leader, and the son of Daddy King — were equally high.

But what few people tell the eager ABD is how completing the doctorate from a distance means wall-to-wall work. There were always meetings with the local NAACP, ministers' organizations, and church committees; or, failing that, the budget and treasury to balance; or, failing that, the sick to visit in their homes, the ordination of deacons to preside over, and a new sermon to write every week. During that first year away from Boston, he delivered forty-six sermons to his congregation, and twenty sermons and lectures at other colleges and churches in the South. And, dutifully, he got up every morning at 5:30 to spend three hours composing the thesis in his parsonage, a white frame house with a railed-in front porch and two oak trees in the yard, after which he devoted another three hours to it late at night, in addition to spending sixteen hours each week on his Sunday sermons.

On the Wednesday night of December first, exactly one year before Rosa Parks refused to give up her bus seat, and after a long day of meetings, writing memos and letters, he sat entrenched behind a roll-top desk in his cluttered den at five minutes past midnight, smoking cigarettes and drinking black coffee, wearing an old fisherman's knit sweater, his desk barricaded in by books and piles of paperwork. Naturally, his in-progress dissertation, "A Comparison of the Conceptions of God in the Thinking of Paul Tillich and Henry Nelson Wieman," was itching at the edge of his mind, but what he really needed this night was a theme for his sermon on Sunday. Usually by Tuesday Martin at least had a sketch, by Wednesday he had his research and citations — which ranged freely over five thousand years of eastern and western philosophy — compiled on note cards, and by Friday he was writing his text on a pad of lined yellow paper. Put bluntly, he was two days behind schedule.

A few rooms away, his wife was sleeping under a blue corduroy bedspread. For an instant he thought of giving up work for the night and climbing into sheets warmed by her body, curling up beside this heartbreakingly beautiful and very understanding woman, a graduate of the New England Conservatory of Music, who had sacrificed her career back East in order to follow him into the Deep South. He remembered their wedding night on June 18 a year ago, in Perry County, Alabama, and how the insanity of segregation meant that he and his new bride could not stay in a hotel operated by whites. Instead they spent their wedding night at a black funeral home and had no honeymoon at all. Yes, he probably should join her in their bedroom. He wondered if she resented how his academic and theological duties took him away from her and their home (many an ABD's marriage ended before the dissertation was done) — work like that infernal, unwritten sermon, which hung over his head like the sword of Damocles.

Weary, feeling guilty, he pushed back from his desk, stretched out his stiff spine, and decided to get a midnight snack.

Now, he knew he shouldn't do that, of course. He often told

friends that food was his greatest weakness. His ideal weight in college was 150 pounds, and he was aware that, at five feet, seven inches tall, he should not eat between meals. His bantam weight ballooned easily. Moreover, he'd read somewhere that the average American will in his (or her) lifetime eat 60,000 pounds of food. To Martin's ethical way of thinking, consuming that much tonnage was downright obscene, given the fact that there was so much famine and poverty throughout the rest of the world. He made himself a promise — a small prayer — to eat just a little, only enough tonight to replenish his tissues.

He made his way cautiously through the dark seven-room house, his footsteps echoing on the hardwood floors as if he were in a swimming pool, scuffing from the smoke-filled den to the living room, where he circled round the baby grand piano his wife practiced on for church recitals, then past her choices in decorations — two African masks on one wall and West Indian gourds on the mantle above the fireplace — to the kitchen. There, he clicked on the overhead light and drew open the door to their refrigerator.

Scratching his stomach, he gazed — and gazed — at four well-stocked shelves of food. He saw a Florida grapefruit and a California orange. On one of the middle shelves he saw corn and squash, both native to North America, and introduced by Indians to Europe in the fifteenth century through Columbus. To the right of that, his eyes tracked bright yellow slices of pineapple from Hawaii, truffles from England, and a half-eaten Mexican tortilla. Martin took a step back, cocking his head to one side, less hungry now than curious about what his wife had found at public market and stacked inside their refrigerator without telling him.

He began to empty the refrigerator and the heavily packed food cabinets, placing everything on the table and kitchen counter and, when those were filled, on the flower-printed linoleum floor, taking things out slowly at first, his eyes squinted, scrutinizing each item like an old woman on a fixed budget at the bargain table in a grocery store. Then he worked quickly, bewitched, chuckling to himself as he tore apart his wife's tidy, well-scrubbed, Christian kitchen. He removed all the beryline olives from a thick glass jar and held each one up to the light, as if perhaps he'd never really seen an olive before, or seen one so clearly. Of one thing he was sure: no two olives were the same. Within fifteen minutes, Martin stood surrounded by a galaxy of food.

From one corner of the kitchen floor to the other, there were popular American items such as pumpkin pie and hot dogs, but also heavy, sour-sweet dishes like German sauerkraut and schnitzel right beside Tibetan rice, one of the staples of the Far East, all sorts of spices, and the macaroni, spaghetti, and ravioli favored by Italians. There were bricks of cheese and wine from French vineyards, coffee from Brazil, and from China and India black and green teas that probably had been carried from fields to faraway markets on the heads of women or the backs of donkeys, horses, and mules.

All of human culture, history, and civilization scrolled at his feet, and he had only to step into his kitchen to discover it. No one people or tribe, living in one place on this planet, could produce the endless riches for the palate that he'd just pulled from his refrigerator. He looked around the disheveled room, and he saw in each succulent fruit, each loaf of bread, and each grain of rice a fragile, inescapable network of mutuality in which all earthly creatures were codependent, integrated, and tied in a single garment of destiny. He recalled Exodus 25:30, and realized that all this before him was showbread. From the floor Martin picked up a Golden Delicious apple, took a bite from it, and instantly he prehended the haze of heat from summers past, the roots of the tree from which the fruit was taken, the cycles of sun and rain and seasons, the earth and even those who tended the orchard. Then he slowly put the apple down, feeling not so much hunger now as a profound indebtedness and thanksgiving — to everyone and everything in Creation. For was not he too the product of infinite causes and the full, miraculous orchestration of Being stretching back to the beginning of time?

At that moment his wife came into the disaster area that was their kitchen, half asleep, wearing blue slippers and an old housecoat over her nightgown. When she saw what her philosopher husband had done, she said *Oh!* and promptly disappeared from the room. A moment later she was back, having composed herself, though her voice was barely above a whisper: "Are you all right?"

"Of course I am! I've never felt better!" he said. "The whole universe is inside our refrigerator!"

She blinked. "Really? You don't mean that, do you? Honey, have you been drinking? I've told you time and again that orange juice and vodka you like so much isn't good for you, and if anyone at church smells it on your breath . . ."

"If you must know, I was hard at work on my thesis an hour ago. I didn't drink a drop of anything — except coffee."

"Well, that explains," she said.

"No, you don't understand! I was trying to write my speech for Sunday, but — but — I couldn't think of anything, and I got hungry . . ."

She stared at food heaped on the floor. "This hungry?"

"Well, no." His mouth wobbled, and now he was no longer thinking about the metaphysics of food but instead how the mess he'd made must look through her eyes. And, more important, how *he* must look through her eyes. "I think I've got my sermon, or at least something I might use later. It's so obvious to me now!" He could tell by the tilt of her head and the twitching of her nose that she didn't think any of this was obvious at all. "When we get up in the morning, we go into the bathroom, where we reach for a sponge provided for us by a Pacific Islander. We reach for soap created by a Frenchman. The towel is provided by a Turk. Before we leave for our jobs, we are beholden to more than half the world."

"Yes, dear." She sighed. "I can see that, but what about my kitchen? You *know* I'm hosting the Ladies' Prayer Circle today at eight o'clock. That's seven hours from now. Please tell me you're going to clean up everything before you go to bed."

"But I have a sermon to write! What I'm saying — trying to say — is that whatever affects one directly affects all indirectly!"

"Oh, yes, I'm sure all this is going to have a remarkable effect on the Ladies' Prayer Circle . . ."

"Sweetheart . . ." He held up a grapefruit and a head of lettuce. "I had a revelation tonight. Do you know how rare that is? Those things don't come easy. Just ask Meister Eckhart or Martin Luther — you know Luther experienced enlightenment on the toilet, don't you? Ministers only get maybe one or two revelations in a lifetime. But you made it possible for me to have a vision when I opened the refrigerator." All at once, he had a discomforting thought. "How much did you spend for groceries last week?"

"I bought extra things for the Ladies' Prayer Circle," she said. "Don't ask how much and I won't ask why you've turned the kitchen inside out." Gracefully, like an angel, or the perfect wife in the Book of Proverbs, she stepped toward him over cans and containers, plates of leftovers and bowls of chili. She placed her hand on his cheek, like a mother might do with her gifted and exasperating child, a prodigy who had just torched his bedroom in a scientific experiment. Then she wrapped her arms around him, slipped her hands under his sweater, and gave him a kiss. Stepping back, she touched the tip of his nose with her finger and turned to leave. "Don't stay up too late," she said. "Put everything back before it spoils. And come to bed — I'll be waiting."

Martin watched her leave and said, "Yes, dear," still holding a very spiritually understood grapefruit in one hand and an ontologically clarified head of lettuce in the other. He started putting back everything on the shelves, deciding as he did so that while his sermon could wait until morning, his new wife definitely should not.

MARIA POGGI JOHNSON

Us and Them

FROM *First Things*

SIX MONTHS OUT OF GRAD SCHOOL and into our first jobs, my husband and I fell in love with a house, a beautiful, eccentric Victorian. It was, of course, a fixer-upper, with a few caved-in ceilings, and it stood on a block that might be called borderline — there were some neglected houses nearby with bad landlords and worse tenants, a certain amount of drug activity, and there had been a shooting across the road the month before. This was why we could afford the house. On the plus side, there were a number of long-established stable families, and on the next block was a synagogue that was the center of a growing community of strictly observant Orthodox Jews. We persuaded ourselves that things couldn't get too bad, took a gamble, and bought the house.

Not only did things not get bad, they got very good indeed. Seven years later, the fixing-up is far from complete, but we have welcomed four babies into our home among the paint pots and half-built bookcases, and the block, now free of trouble spots, has welcomed four new Orthodox Jewish families with twenty-three children among them. There is a thriving and cohesive community on our street, and to our surprise we have been cheerfully welcomed into many aspects of its life. We've been invited to numerous festive meals (of course, we could not return the favor, although my husband's single-malt scotch has been enthusiastically pronounced kosher), we have joined in neighborhood patrols when there was a spate of vandalism against the *succahs,* we have performed the office of what I believe is called a *Shabbos goy,* which involves setting the timer on an Orthodox family's heat and lights for the Sabbath when they forget to do so. We have taken our turn with the scissors when Binyomin had his first haircut at his third birthday party, and we have spent many hours sitting on doorsteps chatting idly and watching children practice riding tricycles. Having become good friends with a couple of families has made us automatically acquaintances of all the Orthodox in the neighborhood: children wave to me and mothers greet me when I walk past the Hebrew day school on my way to the office. We only wish that the sense of community among the Christians we know could rival what we have experienced among Orthodox Jews.

Living on the fringes of such a strong community is intriguing and deeply appealing in itself, and, of course, for us as Christians the fact that it is a Jewish community, intensely and vividly Jewish, is particularly meaningful. My theological views are much what they were — I'm a theologian by profession and had a pretty good handle on the whole law/gospel/covenant thing at a theoretical level — but my grasp of and relation to my own faith has been altered profoundly by living on familiar terms with a religious reality that precedes and underpins my own, even as it differs dramatically. The imaginative and emotional resonances of the Holy Week liturgies and the Eucharist, to give just two examples, are deepened by the fact that I have friends for whom the phrase "paschal lamb" refers to what one eats on Passover.

Another effect has been the way I teach the introductory Bible course that all students at my university are required to take. When teaching about Mount Sinai, the law, and the covenant, for instance, I can fulfill my responsibilities as a Catholic and a scholar, be faithful to the teaching of *Dei Verbum,* and meet the departmental objectives for the course if I (attempt to) help my students to understand the law both as an ancient Near Eastern legal, social, and ritual code and as a revelation of the character and will of God and a key stage in the salvation history that culminates in the coming of Christ. And before living in this neighborhood I might have felt that that was plenty. But now I feel I have not told my students the whole story unless I can get them to see a little of what I have learned from living in a place where the law is not a historical relic or a preliminary stage in the plot of a larger story but something vividly and vigorously alive in every aspect of life.

When possible, I invite a good friend to talk to my students about the law in her daily life. Initially she talked mainly about kosher laws and the Sabbath, but after coming to class a few times she got the measure of the students' reaction and now mischievously enjoys watching their jaws drop in disbelief as she describes dating and marriage, sex and modesty in Orthodox communities. They are fascinated and bewildered by the notion of according such deep and demanding seriousness to such things as time, food, and sex — things that they are used to handling with an eye to speedy self-fulfillment. Some of them would doubtless like to dismiss the whole thing as weirdness or fanaticism, but it is impossible to do that with my friend, who is a thoroughly appealing person — warm, clever, funny, and very obviously sane and happy. "Who's got it right?" she says. "Well, when Moshiach comes, we'll just have to ask him, 'Well then, have you been here before, or is this your first time?'"

My attempt to put my students in touch with the Jewishness of the scriptures is not limited to those scriptures that Christians share with Jews. It is hard enough when we read the Old Testament to keep some students from throwing into their essays wildly anachronistic (rather than properly typological, which is way beyond most of them) references to Jesus and the Church. When we turn to the New Testament and meet the baby Jesus in the manger, they imagine themselves on home ground and they can become lazy. I have to remind them energetically that this is still a book largely by and about Jews; that although we are reading about the roots of the Church to which they belong, the world of the New Testament is very different from the novenas, CCD classes, and parish raffles of our area's deep-rooted Catholic culture. I find that the more I succeed in getting them to "think Jewish," the better readers of the text they become and the more attuned they are to the intense drama of the New Testament. If I can help them to grasp that the apostles and the Pharisees are as passionate about the law and about their Jewishness as that lady in the hat who came to class to talk to us, then Jesus starts to look a lot more exciting and troubling. They can better appreciate what is at stake in the story of Cornelius's conversion if they can identify with Peter, who, tossed a few cryptic clues and forced to think on his feet, must rethink hundreds of years of religious tradition in the course of an afternoon. They must learn to side with the conservatives at the Jerusalem conference in the Acts of the Apostles in order to understand the depth of the debate about whether gentiles must be circumcised in order to become Christians.

If I have to remind my students to think Jewish, I have also to remind myself to think Christian. In my eagerness to help my students see that the decision at Jerusalem against circumcision was a difficult one to make, and in my fascination with the lives of my neighbors (a fascination in part foolish and romantic, I admit), I become half a Judaizer myself, and occasionally find myself musing about how it might be nice to do something with candles on Friday evenings or even keep just a very little bit kosher. When Paul bellows, "You foolish Galatians! Who has bewitched you?" I have to shake myself and remember that this question has already been dealt with, and an answer has been given, with a clarity that it would be more than foolish to second-guess.

What precisely my students make of the heavily Jewish emphasis of my Bible courses or whether they will remember anything at all in the long term I cannot say. But at home the main day-to-day contact with Orthodox Jewish life is still through the children, and I can confidently say that these friendships will have a long-lasting impact. The neighborhood children live, like ours, in homes without video games or cable TV. Our tree house with a slide and our big box of dress-up clothes are enough to render our house a highly desirable venue, and some collection of neighborhood children is at our home most days. They are all a mother could desire in her children's friends — they are friendly, polite, good at sharing, and they are unlikely ever to set undesirable examples with regard to skimpy T-shirts and obnoxious music, or to share unhelpful stories about Mom's new boyfriend.

The religious and cultural difference is always present and often hilarious. Our Adam, blessed with three sisters and quick to latch onto anything male that comes through the door and identify with it for all he is worth, has decided that Real Men wear yarmulkes. We have had to get him his own to stop him from constantly stealing Binyomin's. The occasional rainy-day movie on the VCR is considerably enlivened by Chaya Sara's emphatic editorial comments to the effect that Sleeping Beauty's dress is not *tznius* or that the best part of *Prince of Egypt* is "the bit where Ha-Shem saves the yids and drowns all the goys." This necessitated a stern lecture to my children as soon as their friends had gone home: "Listen, *yid* is a very special word that only Jews are allowed to use, and you must never, ever say it, do you understand?"

The children are allowed in our house because their parents trust that I "get it." I think I do, but still, some amount of vigilance on my part is necessary to ensure that their trust is not betrayed. Batsheva has a liking for rosary beads and has to be routinely frisked before she goes home. I have had to deflect endless arguments along the lines of "Catherine had a banana at my house yesterday so our food is kosher for you, so your food must be kosher for us, so can I have a sandwich, please?" The idea that our food isn't kosher, period, not even for us, is rejected as obviously absurd. The only effective explanation on these occasions, I have reluctantly learned from the children themselves, is to say, "That's not for Jews." This is not a phrase that trips easily off the tongue, as may well be imagined, but it is promptly and cheerfully accepted as permitting no appeal.

Besides having the sort of peer group that many modern parents can only dream of, our children are learning all sorts of things from their familiarity with Jewish life. Some of the lessons are essentially the same as those I try to communicate to my students — Abraham, Isaac, and Jacob are rendered much more interesting than they would be otherwise by virtue of being Moshe Yehuda's great-great-great-great-grandfathers. Our children are bright and curious and very interested in the differences between their lives and their friends' lives, the relationship between church and *shul*, between Jesus and Ha-Shem, between Sunday and Shabbos. They discuss it among themselves from time to time and come to us for clarification when necessary. Having learned Christianity as a story rather than as a series of propositions, they have no trouble understanding that "they have different rules from us because it reminds us that they were God's friends first. The law is how they are friends with God, and Jesus is how we and everybody else can be his friends." Sometimes they push the point a little: If we are friends of the same God after all, and if Jesus really is God's son, then why can't we make them Christmas cards? They are contented for the present with a simple, and truthful, "because they would think it was rude," but it's only a matter of time before that is subjected to the inevitable "why?" When that happens, we will have to decide whether to tackle the question historically or philosophically. Even when one has a Ph.D. in theology, it requires a certain amount of delicacy to maintain the finality of God's self-revelation in Christ while at the same time eschewing supersessionism; it is naturally much harder when one is only eight. On the other hand, I'm in no hurry to explain to my open-hearted innocents the historical reasons that anything remotely like proselytism would be offensive to their friends.

However complex the questions and answers may become, they will arise, if they do arise, among friends who have already dealt with heated debates over whose turn it is to go down the slide and who gets to wear the sparkly shoes. There is a great deal of nonsense written, to be sure, on the subject of diversity and multiculturalism, but the fact remains that the great challenge facing our world is that of maintaining clear convictions and strong commitments while living in peaceful proximity with people with different convictions and commitments, avoiding brittle bigotry on the one hand and soggy relativism on the other. If we are to make it into the next century, we need to figure out how to do this, and I cannot imagine a stronger foundation for doing so than the negotiations that are second nature to our children and their friends: "We've got to have lunch now so you have to go home, but can we come to yours after?" "My mom says I have to have a shower now — I'll come back later, but I'll have my Shabbos clothes on so we'll have to play inside." "We call it a creche — I don't think you're supposed to play with the baby because it's Jesus, but the camels and the sheep are probably OK. Are Jews allowed angels?"

For our part, my husband and I feel at home in the Jewish life around us in large part precisely because there is no attempt to deny the extent of the gulf between us and our neighbors, to pretend that we and they are really all the same. Our neighbors are infinitely tolerant of my no doubt tedious fascination with the details of Torah observance, but they have never attempted to feign interest in what Catholics believe and do. They are both warmly generous in their hospitality and unapologetically clear that all they will accept from us is tap water in a paper cup. My friend cheerfully welcomes my children, who are constantly banging on her door, and openly discusses with me her acute distress about her sister, who is dating a Gentile and whom she will no longer allow in

her home. There is none of the painful embarrassment that at-
tends deliberate attempts at cultural sensitivity; nor, ironically, is
there any of the suspicion or tension that can mar relationships
among our Catholic colleagues, some of whom are inclined to
keep a sharp eye on those whom they suspect of being not quite
Catholic enough, or altogether too Catholic. Because the boundaries between us and our Orthodox neighbors are so unequivocally
clear, they do not spill over into the rest of our dealings; I would
no more waste my time with "Are you sure I can't get you a cup of
tea?" than they would in trying to gauge my level of loyalty to the
Church's magisterium.

The image of Christians as an alien branch engrafted, by the
grace of God, into the vine of the covenant and thus truly of the
Chosen People would probably sound thoroughly absurd, at best,
to our Jewish friends. For us the image expresses not only a theological proposition subject to analysis and interpretation but also a
simple fact of daily life, and as such it makes perfect sense.

HEATHER KING

Wonder Bread

FROM *The Sun*

ALL THAT WINTER — when I was deep into my self-deprivation, self-imposed-poverty phase — I walked the filthy, noisy streets of downtown L.A., my used laptop on my back, toting a Ralph's grocery bag containing my lunch: a quart yogurt container of brown rice and cabbage, a half-rotten apple, and a few crumbled matzos (two boxes for ninety-nine cents at the ninety-nine-cent store). I wore black jeans (orange earplugs in one pocket), a heavy cotton pullover, a polar fleece jacket, and a purple scarf. I walked from Lucas and Sixth (because I could park there for free) half a mile west to the county law library (because it opened at 8:30, compared to 10:00 for the public library), then to the park adjacent to the superior courthouse at lunch (because it had a public bathroom and a fountain), and afterward to the public library at Olive and Fifth. Laden with a backpack full of books, feeling broken and lost and rag-and-bone — gray sky, honking horns, sunless streets hemmed in by grimy buildings — I thought over and over: *Christ nailed to a cross. Christ nailed to a cross.*

With a laptop (albeit a used one) on my back, a roof over my head, and a wage-earning husband at home, I wasn't poor by a long shot, but I did have a particular poverty of spirit. I'd been diagnosed with breast cancer the previous year, and I was still feeling shaken and raw, still grieving the loss of a kind of innocence I'd never known I had. I realized that the rest of my life would be shadowed by the possibility of recurrence. I'd always been anxious about my writing, but now more than ever I was haunted by the fear that I would die without having published a book. And in my anxiety and the twisted thinking that anxiety generates, it seemed the best way to get a book published was to write as much as I could while living off the nest egg I'd set aside while working as a lawyer. I scrimped and saved, especially on food. I focused all my worries on my finances, as if by making my needs smaller, making do with less, I could ensure there'd be less of me to suffer if the cancer came back, less of me to feel the pain of rejection from publishers, less of me to die a failure. I developed an agenda, so deeply buried that it was hidden even from myself: to get through each day spending the least amount of money possible.

I didn't know this, and then again, on some level I did. It flickered in and out of my consciousness like a match in the wind; like my on-again, off-again relationship with my husband, my friends, myself. *Save, save, save; work, work, work.* Why wouldn't the world just leave me alone to write? It was what God wanted me to do, I believed. I thought I was being holy.

Christ had nowhere to lay his head, and neither — or so it felt that winter — did I. I roamed from library to library because my husband was home asleep, having worked the night shift as a nurse, and being too cheap to rent even a tiny office, I had nowhere else to go. Sometimes at noon I'd walk down Flower to Ninth for mass at Our Lady, a narrow, time-lost chapel sandwiched between the Orchid Hotel and American Computer. The foyer smelled of mothballs, and a shiny porcelain bas-relief of Mary, circa 1940 — green velvet cowl, dark lashes, petunia pink lips — gazed down from above the sanctuary door. The sanctuary itself was windowless and claustrophobic. The sort of people who lived in residential hotels and cooked on hotplates sat here and there, clutching plastic rosaries and moaning prayers. Against the back wall rested a wooden crucifix, for those who felt the urge to stroke Jesus' feet or kiss his wounds.

What struck me most about Christ that winter was his smallness, his hiddenness: his unremarkable early life as a carpenter; his ragtag, spiritually undistinguished group of disciples; the way, after the resurrection, nobody had recognized him. Here in this church at least, he remained small and hidden. The little unassuming chapel, with its chintzy tabernacle, was dwarfed by the towering banks and investment firms and lawyers' offices that surrounded it. We fallen, lonely strangers, converging on South Flower, were hardly the kind of people any public-relations-savvy Messiah would have chosen to glorify his cause.

And yet things happened in that little chapel. People with brief-cases and business suits got down on their knees and buried their faces in their hands. The elderly priest talked about his own strug-gles and failures, which made me feel not quite so bad about my own. At the sign of peace, we took each other's hands and some-times even smiled. This is where we found him, among these wax flowers and stifled sighs; this was the church we had built for him. And so we came with our burdens, our fragile flesh, but also with our little spark that the meanness of the world had not quite extin-guished, our little flame of obedience, our ridiculous stubborn be-lief that the body of Christ was not a symbol but food, real food. Each tiny, broken piece of bread might enable us broken people to go out — anonymous, small, hidden — and transform the world.

I wasn't the only one who needed a place to hang out during the day. At the county law library, where I spent my mornings, there were several other regulars: the guy with a white ponytail who sat talking to himself by the *Southwest Reporter*s; the woman with the glazed-over eyes who stood for hours at the Xerox machine with the exact same page poised over the glass. We never exchanged words — we were all in our own little worlds — but in a strange way I felt more connected to these outcasts than I did to the people with cell phones and expensive haircuts who were technically my peers. I wrote at an isolated desk on the west wall reserved "For Computer Use Only," my nearest neighbor a fellow in the Federal Supplements alcove who had a tubercular cough and a notebook full of unintelligible scribbles.

The L.A. Central Library, where I spent my afternoons, had a whole community of folks who made it their daytime home. It was much noisier than the law library. On Lower Level 4 — history and travel — a guard in a blue satin bomber jacket patrolled the stacks, reminding people they weren't allowed to sleep, or telling some nutcase to keep it down, or cautioning me to take my laptop with me when I went to the bathroom. I jammed in my orange earplugs and wrote for another couple of hours, after which I trolled the stacks for books: music and art on the second floor, popular litera-ture on the mezzanine, spirituality and religion on Lower Level 3.

One of the books I read that winter was *The Diary of a Country*

Priest, by Georges Bernanos. This priest has deep faith, but he's an utter failure: sickly, weak, ineffective, an object of scorn even in his own parish. One day his only friend, the Curé de Torcy, reminds him that it's through poverty and suffering that we find God. This doesn't mean turning our backs on our poor brothers and sisters — out duty is always to treat our neighbors as ourselves — only that our deepest poverty is spiritual. "Poverty is the image of your own fundamental illusion," the curé says. ". . . the emptiness in your hearts and in your hands."

"Your own fundamental illusion": what was mine? That the point of writing — of any work worth doing — is ever anything besides the work itself? That I couldn't be happy till I sold a book? That the success I longed for would fix me? I was on the right track, but it didn't occur to me that my fundamental illusion might literally have been reflected in my approach: holding on as hard as the stingiest millionaire to the money I already had.

I kept thinking of a Richard Rohr essay in which he described going to a monastery and meeting one particular monk, a hermit who lived in a hut in the mountains. They met only once and chatted briefly. Twenty years later, Rohr returned to this same monastery and, by chance, ran into the same monk while walking in the woods. Thinking there was no way the hermit would recognize him after all that time, and not wanting to disturb his solitude, Rohr was prepared to pass silently by. Instead, the hermit stopped, embraced him, and began talking as if they'd broken off a conversation not five minutes before. "Richard!" he said. "You must tell them! Tell them God is not . . . out there. He's *in here.*" He pointed to his heart, and then he continued on his way.

Every day on the streets I saw someone I recognized from the Skid Row soup kitchen where I'd volunteered a couple of years before: a thirtyish man in a frayed sports coat and K-Swiss sneakers who paced outside the Y; a fat guy with thick black glasses and mad-scientist hair snoozing on a bench near City Hall, his pockets stuffed with what he claimed were CIA papers.

One afternoon down by Our Lady, a toothless woman in white go-go boots tottered up to me, her palm out. With a sigh, I took out my wallet.

"Oh, look, she gave all she had," she crooned, as I extracted a one from a wad of fives and tens.

Is she mocking me? I thought, remembering Luke's parable of the widow who gave her last coin: how the Pharisees had given from their excess, while she had given from her want. I was giving from my excess, and the woman and I both knew it.

"All she had," she murmured lovingly, and she walked away.

Biblical scenes coming to life on the streets of twenty-first-century L.A.? This was getting creepy. Why didn't I have a country cottage with a fireplace to write in front of? Why didn't I have a room of my own, like Virginia Woolf? Why, after working my ass off for eight years, was I instead wandering around downtown having encounters with the modern-day equivalents of lepers and mutes? If something didn't break pretty soon, I thought, I'd end up standing on a street corner myself, croaking "Pick up your mat and walk!" or "By his stripes, you were healed!" to random passersby.

Another book that made an impression on me that winter was by Margaret Wertheim. Titled *The Pearly Gates of Cyberspace: A History of Space from Dante to the Internet,* it describes the fascinating world of quantum physics in terms even a science ignoramus like me can understand. One part I found particularly gripping was the 1920 discovery, by a Russian named Theodr Kaluza, of a fifth dimension. I'd always assumed a dimension would be unimaginably huge. Instead, Wertheim writes, it is absolutely minute: "Its circumference was just 10 to the minus 23rd power centimeters — a hundred billion billion times smaller than the nucleus of an atom! . . . So small was Kaluza's dimension that even if we ourselves were the size of atoms we would *still* not notice it. Yet this tiny dimension could be responsible for all electromagnetic radiation."

Could there be a more exciting metaphor for the smallness, the poverty, the hiddenness of Christ? After the resurrection, he had gone on to reside invisibly in all of us. Each thought, word, and deed counted. The smallest act of charity helped: every perfunctory smile at the sign of peace, every plastic-rosary prayer, every reluctantly coughed-up dollar. Biblical scenes took place on the streets of twenty-first-century L.A. as they had taken place everywhere for thousands of years, opening our hearts, confounding every expectation; surprising us, waking us up.

One drizzly morning not long afterward, I was walking east on First on my way to the law library. For lunch I'd packed some rice cakes with hummus, an orange, and a yogurt container of white beans with kale. I was just wishing I'd thrown in an oatmeal cookie or two when I passed a grimy sleeping bag with a person-shaped lump inside. *Poor bastard,* I thought — the air was raw that morning — and though homeless people were all too common in downtown L.A., I was seized with the conviction that I should give this one my lunch.

I can't describe how out of character this was for me. Ordinarily my mind would have raised a host of objections: one meal would change nothing for this man, who probably wouldn't even want my hippy-dippy food; if I was going to give anything to this person, who hadn't even asked for a handout, why not money? I'll never understand why I stopped and turned around. A misfired synapse? Every one of the trillions of choices I had made in my life converging to bring me to this point? The ten-to-the-minus-twenty-third-power-centimeter-in-circumference fifth dimension leading me to, for once, cede reason and offer my actions up to the universe? Whatever the cause, I walked back to the sleeping bag.

"I'm going to leave some food out here," I said. "There's a fork and a napkin and everything."

I'd pictured a wraithlike being, half dead, far too exhausted to rouse him- or herself from slumber. Instead, the figure sat bolt upright, as if a spring had been released. He was a handsome, healthy-looking African American man in his early thirties. "Why, thank you, ma'am. That's very kind of you," he said cheerfully, peering into the bag. "I'll eat it right away!"

Somehow I knew we were both going to make it.

And the next day I started looking for an office.

PHILIP LEVINE

The Genius

FROM *Georgia Review*

When Jake gave up his job on afternoons,
who took up his magical tools so the line
would never stop? Think of the Packard sixteens,
rolling and rolling toward paradise or

Toledo without their upholstery
perfected. Think of it in human terms,
the want of a stitch, the want of a tuck,
Lonnie the foreman howling, "Where's my kike

when I need him?" the heads of the sewers
bowed before the cloth they'll puzzle over
forevermore on earth or in heaven.
Let the whole shop know, he won't arrive;

Jacob the cutter missed the streetcar
this very afternoon and no one cried out,
"We're short a passenger, the little kike
whose bad left shoulder tilts to the right."

No one noticed, not even the conductor
busy short-changing & punching transfers,
nor the blank assembler nor the typist,
her scalded fingers the color of cinders.

No doubt the god of Detroit looked down
or up, however such a god might look,
and found things as usual, green
the sweet rivers of home, green as raw beer

pissed out, and the air was lavender
and the little kike with a lilt to the right
nowhere in sight. All that afternoon
the men in upholstery did as they might

and nothing got done. The angels of Detroit,
among the silent choirs of engineers,
wept to see their industry unhoused
after so many profitable years.

The answer is: no one took up the tools,
no one took up the craft. The handmade awls,
the cruel needles, scissors, knives, all he'd sewn,
vanished with him at four in the afternoon.

This has been a short chapter in the tragedy
of my country, one without beginning,
middle, or end, as Aristotle wrote
such tales require — not having lived in Detroit —

and yet among these details abides a truth
that defines the nature of events on earth,
the perfection of the life or of the work,
and has nothing to do with Uncle Jake.

THOMAS LYNCH

Passed On

FROM *Christian Century*

THE PHOTO of the new priest among his people is an old one. "First Solemn High Mass," it reads in white handprint in the top right corner, "of Rev. Thomas P. Lynch," and on the next line, "St. John's Church, Jackson, Mich., June 10, 1934." It is a panoramic, 17″ × 7″ black-and-white glossy.

Up on the steps in the middle background at the arching doorway of the church stands the celebrant, flanked by deacon and subdeacon, vested in albs and chasubles, with two cassocked and surpliced men off to the right who must have been the altar servers on the day. They are surrounded by a crescent of family and well-wishers, five dozen or more, the front row seated on folding chairs in the foreground, all posed, looking at the photographer with that same grin folks get on their faces when they say "Cheese!"

Thomas P. Lynch is two months shy of his thirtieth birthday. Though he survived the Spanish flu in 1918, he's been sickly and susceptible ever since. He has been to seminary in Detroit, but because he was croupy and tubercular, his archbishop sent him to Denver and then Santa Fe to finish his training in those high, dry western climates. He has come home at long last, fully fledged, anointed, and ordained, to say a solemn high mass for his people — the family and neighbors of his childhood. He will die in two years of influenza and pneumonia, ten days short of his thirty-second birthday.

In front of him, smack in the middle of this assemblage, seated at the right hand of my grandfather, is my father, the priest's only nephew. It is the second Sunday in June, the middle of the Great

Depression, and my father is ten years old, the only young boy in the frame, dressed in saddle shoes, knee britches, white shirt, and tie, looking for all the world like his grandson, my eldest boy, when he was ten.

Father Lynch will be stationed in Taos, New Mexico, at Nuestra Señora de Guadalupe. He will marry and bury and baptize and teach young Apache and Hispanic children how to play baseball and avoid the deadly sins. After two years his health will turn and he'll be taken to Santa Fe, where, after three days in St. Vincent's Sanatorium, he will die on July 31, 1936. His body will be sent home in a box by train to Jackson, Michigan, where the people in this photo will follow him back into this church for the funeral mass and out to St. John's Cemetery, where he'll be buried next to his father and mother.

When his brother, my grandfather, E. J. Lynch, goes to the funeral home to organize the local obsequies, he takes my father, now twelve years old, along for the ride. While the men talk, the boy wanders through the old house until he makes it to the basement, where he sees his uncle, the dead priest, being dressed in his liturgical vestments by two men in shirtsleeves, black slacks, and gray-striped ties. They lift the priest's body into a casket, place his biretta in the corner of the casket lid, and turn to find the young boy standing in the doorway, watching.

It is to this moment in the first week of August 1936, standing in the basement of Desnoyer Funeral Home in Jackson, Michigan, that my father will always trace his decision to become a funeral director.

"I knew right away," he would always recount it, "that was the thing I was meant to do."

Why, I've often wondered, did he not decide to be a priest? But speaking for my brothers and my sisters, we're pleased he chose the course in life he did.

In the next ten years my father will play right tackle for the St. Francis de Sales High School, learn to drive a car, fall in love with the red-headed Rosemary O'Hara, enlist in the Marine Corps, and spend four years in the South Pacific shooting a light machine gun at Japanese foot soldiers. He will return, a skinny and malarial hero, to Detroit, wed Rosemary, enroll in mortuary school at Wayne State University, and go to work for a local funeral home.

He promises his new bride that someday, just wait and see, they'll have a funeral home of their own, a house in the suburbs, "and maybe a couple of junior partners!" Within two months she is pregnant with the first of nine children.

Two generations later, their grandsons and granddaughters are graduating from mortuary school and joining the family firm of funeral directors, which operates five mortuaries in the suburbs of Detroit, serving more than a thousand families a year. They trace their calling to their parents. Their parents trace their calling to their father, who traced his calling to the priest in this photo, who died young and was sent home to Michigan and prepared for burial. Such are the oddities of chance and happenstance. Or such are the workings of the will of God.

Lately I've been thinking about vocations — the calling we were always told to listen for that would tell us what God had in mind for us. I wonder if the young priest heard it, or my father, or if, out of the ordinary silence, they discerned by faith just what it was God wanted them to do. In this, I think we are fellow pilgrims, we sometimes doubting Thomases who wonder still but live our lives by faith.

"All things work together toward some good" is what Saint Paul has to say about such things. "God works in strange ways," my mother said.

BILL MCKIBBEN

High Fidelity

FROM *Christian Century*

I LIVE in the north country mountains, where winter begins in late October and gives up, some years, in early May. That means you come to church half the year in boots — heavy boots, in case you get stuck in a snow bank on the way. Which means, in turn, that the carpet on the floor better be some shade of brown.

Two or three times in my years there I've vacuumed the church. (Not very often, because we tend to divide up jobs along traditional gender lines. Men make sure the furnace is turned up, change the storm windows, lift heavy things, paint, put away folding chairs, shovel the stairs. Women do everything else.) The first time I vacuumed I was merrily buzzing away between the pews, listening to the random click-clack of sand disappearing up the hose, when all of a sudden the noise trebled — click-click-click, like a Geiger counter in a uranium mine.

At that moment I was vacuuming beneath the third pew right along the center aisle. Right where Frank and Jean have been sitting every single Sunday that I can remember. I believe that Frank and Jean began attending our congregation the Sunday after the Council of Nicea. Each time they claim the same spot.

I kept vacuuming, hoovering up the same steady background level of sand, until I reached the sixth pew, against the right wall, where Velda and Don sit each Sunday — each Sunday they possibly can, that is, as both of them have been as much in the hospital as out lately. Again my Geiger counter went off. I decided that instead of radioactivity, it was measuring something else. Fidelity.

"Spirituality" is our watchword at the moment, of course. And rightly so. But Woody Allen had a point when he said that 90 percent of life consists of just showing up.

Consider what it means to belong to the same rural Methodist church for sixty or seventy years. Because Methodist central command insists on changing preachers about as frequently as Sheraton changes sheets, and because small, poor, rural congregations serve as practice ground for the rawest seminary graduates, anyone sitting in the pews for a decade or two sees a head-spinning mix of styles, theologies, and talents.

When I first arrived, the incumbent pastor was a jailhouse convert — a holy roller with a pinkie ring who returned whence he had come after embezzling a widow's insurance. Since then we've had wonderful people in the pulpit — some conservatives, some progressives. Some of them illustrated their sermons with examples taken from some preacher's helper that must have been published in 1921, because the anecdotes all involved World War I. We've taken communion by every method short of scuba diving into a tank of wine. We had one truly great preacher. She was young, smart, funny, full of love, able to talk to young and old, able to afflict the few of us who were comfortable while simultaneously comforting the many afflicted. And she hadn't been there a month before we were, all of us, worried sick about what it was going to be like when, inevitably, she would have to leave. Though none of us would have traded her years for anything, in certain ways it was the hardest passage of all.

Through it all Don and Velda and Frank and Jean never wavered. They might not have liked some new theological twist or liturgical gambit, but they didn't complain very much. (Not even when every other pastor would reinstitute the Greeting of the Neighbors, or the Passing of the Peace, or whatever they called it — a practice that makes less sense when the same fifteen people are there every week, and you've greeted them when you came in, and you're going to greet them again at coffee hour.) And they kept doing the fairly awesome amount of labor even a poor small church requires if it is to keep going.

It's easy to say that all this doesn't add up to a daring relationship with God, that it's Mary and Martha come to life, that routine can suck the meaning out of something as bracing as the gospel. But those of us who've claimed this place were attracted by the sheer dogged devotion of the regulars.

My generation has been good at many things, but tenacity —
faithfulness — is not one of them. Sometimes, in fact, we simply
want too much. Like marriages that complete us, fulfill us in every
way, make us whole, instead of marriages where, on most days, it's
enough to be living faithfully together, adding another increment
of quotidian devotion, giving each other the benefit of the doubt.
Or like religious *experiences,* instead of the experience of being religious. I have no real sense of what it might have felt like to inhabit the medieval world, when the church was simply the air one
breathed, the environment in which one lived. Or rather, what
sense of that world I have comes from watching people like Frank
and Jean and Don and Velda.

One spring day some years ago, when Don and I had finished
taking down the storm windows, we decided to climb up into the
steeple on a rickety ladder so that we could take in the view across
our small town. We could see the house where he'd grown up and
the graveyard where many generations of his ancestors were buried. And while we were up there, Don showed me something else
— the place he had carved his initials, and Velda's. Sometime in
the 1920s, when they were in grade school.

W. S. MERWIN

To the Gods

FROM *American Poetry Review*

When did you stop
telling us what we could believe

when did you take that one step
only one
above
all that
as once you stepped
out of each of the stories
about you one after the other
and out of whatever
we imagined we knew
of you

who were the light
to begin with
and all of the darkness
at the same time
and the voice in them
calling crying
and the enormous answer
neither coming nor going
but too fast to hear

you let us believe
the names for you
whenever we heard them

you let us believe the stories
how death came to be
how the light happened
how the beginning began
you let us believe
all that

then you let us believe
that we had invented you
and that we no longer
believed in you
and that you were only stories
we did not believe

you with no
moment for beginning
no place to end
one step above
all that

listen to us
wait
believe in us

To the Tongue

Whatever we say
we know there is another

RICHARD JOHN NEUHAUS

Kierkegaard for Grownups

FROM *First Things*

THAT EXTRAORDINARY WRITER of stories about the "Christ-haunted" American South, Flannery O'Connor, was frequently asked why her people and plots were so often outlandish, even grotesque. She answered, "To the hard of hearing you shout, and for the almost-blind you have to draw large and startling figures." I expect Søren Kierkegaard, had he lived a century later, would have taken to Flannery O'Connor and would have relished her affirmation of the necessarily outlandish. But then he would immediately be on guard lest anyone think that he does not really mean what he says, that he is anything less than utterly, indeed deadly, serious. He exaggerates for effect and witheringly attacks his opponents who suggest that his exaggeration is anything less than the truth of the matter. He writes, as he repeatedly says, for that one reader — the singular individual who has the courage to understand him — while at the same time describing in detail, and often with hilarious parody, the many readers who refuse to take him at his word. Kierkegaard was keenly (some would say obsessively) attentive to the ways in which he was misunderstood, even as he persistently and defiantly courted misunderstanding. This, as readers beyond numbering have discovered, can be quite maddening. It is also at least part of the reason that Kierkegaard is so widely read.

There are circles of Kierkegaard scholarship, some of it academically solemn and much of it more in the nature of fan clubs. One can only guess what he would make of professors who lecture on his contempt for professors and lecturing, or of admirers who have made him, of all things he unremittingly despised, popular. Apart

from the stolid academics and enthusiastic fans, reading Kierkegaard is for many people an "experience," preferably to be indulged early in life before moving on to the ambiguities and com-
promises of adulthood that we resign ourselves to believing is the
real world. A well-read acquaintance of a certain age says that he re-
members fondly his "Kierkegaard period." He was about nineteen
at the time, and it followed closely upon his "Holden Caulfield period," referring to the young rebel of J. D. Salinger's *Catcher in the
Rye*. In his view — shared, I have no doubt, by many others — Kierkegaard provides a spiritual and intellectual rush, a frisson of
youthful rebellion, a flirtation with radical refusal of the world as it
is. Kierkegaard is, in sum, a spiritually and intellectually complexi-
fied way of joining Holden Caulfield in declaring that established
ways of thinking and acting are "phony" to the core, which declara-
tion certifies, by way of dramatic contrast, one's most singular
"authenticity." Such certification does wonders for what today is
called self-esteem. It is a way of thinking and acting that has the further cachet of coming with an impressive philosophical title: existentialism.

As it happened, Kierkegaard's writings were gaining currency in
the English-speaking world about the same time as the appearance
of *Catcher in the Rye* and other "demythologizings" of all things conventional. For many readers, especially younger readers, the encounter with Kierkegaard was part of a cultural moment marked by
the beginnings of disillusionment with the American Way of Life
that was so triumphantly celebrated after the Second World War.
Those beginnings would build into what was later dubbed the
youth culture or the counterculture, which we loosely associate
with "the '6os," a curious mix of social, sexual, political, and religious liberationisms that made, as it was said, their long march
through the institutions and still shape and misshape the way we
think and the way we live today. Many Americans now reaching re-
tirement age nostalgically recall, and maybe could still find somewhere around the house, the paperbacks that were the vademe-
cums of that time: Marcuse on one-dimensional man, Charles
Reich on the greening of America, C. Wright Mills on the power
elite, Malcolm X on revolutionary violence, Jean-Paul Sartre on the
nausea of society — and, among those and many others, Kierkegaard on authentic existence. The arguments of these books were
dramatically different and often contradictory, but they had in

common what was taken to be a relentless hostility to the establishment.

Walter Lowrie was a prime mover, if not the prime mover, in bringing Kierkegaard to an American readership. As early as the 1940s, he had misgivings about how Kierkegaard would be understood and misunderstood, used and misused. In his preface to Kierkegaard's *Training in Christianity,* he deplores the ways in which Europeans, who were reading Kierkegaard long before he was translated into English, deeply distorted the man and his message. They published first those writings that lent themselves to anticlerical and anti-Christian purposes, and even items of salacious interest, such as "The Diary of the Seducer," torn from its context in *Either/Or.* The result was a grave misrepresentation of — among other things, but the most important thing — Kierkegaard's profound Christian faith and commitment to the renewal of the church. As he repeatedly says in *Training,* that renewal entails "introducing Christianity to Christendom." What Lowrie feared might happen has to a significant extent, and despite his best efforts, happened among readers of Kierkegaard in English. The result is Kierkegaard experienced as an intellectually upmarket Holden Caulfield, or as an "existentialist" compatriot of atheists such as Sartre.

Lowrie rightly notes that *Training in Christianity* is Kierkegaard's most mature and self-revealing text. It is also his last major work, written after his "conversion experience" during Holy Week of 1848. After this work and until his death in 1855, we have only the typically strident polemical tracts from his last years of open warfare with church authorities who, in his view, were determined to preserve Christendom at the price of denying true Christianity. From beginning to end, Kierkegaard's writings are marked by an intensity of argument and expression that can only be explained — if *explain* is the right word — by his uncompromisable passion for the truth. He was convinced that almost everyone — maybe everyone except Jesus Christ and a few spiritual "virtuosi" who have honestly followed Jesus — had settled for something less than the truth. Kierkegaard's many readers are fascinated, perhaps even spiritually titillated, by his pressing every question to the limits, and then beyond the limits. The pressing, the fearless exploration, never ends.

There are Christians who call themselves Kierkegaardians, much as others call themselves Augustinians or Thomists or Barthians. But Kierkegaard provides no school of thought, and most emphatically no "system," that can be a secure resting place for one's Christian identity. Kierkegaard offers only a mode of being, of thinking, of living that has no end other than the end of being "contemporaneous" with Jesus Christ, true man and true God, who has no end. The certifying mark that one has accepted what he offers — or, more precisely, what Christ offers — is martyrdom, and Kierkegaard yearned to be a martyr. The word *martyr,* one recalls, means witness. If Kierkegaard was not to be given the privilege of literally shedding his blood, he would bear witness in other ways. He welcomed the derision of those surrounding him, recognizing in them the same crowd that surrounded the cross of his contemporary, Jesus Christ.

To understand Søren Kierkegaard it is helpful to know something of his life. I say that hesitantly, being mindful of today's propensity for "biopathology," for psychologizing thinkers in order to fit them into the patterns that we think we know. Actually, that propensity is not so new. Kierkegaard takes obvious pleasure in skewering those who evade what he is saying by speaking knowingly about "the problem" with poor Søren Kierkegaard. Yet it is necessary to say something about his life and times.

Søren Aabye Kierkegaard was born in Copenhagen, Denmark, on May 5, 1813, and died there on November 11, 1855. As is, I think, typically the case with men, his character was powerfully formed by his father; indeed, his life was in crucial respects a conflicted recapitulation of his father's. His father had been an embittered hired hand to a poor tenant farmer in the forsaken moorlands of Jutland. One day, in a rage at his unhappy state, he climbed a hill and cursed God for his mistreatment. He would later relate this incident to his son, when the latter was in his early twenties, and it made a deep and permanent impact that was to haunt Søren for the rest of his life. He never entirely set aside the question of whether he and his family were cursed by God because of his father's blasphemy. The suspicion was reinforced by the early death of his mother and the deaths of five of his six siblings. Kierkegaard described his learning of his father's blasphemy as "the great earthquake" of his life.

Shortly after that dramatic act of defiance, his father went to live with an uncle in Copenhagen, where, over time, he built a very considerable fortune by dealing in woolen goods. At his death in 1838, he left Søren and his brother a handsome legacy that relieved Kierkegaard of the need to make a living, although the money had almost run out toward the end of his life. From early on, Søren's brilliance was obvious to his father, who relished forming the boy in his strictly orthodox Lutheranism, combined — as will not surprise those familiar with the period of Lutheran orthodoxy — with a passion for formal logic. He also passed on a spirit of melancholy, closely associated with a sense of guilt joined to an intimation — or perhaps conviction — of the family curse. When it came time for university, young Kierkegaard was in a conflicted state of mind about what to do with his life, or whether anything worthwhile could be done with it, and sought relief by throwing himself into a life of general dissipation. At the University of Copenhagen, he enrolled in theology but increasingly turned his divided attention toward philosophy. Deeply shaken by the death of his father, he resumed his theological studies and two years later obtained the master's degree.

His restored sense of purpose was closely connected to another development. He had fallen in love with Regine Olsen and became engaged to marry. Very soon, however, he realized that he would never be able to communicate with such a young and inexperienced person the storm of complex and conflicted ideas raging in his mind. He broke the engagement and went off to seek refuge in Berlin, where he lived for half a year. Thereafter, Regine and the broken engagement would never be far from his thoughts. In his 1845 book *Stages on Life's Way*, the last section is titled "Guilty?/Not Guilty?" and there he examines the relationship with Regine in terms of his distinction between the aesthetic, the ethical, and the religious. This three-part distinction began to emerge earlier in *Either/Or: A Fragment of Life*, which was the huge manuscript he brought back from his months in Berlin and is probably the book that most commonly serves as an introduction to Kierkegaard today. In *Either/Or* the distinction is between the aesthetic and the ethical-religious, while two years later the ethical and the religious were more sharply distinguished.

The reader will want to keep in mind the three stages of life while reading *Training in Christianity*, since all three "types" appear in various forms. His opponents, as he depicts them, represent both the aesthetic and moral stages, while Kierkegaard is, of course, the champion of the authentically religious. Each stage of life has its own dynamic and is totally — one might say existentially — different from the others. Each assumes that man is confronted by a radical decision — radical in the sense of going to the roots — between God and the world. The aesthetic life is one of pleasure, of sophisticated humanism, of a refusal to make life-determining decisions that might set limits on all that seems possible. The word *decide* is derived from the Latin for "cut," and the aesthetic life is averse to cutting off options. In the ethical stage of life, one "grows up" and accepts responsibilities as defined by general principles of moral conduct. It is only in the religious stage, however, that one becomes a "knight of faith" who makes the ultimate leap beyond unending complexifications and beyond the despair induced by unending complexifications to a true actualization of his existence before God.

A rush of writing followed, and 1844 saw the appearance of both *Philosophical Fragments* and *The Concept of Dread*. The latter has been called history's first work of what would come to be known as depth psychology. These and other works were building toward Kierkegaard's frontal assault on Hegel and Hegelianism. Georg Wilhelm Friedrich Hegel had died only a few years earlier, in 1831, but the influence of the monumental achievement that was his life's work was everywhere evident among educated people, and not least in the leadership of the Protestant churches. Kierkegaard's direct assault began in 1846 with a book bearing the remarkable title *Concluding Unscientific Postscript to the Philosophical Fragments. A Mimic-Pathetic-Dialectic Composition, an Existential Contribution*. The author was named as Johannes Climacus, and S. Kierkegaard was listed as the publisher.

Hegel was the great system-maker. What others viewed as his grand achievement Kierkegaard viewed as his unforgivable crime, the attempt to rationally systematize the whole of existence. The whole of existence cannot be systematized, Kierkegaard insisted, because existence is not yet whole; it is incomplete and in a state of constant development. Hegel attempted to introduce mobility into logic, which, said Kierkegaard, is itself an error in logic. The greatest of Hegel's errors, however, was his claim that he had established the objective theory of knowledge. Kierkegaard countered with the argument that subjectivity is truth. As he put it, "The objective uncertainty maintained in the most passionate spirit of dedication is truth, the highest truth for one existing." Bringing us closer to the central concerns of *Training in Christianity,* Hegel thought it was possible to understand existence intellectually; he equated existence with thought and thus left no room for faith. In this understanding, Kierkegaard protested, Christianity — and Christ! — were reduced to being no more than part of the System. The apparently harmonious but demonically seductive synthesis of history, thought, morality, society, church, and Christ that characterized establishment Protestantism was condemned by Kierkegaard as "Christendom," and against it he intends to make the argument for true Christianity.

He does not expect to persuade everyone. Far from it. What would persuade everyone is almost by definition false. He writes for *Hiin Enkelte,* the emphatically singular individual. *Hiin Enkelte* — those were the words he wanted inscribed on his tombstone. In an 1843 preface he describes watching how his publication fares: "I let my eye follow it a little while. I saw then how it fared forth along lonely paths or alone upon the highway. After one and another little misunderstanding . . . it finally encountered that single individual whom I with joy and gratitude call my reader, that single individual whom it seeks, towards whom it stretches out its arms, that single individual who is willing enough to let himself be found, willing enough to encounter it."

In our day the French philosopher Paul Ricoeur has written powerfully about the "second naiveté" that is the mark of true faith. A century earlier, Kierkegaard wrote about "the second immediacy," the possibility of being a child or youth for the second time. "To become again a child, to become as nothing, without any selfishness, to become again a youth, notwithstanding one has become shrewd, shrewd by experience, shrewd in worldly wisdom, and then to despise the thought of behaving shrewdly, to *will* to be a youth, to *will* to retain youth's enthusiasm with its spontaneity unabated, to *will* to reacquire it by valiant effort, more apprehensive and shamefaced at the thought of equivocating and bargaining to win earthly advantage than a modest maiden is made by an indecent action — yes, that is the task."

The grownups, those who are shrewd in worldly wisdom, have built secure defenses against being encountered by Christ, and they will not let him become their contemporary. With caustic wit Kierkegaard gives voice to the reasoning of the worldly wise. Of Christ the worldly wise say: "His life is simply fantastic. Indeed, this is the mildest expression one can use to describe it, for in passing that judgment one is good-humored enough to ignore altogether this sheer madness of conceiving Himself to be God. It is fantastic. At the most one can live like that for a few years in one's youth. But He is already more than thirty years of age. And literally He is nothing." Another worldling says: "That one should push through the crowd in order to get to the spot where money is dealt out, and honor, and glory — that one can understand. But to push oneself forward in order to be flogged — how sublime, how Christian, how stupid!" (A little later, Friedrich Nietzsche will write with withering scorn of Christianity's "slave morality.") The anti-Hegelian barbs are scarcely hidden in the words of yet another worldling: "We all look forward to an Expected One, in this we are all agreed. But the regiment of this world does not move forward tumultuously by leaps, the world development is (as the word itself implies) *evolutionary* not *revolutionary*." The cultural Protestantism that German theologians call *Kulturprotestantismus* and Kierkegaard calls Christendom is as hostile to Christ as was the religious establishment of first-century Judaism. Indeed, the hostility is stronger, since the Pharisees did expect a radically new thing in the coming of the true Messiah, whereas Christendom thinks it has smoothly subsumed what it formally acknowledges as the true Messiah into the all-inclusive synthesis that is the System.

Christendom is the enemy of Christianity — it is, Kierkegaard says repeatedly, the "blasphemy" — that stands in the way of encountering Christ as our contemporary. Christendom assumes that Christ is far in the past, having laid the foundation for the wonderful thing that has historically resulted, Christendom. Of course we are all good Christians because we are all good Danes. It is a package deal, and Christ and Christianity are part of the package. If we are good Danes (or good Americans), if we work hard and abide by the rules, the church, which is an integral part of the social order, will guarantee the delivery to heaven of the package that is our lives. But Christ is not in the distant past, protests Kierkegaard. He confronts us now, and a decision must be made. "In relation to the absolute there is only one tense: the present. For him who is not contemporary with the absolute — for him it has no existence."

This encounter with Christ the contemporary is not to be confused with today's evangelical Protestant language about conversion as a decisive moment in which one "accepts Jesus Christ as one's personal Lord and Savior." Kierkegaard did not, of course, know about the nineteenth-century American revivalism from which today's evangelicalism issues, but he had some acquaintance with the enthusiasms that were in his day associated with "pietism." As he inveighed against Christendom, it seems likely he would also inveigh against Evangelicaldom today. As he would inveigh against Christianity of any sort — whether it calls itself liberal or conservative, orthodox or progressive — that neatly accommodates itself to its cultural context. To decide for Christ our contemporary is always a decision to be a cultural alien, to join Christ on his way of suffering and death as an outsider.

Once the established order has "deified" itself by claiming to have subsumed the absolute to itself, there is nothing that it cannot presume to do. A person asks, "Do you mean the established order can assure my eternal salvation?" In one of the most scathing passages in *Training*, Kierkegaard lets the established order answer that question. "Why certainly. And if with regard to this matter you encounter in the end some obstacle, can you not be contented like all the others, when your last hour has come, to go well baled and crated in one of the large shipments which the established order sends straight through to heaven under its own seal and plainly addressed to 'The Eternal Blessedness,' with the assurance that you will be exactly as well received and just as blessed as 'all the others'? In short, can you not be content with such reassuring security and guaranty as this, that the established order vouches for your blessedness in the hereafter? Very well then. Only keep this to yourself. The established order has no objection. If you keep as still as a mouse about it, you will nevertheless be just as well off as the others." But of course, Kierkegaard would not keep it to himself. And that is why, as he understood it, he was defamed, derided, and dismissed as an eccentric and malcontent.

Kierkegaard's relentless polemic is not, in the first place, against what is today called "institutional religion." It is, in the first place, a polemic against the deifying of the social order, which can happen with or without Hegelian philosophy. It is, in the second place, a polemic against the church for letting itself become party to this blasphemous fraud and thus betraying Christianity for the sake of Christendom. Since a person's relationship with Christ, however, is of infinitely greater importance than his relationship with his society, the main fire of Kierkegaard's polemic is directed against the treason of the church. In this connection, Kierkegaard makes a lasting contribution to the endless — or at least unending until Christ returns in glory — debate over the proper relationship between, as the twentieth-century American theologian H. Richard Niebuhr titled his classic book, "Christ and Culture." Niebuhr proposed five main "types" of that relationship as Christians have thought about these things over the centuries. Kierkegaard, one might suggest, is polemicizing against the type of Christ *as* culture and is arguing for the type of Christ *against* culture.

Even more telling, I believe, is the similarity of Kierkegaard's argument with the chilling "Legend of the Grand Inquisitor" in Dostoyevsky's *The Brothers Karamazov*. I have sometimes suggested, half tongue-in-cheek, that if anything might be added to the canon of the New Testament, it should be "The Legend of the Grand Inquisitor." Although Ivan Karamazov tells the story against the Catholic Church, it is the story of all Christians and the subtle ways in which Christianity can be displaced by Christendom, in which people can be seduced into surrendering their souls to the established order. When Jesus appears in the public square of medieval Spain, the Grand Inquisitor has him put in jail and explains to him, with sophisticated reasons, why he has no right to come back, why people do not need him and cannot bear him as their contemporary. The established order has now taken over the business of salvation, the Inquisitor tells Jesus, and it is simply intolerable that he should return to interfere. After the long night's monologue, in which Jesus says not a word, the Inquisitor opens the prison door and says, "Go, and come never again." Kierkegaard, I am convinced, would relish the tale.

Kierkegaard's influence on contemporary Christian thought is considerable, and aspects of his "existentialism" play a role in that multifaceted phenomenon called postmodernism, although usually stripped of his radical faith in the God-man, Jesus Christ. Apart from the absolute, which was the object of his decision, today's interest in the existentialist mode of his thinking and deciding would, I expect, be of little interest to Kierkegaard. His impact on theology proper has been, in very large part, through the most influential Protestant theologian of the past century, Karl Barth. Kierkegaard's accent on "the infinite qualitative distinction" between God and man, time and eternity, was decisive for Barth's radical break with the liberal theology and *Kulturprotestantismus* of the nineteenth century. At the same time, and despite Kierkegaard's frequent identification with Luther, Barth thought Kierkegaard betrayed authentic Reformation teaching by his "legalistic" notion that *sola fide* (faith alone) is not enough, that salvation is a matter of open-ended "becoming" through authentic encounter with Christ.

Another figure pertinent to Kierkegaard's legacy, and especially to the argument of *Training in Christianity*, is Dietrich Bonhoeffer. Kierkegaard was convinced that an honest following of "Christ the contemporary" necessarily entailed suffering and aspired toward the ultimate sharing in his suffering which is martyrdom. Bonhoeffer, a Lutheran pastor in Germany, actually was a martyr, being executed upon the direct orders of Hitler on April 9, 1945, for his resistance activities and aid to Jews. Bonhoeffer's thought is indebted to Kierkegaard, and he wrote a powerful little book that is in some respects very similar to *Training in Christianity*. In *The Cost of Discipleship*, Bonhoeffer wrote, "When Jesus calls a man, he calls him to come and die." At the same time, Bonhoeffer was critical of Kierkegaard's sharp divisions of the aesthetic, ethical, and religious life. An editorial footnote in Bonhoeffer's *Ethics* cites a 1944 letter from prison in which he writes, "Perhaps, then, what Kierkegaard calls the 'aesthetic existence,' far from being excluded from the domain of the Church, should be given a new foundation within the Church . . . Who, for example, in our time can still with an easy mind cultivate music or friendship, play games and enjoy himself? Certainly not the 'ethical' man, but only the Christian." For Bonhoeffer, the cost of discipleship was attended by a Christian liberty that frees a person to engage the aesthetic, as well as one's responsibilities in church, marriage and family, culture and government.

The comparison between Kierkegaard and Bonhoeffer is instructive. Both were radically opposed to *Kulturprotestantismus*. Kierkegaard sought to expose it for the sham Christianity (i.e., Christendom) that it was. A hundred years later, in Germany, the corruption and consequent weakness of *Kulturprotestantismus* were exposed under the terror of National Socialism. Both Kierkegaard and Bonhoeffer railed against the smooth synthesis of Christ and culture, contending for the courage of personal decision and a costly form of discipleship. In the actual situation of the collapse of cultural-religious securities, however, Bonhoeffer discovered a new freedom for vibrant engagement with questions of church, culture, politics, marriage, family, and friendship, and also with the celebration of the aesthetic. By circumstance as well as by personal disposition and decision, such engagement and celebration were largely absent from Kierkegaard's life and thought. These two apostles of radical discipleship were very different personalities, but one cannot help but wonder what Kierkegaard would have thought of Bonhoeffer's existential decision and consequent martyrdom, or how Kierkegaard would have envisioned the imperatives of discipleship if Denmark's Christ-as-culture synthesis had been shattered in his time as thoroughly — although no doubt under very different circumstances — as it was shattered a century later in Germany.

Catholic thinkers, when they have engaged Kierkegaard at all, have been ambivalent about him. This is not surprising, since he seems to be hyper-Protestant in his relentless individualism and antipathy to ecclesiastical authority, even if, in Denmark, it was to Protestant ecclesiastical authority. One Catholic who took Kierkegaard very seriously was Hans Urs von Balthasar, probably one of the two most influential Catholic theologians of the past century (the other being Karol Wojtyla, later to be John Paul II, who also wrote insightfully about Kierkegaard). Balthasar, however, was like Bonhoeffer in wanting to rethink the aesthetic and to place it upon authentically Christian foundations. He wrote several thick volumes on the theology of the aesthetic (not, it is important to note, on aesthetic theology). I have already alluded to Karl Barth's relation to Kierkegaard, and the following passage from Balthasar on Barth's devotion to music, especially to Mozart, brings together a number of pertinent considerations:

> This refutation of Kierkegaard, already evident and fully formed in the early Barth, is attributable to a final contrast: for Kierkegaard Christianity is unworldly, ascetic, polemic; for Barth it is the immense revelation

of the eternal light that radiates over all of nature and fulfills every promise; it is God's Yes and Amen to himself and his creation. Nothing is more characteristic of these two men than the way they stand in relation to Mozart. For Kierkegaard, Mozart is the very quintessence of the aesthetic sphere and therefore the very contrast to a religious existence. He had no choice but to interpret him demonically, from the perspective of Don Juan. Quite different is that view of Mozart by one of his greatest devotees, Karl Barth.

Barth wrote that although Mozart lived a rather frivolous life when he was not working at his music, and was a Roman Catholic to boot, he has an important place in theology, especially in the doctrine of creation, "because he had heard, and causes those who have ears to hear, even today, what we shall not see until the end of time — the whole context of Providence." While the aesthetic can, in its sickly form so powerfully depicted by Kierkegaard, lead to despair, it can also, as in the case of Mozart's music, lead us beyond despair, not so much by a religious leap of faith as by an eschatological prolepsis, an anticipation of the promised wholeness of creation that is to be. As with Bonhoeffer, so also with Balthasar and Barth, we can only speculate about what Kierkegaard would make of their quite different understanding of the "infinite qualitative distinction" between God and man, between time and eternity, as it applies to the aesthetic, ethical, and religious in the life of radical Christian discipleship.

Although it may seem surprising, some have entered the Catholic Church under the influence of Kierkegaard. After Kierkegaard succeeds in demolishing the false securities of every form of Christendom, one's only resort is to a church that is unqualifiedly and without remainder the Church. In his 1963 study, *Kierkegaard as Theologian,* the Catholic philosopher Louis Dupré argued that these converts to Catholicism misunderstood Kierkegaard. "He is a person who kept protesting, who could never accept a church which had become established, even if on the basis of protest itself. The Protestant principle has been abandoned as soon as it has developed itself to the point of becoming a church. [Kierkegaard] protested against everything, even against the protest itself. Therefore his attitude was not purely negative but [dialectically] made itself positive again." It is very different for the Catholic, says Dupré, "for the Catholic Church cannot accept the dialectical principle except in her own bosom." Kierkegaard could never be content with a dialectic operating within an ambiance of rest, with a dialectic that had found its home, and therefore, says Dupré, Kierkegaard's own relation to Catholicism was always one of "an antipathetic sympathy and a sympathetic antipathy." I am not convinced Dupré is right and therefore have greater sympathy for those who have found Catholicism on the far side of Kierkegaard. From long and hard wrestling with Kierkegaard, one may come to see the ways in which the Church is "Christ the contemporary," but that is a reflection for another time.

Kierkegaard, it remains to be said, is not a systematic theologian. We know what he thought of systems and system makers, of which Hegel was the prime example. There is hardly a page in his writings that does not prompt from the systematically minded reader a protest against disconnections and apparent contradictions. Like Flannery O'Connor, he shouted to the hard of hearing and drew startling pictures for the almost blind. Kierkegaard was eccentric in the precise meaning of that word — off center, even out of the center. He believed that the center of his time and place, and of any time and place, is where the easy lies are told. He was *Hiin Enkelte* writing for the singular individual who might understand him. Many have read him to experience the frisson of youthful dissent from establishment ways of thinking and being, and have then set him aside upon assuming what are taken to be the responsibilities of adulthood. That, I believe, is a grave mistake. Kierkegaard is for the young, but he is also for grownups who have attained the wisdom of knowing how fragile and partial is our knowing in the face of the absolute, who are prepared to begin ever anew the lifelong discipline that is training in Christianity.

OLIVER SACKS

Speed

FROM *The New Yorker*

As a boy, I was fascinated by speed, the wild range of speeds in the world around me. People moved at different speeds; animals much more so. The wings of insects moved too fast to see, though one could judge their frequency by the tone they emitted — a hateful noise, a high E, with mosquitoes, or a lovely bass hum with the fat bumblebees that flew around the hollyhocks each summer. Our pet tortoise, which could take an entire day to cross the lawn, seemed to live in a different time frame altogether. But what then of the movement of plants? I would come down to the garden in the morning and find the hollyhocks a little higher, the roses more entwined around their trellis, but however patient I was, I could never catch them moving.

Experiences like this played a part in turning me to photography, because it allowed me to alter the rate of motion, speed it up, slow it down, so I could see, adjusted to a human perceptual rate, the details of movement or change otherwise beyond the power of the eye to register. Being fond of microscopes and telescopes — my older brothers, medical students and bird watchers, kept theirs in the house — I thought of the slowing down or the speeding up of motion as a sort of temporal equivalent: slow motion as an enlargement, a microscopy of time, and speeded-up motion as a foreshortening, a telescopy of time.

I experimented with photographing plants. Ferns, in particular, had many attractions for me — not least in their tightly wound crosiers or fiddleheads, tense with contained time, like watch springs, with the future all rolled up in them. So I would set my camera on a

tripod in the garden and take photographs of fiddleheads at intervals of an hour; I would develop the negatives, print them up, and
bind a dozen or so prints together in a little flick-book. And then,
as if by magic, I could see the fiddleheads unfurl like the curled-up
paper trumpets one blew into at parties, taking a second or two for
what, in real time, took a couple of days.

Slowing down motion was not so easy as speeding it up, and here
I depended on my cousin, a photographer, who had a cinecamera
capable of taking more than a hundred frames per second. With
this I was able to catch the bumblebees at work, as they hovered in
the hollyhocks, and to slow down their time-blurred wingbeats so
that I could see each up-and-down movement distinctly.

My interest in speed and movement and time, and in possible
ways to make them appear faster or slower, made me take a special
pleasure in two of H. G. Wells's stories, *The Time Machine* and "The
New Accelerator," with their vividly imagined, almost cinematic descriptions of altered time.

"As I put on pace, night followed day like the flapping of a black
wing," Wells's Time Traveller relates:

> I saw the sun hopping swiftly across the sky, leaping it every minute, and
> every minute marking a day . . . The slowest snail that ever crawled
> dashed by too fast for me . . . Presently, as I went on, still gaining velocity,
> the palpitation of day and night merged into one continuous greyness
> . . . the jerking sun became a streak of fire . . . the moon a fainter
> fluctuating band . . . I saw trees growing and changing like puffs of
> vapour . . . huge buildings rise up faint and fair, and pass like dreams.
> The whole surface of the earth seemed changed — melting and flowing
> under my eyes.

The opposite of this occurs in "The New Accelerator," the story
of a drug that accelerates one's perceptions, thoughts, and metab-
olism several thousand times or so. Its inventor and the narrator,
who have taken the drug together, wander out into a glaciated
world, watching

> people like ourselves and yet not like ourselves, frozen in careless atti-
> tudes, caught in mid-gesture . . . and sliding down the air with wings
> flapping slowly and at the speed of an exceptionally languid snail — was
> a bee.

The Time Machine was published in 1895, when there was intense
interest in the new powers of photography and cinematography

to reveal details of movements inaccessible to the unaided eye. Étienne-Jules Marey, a French physiologist, had been the first to show that a galloping horse at one point had all four hooves off the ground. His work, as the historian Marta Braun brings out, was instrumental in stimulating Eadweard Muybridge's famous photographic studies of motion. Marey, in turn stimulated by Muybridge, went on to develop high-speed cameras which could slow and almost arrest the movements of birds and insects in flight; and, at the opposite extreme, to use time-lapse photography to accelerate the otherwise almost imperceptible movements of sea urchins, starfish, and other marine animals.

I wondered sometimes whether the speeds of animals and plants could be very different from what they were: how much they were constrained by internal limits, how much by external — the gravity of the earth, the amount of energy received from the sun, the amount of oxygen in the atmosphere, and so on. So I was fascinated by yet another Wells story, *The First Men in the Moon,* with its beautiful description of how the growth of plants was dramatically accelerated on a celestial body with only a fraction of the earth's gravity:

> With a steady assurance, a swift deliberation, these amazing seeds thrust a rootlet downward to the earth and a queer little bundle-like bud into the air . . . The bundle-like buds swelled and strained and opened with a jerk, thrusting out a coronet of little sharp tips . . . that lengthened rapidly, lengthened visibly even as we watched. The movement was slower than any animal's, swifter than any plant's I have ever seen before. How can I suggest it to you — the way that growth went on? . . . Have you ever on a cold day taken a thermometer into your warm hand and watched the little thread of mercury creep up the tube? These moon plants grew like that.

Here, as in *The Time Machine* and "The New Accelerator," the description was irresistibly cinematic, and made me wonder if the young Wells had seen, or experimented with, time-lapse photography of plants, as I had.

A few years later, when I was a student at Oxford, I read William James's *Principles of Psychology,* and there, in a wonderful chapter on "The Perception of Time," I found this description:

> We have every reason to think that creatures may possibly differ enormously in the amounts of duration which they intuitively feel, and in the

fineness of the events that may fill it. Von Baer has indulged in some interesting computations of the effect of such differences in changing the
aspect of Nature. Suppose we were able, within the length of a second,
to note 10,000 events distinctly, instead of barely 10, as now; if our life
were then destined to hold the same number of impressions, it might be
1000 times as short. We should live less than a month, and personally
know nothing of the change of seasons. If born in winter, we should believe in summer as we now believe in the heats of the Carboniferous era.
The motions of organic beings would be so slow to our senses as to be in-
ferred, not seen. The sun would stand still in the sky, the moon be almost free from change, and so on. But now reverse the hypothesis and
suppose a being to get only one 1000th part of the sensations that we get
in a given time, and consequently live 1000 times as long. Winters and
summers will be to him like quarters of an hour. Mushrooms and the
swifter-growing plants will shoot into being so rapidly as to appear instantaneous creations; annual shrubs will rise and fall from the earth
like restlessly boiling-water springs; the motions of animals will be as invisible as are to us the movements of bullets and cannon-balls; the sun
will scour through the sky like a meteor, leaving a fiery trail behind him,
etc. That such imaginary cases (barring the superhuman longevity) may
be realized somewhere in the animal kingdom, it would be rash to deny.

This was published in 1890, when Wells was a young biologist
(and writer of biology texts). Could he have read James, or, for that
matter, the original computations of Von Baer, from the 1860s? Indeed, one might say that a cinematographic model is implicit in all
these descriptions, for the business of registering larger or smaller
numbers of events in a given time is exactly what cinecameras do
if they are run faster or slower than the usual twenty-four or so
frames per second.

It is often said that time seems to go more quickly, the years rush
by, as one grows older — either because when one is young one's
days are packed with novel, exciting impressions or because as one
grows older a year becomes a smaller and smaller fraction of one's
life. But if the years appear to pass more quickly, the hours and
minutes do not — they are the same as they always were.

At least, they seem so to me (in my seventies), although experi-
ments have shown that while young people are remarkably accu-
rate at estimating a span of three minutes by counting internally, elderly subjects apparently count more slowly, so that their perceived

three minutes is closer to three and a half or four minutes. But it is still not clear that this phenomenon has anything to do with the existential or psychological feeling of time passing more quickly as one ages.

The hours and minutes still seem excruciatingly long when I am bored, and all too short when I am engaged. As a boy, I hated school, being forced to listen passively to droning teachers. When I looked at my watch surreptitiously, counting the minutes to my liberation, the minute hand, and even the second hand, seemed to move with infinite slowness. There is an exaggerated consciousness of time in such situations; indeed, when one is bored there may be no consciousness of anything *but* time.

In contrast were the delights of experimenting and thinking in the little chemical lab I set up at home, and here, on a weekend, I might spend an entire day in happy activity and absorption. Then I would have no consciousness of time at all, until I began to have difficulty seeing what I was doing and realized that evening had come. When, years later, I read Hannah Arendt, writing in *The Life of the Mind* of "a timeless region, an eternal presence in complete quiet, lying beyond human clocks and calendars altogether . . . the quiet of the Now in the time-pressed, time-tossed existence of man . . . This small non-time space in the very heart of time," I knew exactly what she was talking about.

There have always been anecdotal accounts of people's perception of time when they are suddenly threatened with mortal danger, but the first systematic study was undertaken in 1892 by the Swiss geologist Albert Heim; he explored the mental states of thirty subjects who had survived falls in the Alps. "Mental activity became enormous, rising to a hundred-fold velocity," Heim noted. "Time became greatly expanded . . . In many cases there followed a sudden review of the individual's entire past." In this situation, he wrote, there was "no anxiety" but rather "profound acceptance."

Almost a century later, in the 1970s, Russell Noyes and Roy Kletti, of the University of Iowa, exhumed and translated Heim's study and went on to collect and analyze more than two hundred accounts of such experiences. Most of their subjects, like Heim's, described an increased speed of thought and an apparent slowing of time during what they thought to be their last moments.

A race-car driver who was thrown thirty feet into the air in a crash said, "It seemed like the whole thing took forever. Everything was in slow motion, and it seemed to me like I was a player on a stage and could see myself tumbling over and over . . . as though I sat in the stands and saw it all happening . . . but I was not frightened." Another driver, cresting a hill at high speed and finding himself a hundred feet from a train which he was sure would kill him, observed, "As the train went by, I saw the engineer's face. It was like a movie run slowly, so that the frames progress with a jerky motion. That was how I saw his face."

While some of these near-death experiences are marked by a sense of helplessness and passivity, even dissociation, in others there is an intense sense of immediacy and reality and a dramatic acceleration of thought and perception and reaction, which allow one to negotiate danger successfully. Noyes and Kletti describe a jet pilot who faced almost certain death when his plane was improperly launched from its carrier: "I vividly recalled, in a matter of about three seconds, over a dozen actions necessary to successful recovery of flight attitude. The procedures I needed were readily available. I had almost total recall and felt in complete control."

Many of their subjects, Noyes and Kletti said, felt that "they performed feats, both mental and physical, of which they would ordinarily have been incapable."

It may be similar, in a way, with trained athletes, especially those in games demanding fast reaction times. A baseball may be approaching at close to a hundred miles per hour, and yet, as many people have described, the ball may seem to be almost immobile in the air, its very seams strikingly visible, and the batter finds himself in a suddenly enlarged and spacious timescape, where he has all the time he needs to hit the ball.

In a bicycle race, cyclists may be moving at nearly forty miles per hour, separated only by inches. The situation, to an onlooker, looks precarious in the extreme, and indeed, the cyclists may be mere milliseconds away from each other. The slightest error may lead to a multiple crash. But to the cyclists themselves, concentrating intensely, everything seems to be moving in relatively slow motion, and there is ample room and time, enough to allow improvisation and intricate maneuverings.

The dazzling speed of martial arts masters, the movements too fast for the untrained eye to follow, may be executed in the performer's mind with an almost balletic deliberation and grace, what trainers and coaches like to call "relaxed concentration." This alteration in the perception of speed is often conveyed in movies like *The Matrix* by alternating accelerated and slowed-down versions of the action.

The expertise of athletes (whatever their innate gifts) is only to be acquired by years of dedicated practice and training. At first, an intense conscious effort and attention are necessary to learn every nuance of technique and timing. But at some point the basic skills and their neural representation become so ingrained in the nervous system as to be almost second nature, no longer in need of conscious effort or decision. One level of brain activity may be working automatically, while another, the conscious level, is fashioning a perception of time, a perception that is elastic and can be compressed or expanded.

In the 1960s, the American neurophysiologist Benjamin Libet, investigating how simple motor decisions were made, found that brain signals indicating an act of decision could be detected several hundred milliseconds *before* there was any conscious awareness of it. A champion sprinter may be up and running and already sixteen or eighteen feet into the race before he is consciously aware that the starting gun has fired. (He can be off the blocks in 130 milliseconds, whereas the conscious registration of the gunshot requires 400 milliseconds or more.) The runner's belief that he consciously heard the gun and then immediately exploded off the blocks is an illusion made possible, Libet would suggest, because the mind "antedates" the sound of the gun by almost half a second.

Such a reordering of time, like the apparent compression or expansion of time, raises the question of how we normally perceive time. William James speculated that our judgment of time, our speed of perception, depends on how many "events" we can perceive in a given unit of time.

There is much to suggest that conscious perception (at least, visual perception) is not continuous but consists of discrete moments, like the frames of a movie, which are then blended to give an appearance of continuity. No such partitioning of time, it would seem, occurs in rapid, automatic actions, such as returning a tennis shot or hitting a baseball. Christof Koch, a neuroscientist at

Caltech, distinguishes between "behavior" and "experience" and proposes that "behavior may be executed in a smooth fashion, while experience may be structured in discrete intervals, as in a movie." This model of consciousness would allow a Jamesian mechanism by which the perception of time could be speeded up or slowed down. Koch speculates that the apparent slowing of time in emergencies and athletic performances (at least when athletes find themselves "in the zone") may come from the power of intense attention to reduce the duration of individual frames.

The subject of space and time perception is becoming a popular topic in sensory psychology, and the reactions and perceptions of athletes, and of people facing sudden demands and emergencies, would seem to be an obvious field for further experiment, especially now that virtual reality gives us the power to simulate action under controlled conditions and at ever more taxing speeds.

For William James, the most striking departures from "normal" time were provided by the effects of certain drugs. He tried a number of them himself, from nitrous oxide to peyote, and in his chapter on the perception of time he immediately followed his meditation on Von Baer with a reference to hashish. "In hashish-intoxication," he writes, "there is a curious increase in the apparent time-perspective. We utter a sentence, and ere the end is reached the beginning seems already to date from indefinitely long ago. We enter a short street, and it is as if we should never get to the end of it."

James's observations are an almost exact echo of Jacques-Joseph Moreau's, fifty years earlier. Moreau, a physician, was one of the first to make hashish fashionable in the Paris of the 1840s — indeed, he was a member, along with Gautier, Baudelaire, Balzac, and other savants and artists, of Le Club des Hachichins. Moreau wrote:

> Crossing the covered passage in the Place de l'Opéra one night, I was struck by the length of time it took to get to the other side. I had taken a few steps at most, but it seemed to me that I had been there two or three hours . . . I hastened my step, but time did not pass more rapidly . . . It seemed to me . . . that the walk was endlessly long and that the exit towards which I walked was retreating into the distance at the same rate as my speed of walking.

Going along with the sense that a few words, a few steps, may last an unconscionable time, there may be the sense of a world profoundly slowed, even suspended. L. J. West, in the 1970 book *Psychotomimetic Drugs,* relates this anecdote: "Two hippies, high on pot, are sitting in the Golden Gate Park in San Francisco. A jet aircraft goes zooming overhead and is gone; whereupon one hippie turns to the other and says, 'Man, I thought he'd never leave.'"

But while the external world may appear slowed, an inner world of images and thoughts may take off with great speed. One may set out on an elaborate mental journey, visiting different countries and cultures, or compose a book or a symphony, or live through a whole life or an epoch of history, only to find that mere minutes or seconds have passed. Gautier described how he entered a hashish trance in which "sensations followed one another so numerous and so hurried that true appreciation of time was impossible." It seemed to him, subjectively, that the spell had lasted "three hundred years," but he found, on awakening, that it had lasted no more than a quarter of an hour.

The word *awakening* may be more than a figure of speech here, for such "trips" have surely to be compared with dreams. I have occasionally, it seems to me, lived a whole life between my first alarm, at 5 A.M., and my second alarm, five minutes later.

Sometimes, as one is falling asleep, there may be a massive, involuntary jerk — a myoclonic jerk — of the body. Though such jerks are generated by primitive parts of the brain stem (they are, so to speak, brain-stem reflexes) and as such are without any intrinsic meaning or motive, they may be given meaning and context, turned into acts, by an instantly improvised dream. Thus the jerk may be associated with a dream of tripping, or stepping over a precipice, lunging forward to catch a ball, and so on. Such dreams may be extremely vivid and have several "scenes." Subjectively, they appear to start *before* the jerk, and yet presumably the entire dream mechanism is stimulated by the first, preconscious perception of the jerk. All of this elaborate restructuring of time occurs in a second or less.

There are certain epileptic seizures, sometimes called "experiential seizures," when a detailed recollection or hallucination of the past suddenly imposes itself upon a patient's consciousness and pursues a subjectively lengthy and unhurried course, to complete itself in what, objectively, is only a few seconds. These seizures are typically associated with convulsive activity in the brain's temporal lobes, and can be induced in some patients by electrical stimulation of certain trigger points on the surface of the lobes. Sometimes such epileptic experiences are suffused with a sense of metaphysical significance, along with their subjectively enormous duration. Dostoyevsky wrote of such seizures:

> There are moments, and it is only a matter of a few seconds, when you feel the presence of the eternal harmony . . . A terrible thing is the frightful clearness with which it manifests itself and the rapture with which it fills you . . . During these five seconds I live a whole human existence, and for that I would give my whole life and not think that I was paying too dearly.

There may be no inner sense of speed at such times, but at other times — especially with mescaline or LSD — one may feel hurtled through thought-universes at uncontrollable, supraluminal speeds. In *The Major Ordeals of the Mind,* the French poet and painter Henri Michaux writes, "Persons returning from the speed of mescaline speak of an acceleration of a hundred or two hundred times, or even of five hundred times that of normal speed." He comments that this is probably an illusion, but that even if the acceleration were much more modest — "even only six times" the normal — the increase would still feel overwhelming. What is experienced, Michaux feels, is not so much a huge accumulation of exact literal details as a series of overall impressions, dramatic highlights, as in a dream.

But, this said, if the speed of thought could be significantly heightened, the increase would readily show up (if we had the experimental means to examine it) in physiological recordings of the brain, and would perhaps illustrate the limits of what is neurally possible. We would need, however, the right level of cellular activity to record from, and this would be not the level of individual nerve cells but a higher level, the level of interaction between *groups* of neurons in the cerebral cortex, which, in their tens or hundreds of thousands, form the neural correlate of consciousness.

The speed of such neural interactions is normally regulated by a delicate balance of excitatory and inhibitory forces, but there are certain conditions in which inhibitions may be relaxed. Dreams can take wing, move freely and swiftly, precisely because the activity of the cerebral cortex is not constrained by external perception or reality. Similar considerations perhaps apply to the trances induced by mescaline or hashish.

Other drugs — depressants, by and large, like opiates and barbiturates — may have the opposite effect, producing an opaque, dense inhibition of thought and movement, so that one may enter a state in which scarcely anything seems to happen and then come to, after what seems to have been a few minutes, to find that an entire day has been consumed. Such effects resemble the action of the Retarder, a drug that Wells imagined as the opposite of the Accelerator:

> The Retarder . . . should enable the patient to spread a few seconds over many hours of ordinary time, and so to maintain an apathetic inaction, a glacier-like absence of alacrity, amidst the most animated or irritating surroundings.

That there could be profound and persistent disorders of neural speed lasting for years or decades first hit me when, in 1966, I went to work in the Bronx at Beth Abraham, a hospital for chronic illness, and saw the patients whom I was later to write about in my book *Awakenings*. There were dozens of these patients in the lobby and corridors, all moving at different tempos — some violently accelerated, some in slow motion, some almost glaciated. As I looked at this landscape of disordered time, memories of Wells's Accelerator and Retarder suddenly came back to me. All of these patients, I learned, were survivors of the great pandemic of encephalitis lethargica that swept the world from 1917 to 1928. Of the millions who contracted this "sleepy sickness," about a third died in the acute stages, in states of coma sleep so deep as to preclude arousal, or in states of sleeplessness so intense as to preclude sedation. Some of the survivors, though often accelerated and excited in the early days, had later developed an extreme form of parkinsonism that had slowed or even frozen them, sometimes for decades. A few of the patients at Beth Abraham continued to be accelerated, and one, Ed M., was actually accelerated on one side of his body and slowed on the other.

Dopamine, a neurotransmitter essential for the normal flow of movement and thought, is drastically reduced in ordinary Parkinson's disease, to less than 15 percent of normal levels. In post-encephalitic parkinsonism, dopamine levels may become almost undetectable. In ordinary Parkinson's disease, in addition to tremor or rigidity, one sees moderate slowings and speedings; in post-encephalitic parkinsonism, where the damage in the brain is usually far greater, there may be slowings and speedings to the utmost physiological and mechanical limits of the brain and body.

The very vocabulary of parkinsonism is couched in terms of speed. Neurologists have an array of terms to denote this: if movement is slowed, they talk about "bradykinesia"; if brought to a halt, "akinesia"; if excessively rapid, "tachykinesia." Similarly, one can have bradyphrenia or tachyphrenia — a slowing or accelerating of thought.

In 1969, I was able to start most of these frozen patients on the drug L-dopa, which had recently been shown to be effective in raising dopamine levels in the brain. At first this restored a normal speed and freedom of movement to many of the patients. But then, especially in the most severely affected, it pushed them in the opposite direction. One patient, Hester Y., I observed in my journal, showed such acceleration of movement and speech after five days on L-dopa that "if she had previously resembled a slow-motion film, or a persistent film frame stuck in the projector, she now gave the impression of a speeded-up film, so much so that my colleagues, looking at a film of Mrs. Y. which I took at the time, insisted that the projector was running too fast."

I assumed at first that Hester and other patients realized the unusual rates at which they were moving or speaking or thinking but were simply unable to control themselves. I soon found that this was by no means the case. Nor is it the case in patients with ordinary Parkinson's disease, as William Gooddy, a neurologist in England, remarks at the beginning of his book *Time and the Nervous System.* An observer may note, he says, how slowed a parkinsonian's movements are, but "the patient will say, 'My own movements . . . seem normal unless I see how long they take by looking at a clock. The clock on the wall of the ward seems to be going exceptionally fast.'"

Gooddy refers here to "personal" time, as contrasted with "clock" time, and the extent to which personal time departs from clock

time may become almost unbridgeable with the extreme bradykinesia common in post-encephalitic parkinsonism. I would often
see my patient Miron V. sitting in the hallway outside my office. He
would appear motionless, with his right arm often lifted, sometimes an inch or two above his knee, sometimes near his face.
When I questioned him about these frozen poses, he asked indig-
nantly, "What do you mean, 'frozen poses'? I was just wiping my
nose."

I wondered if he was putting me on. One morning, over a period
of hours, I took a series of twenty or so photos and stapled them together to make a flick-book, like the ones I used to make to show
the unfurling of fiddleheads. With this I could see that Miron actually *was* wiping his nose but was doing so a thousand times more
slowly than normal.

Hester too seemed unaware of the degree to which her personal
time diverged from clock time. I once asked my students to play
ball with her, and they found it impossible to catch her lightning-
quick throws. Hester returned the ball so rapidly that their hands,
still outstretched from the throw, might be hit smartly by the returning ball. "You see how quick she is," I said. "Don't underesti-
mate her — you'd better be ready." But they could not be ready,
since their best reaction times approached a seventh of a second,
whereas Hester's was scarcely more than a tenth of a second.

It was only when Miron and Hester were in normal states, neither excessively retarded nor accelerated, that they could judge
how startling their speed or slowness had been, and it was sometimes necessary to show them a film or a tape to convince them.

(Disorders of spatial scale are as common in parkinsonism as disorders of time scale. An almost diagnostic sign of parkinsonism is
micrographia — minute, and often diminishingly small, handwrit-
ing. Typically, patients are not aware of this at the time; it is only
later, when they are back in a normal spatial frame of reference,
that they are able to judge that their writing was smaller than
usual. Thus there may be, for some patients, a compression of
space which is comparable to the compression of time. One of my
patients, a post-encephalitic woman, used to say, "My space, our
space, is nothing like your space.")

With disorders of time scale, there seems almost no limit to the
degree of slowing that can occur, and the speeding up of move-

ment sometimes seems constrained only by the physical limits of articulation. If Hester tried to speak or count aloud in one of her very accelerated states, the words or numbers would clash and run into each other. Such physical limitations were less evident with thought and perception. If she was shown a perspective drawing of the Necker cube — an ambiguous drawing which normally seems to switch perspective every few seconds — she might, when slowed, see switches every minute or two (or not at all, if she was "frozen"), but when speeded up she would see the cube "flashing," changing its perspective several times a second.

Striking accelerations may also occur in Tourette's syndrome, a condition characterized by compulsions, tics, and involuntary movements and noises. Some people with Tourette's are able to catch flies on the wing. When I asked one man with Tourette's how he managed this, he said that he had no sense of moving especially fast but, rather, that to him the flies moved slowly.

If one reaches out a hand to touch or grasp something, the normal rate is about one meter per second. Normal experimental subjects, when asked to do this as quickly as possible, reach at about 4.5 meters per second. But when I asked Shane F., an artist with Tourette's, to reach as quickly as he could, he was able to achieve a rate of 7 meters per second with ease, without any sacrifice of smoothness or accuracy. When I asked him to stick to normal speeds, his movements became constrained, awkward, inaccurate, and tic-filled.

Another patient with severe Tourette's and very rapid speech told me that in addition to the tics and vocalizations I could see and hear, there were others of which — with my "slow" eyes and ears — I might be unaware. It was only with videotaping and frame-by-frame analysis that the great range of these "micro-tics" could be seen. In fact, there could be several trains of micro-tics proceeding simultaneously, apparently in complete dissociation from one another, adding up to perhaps dozens of micro-tics in a single second. The complexity of all this was as astonishing as its speed, and I thought that one could write an entire book, an atlas of tics, based on a mere five seconds of videotape. Such an atlas, I felt, would provide a sort of microscopy of the brain-mind, for all tics have determinants, whether inner or outer, and every patient's repertoire of tics is unique.

The blurted-out tics that may occur in Tourette's resemble what the great British neurologist John Hughlings Jackson called "emotional" or ejaculate speech (as opposed to complex, syntactically elaborate "propositional" speech). Ejaculate speech is essentially reactive, preconscious, and impulsive; it eludes the monitoring of the frontal lobes, of consciousness, and of ego, and it escapes from the mouth before it can be inhibited.

Not just the speed but the quality of movement and thought is altered in tourettism and parkinsonism. The accelerated state tends to be exuberant in invention and fancy, leaping rapidly from one association to the next, carried along by the force of its own impetus. Slowness, in contrast, tends to go with care and caution, a sober and critical stance, which has its uses no less than the "go" of effusion. This was brought out by Ivan Vaughan, a psychologist with Parkinson's disease, who wrote a memoir about his experiences (*Ivan: Living with Parkinson's Disease*, 1986). He sought to do all his writing, he told me, while he was under the influence of L-dopa, for at such times his imagination and his mental processes seemed to flow more freely and rapidly and he had rich, unexpected associations of every sort (though if he was too accelerated, this might impair his focus and lead him to tangents in all directions). But when the effects of L-dopa wore off, he turned to editing, and would find himself in a perfect state to prune the sometimes too exuberant prose he had written while he was "on."

My tourettic patient Ray, while often beleaguered and bullied by his Tourette's, also managed to exploit it in various ways. The rapidity (and sometimes oddness) of his associations made him quick-witted — he spoke of his "ticcy witticisms" and his "witty ticcicisms" and referred to himself as Witty Ticcy Ray. This quickness and wittiness, when combined with his musical talents, made him a formidable improviser on the drums. He was almost unbeatable at Ping-Pong, partly because of his sheer speed of reaction and partly because his shots, though not technically illegal, were so unpredictable (even to himself) that his opponents were flummoxed and unable to answer them.

People with extremely severe Tourette's syndrome may be our closest approximation to the sorts of speeded-up beings imagined by Von Baer and James, and people with Tourette's sometimes describe themselves as being "supercharged." "It's like having a five-hundred-horsepower engine under the hood," one of my patients says. Indeed, there are a number of world-class athletes with Tourette's — among them Jim Eisenreich and Mike Johnston, in baseball; Mahmoud Abdul-Rauf, in basketball; and Tim Howard, in soccer.

If the speed of Tourette's can be so adaptive — a neurological gift of sorts — then what is the sense of being relatively sluggish, staid, and "normal"? Why has natural selection not served to increase the number of "speeders" in our midst? The disadvantages of excessive slowness are obvious, but it may be necessary (since we sometimes think of speed as unreservedly good) to point out that excessive speed is equally freighted with problems. Tourettic or post-encephalitic speed goes with disinhibition, an impulsiveness and impetuosity that allow "inappropriate" movements and impulses to emerge precipitately. In such conditions, then, dangerous impulses such as putting a finger in a flame or darting in front of traffic, usually inhibited in the rest of us, may be released and acted on before consciousness can intervene.

And, in extreme cases, if the stream of thought is too fast, it may lose itself, break into a torrent of superficial distractions and tangents, dissolve into a brilliant incoherence, a phantasmagoric, almost dreamlike delirium. People with severe Tourette's, like Shane, may find the movements and thoughts and reactions of other people unbearably slow for them, and we "neuro-normals" may at times find the Shanes of this world disconcertingly fast. "Monkeys these people seem to us," James wrote in another context, "whilst we seem to them reptilian."

In the famous chapter in *The Principles of Psychology* on "Will," James speaks of what he calls the "perverse" or pathological will, and of its having two opposite forms: the "explosive" and the "obstructed." He used these terms in relation to psychological dispositions and temperaments, but they seem equally apposite in speaking of such physiological disorders as parkinsonism, Tourette's syndrome, and catatonia. It seems strange that James never speaks of these opposites, the "explosive" and "obstructed" wills, as having, at least sometimes, a relation with each other, for he must have seen people with what we now call manic-depressive or bipolar disorder being thrown, every few weeks or months, from one extreme to the other.

One parkinsonian friend of mine says that being in a slowed state is like being stuck in a vat of peanut butter, while being in an accelerated state is like being on ice, frictionless, slipping down an ever-steeper hill, or on a tiny planet, gravity-less, with no force to hold or moor him.

Though such jammed, impacted states would seem to be at the opposite pole from accelerated, explosive ones, patients can move almost instantaneously from one to the other. The term *kinesia paradoxa* was introduced by French neurologists in the 1920s to describe these remarkable, if rare, transitions in post-encephalitic patients, who had scarcely moved for years but might suddenly be "released" and move with great energy and force, only to return after a few minutes to their previously motionless states. When Hester Y. was put on L-dopa, such alternations reached an extraordinary degree, and she was apt to make dozens of abrupt reversals a day.

Similar reversals may be seen in patients with extremely severe Tourette's syndrome, who can be brought to an almost stuporous halt by the most minute dose of certain drugs. Even without medication, states of motionless and almost hypnotic concentration tend to occur in Touretters, and these represent the other side, so to speak, of the hyperactive and distractible state.

In catatonia, there may also be dramatic, instantaneous transformations from immobile, stuporous states to wildly active, frenzied ones. The great psychiatrist Eugen Bleuler described this in 1911:

> At times the peace and quiet is broken by the appearance of a catatonic raptus. Suddenly the patient springs up, smashes something, seizes someone with extraordinary power and dexterity . . . A catatonic arouses himself from his rigidity, runs around the streets in his nightshirt for three hours, and finally falls down and remains lying in a cataleptic state in the gutter. The movements are often executed with great strength, and nearly always involve unnecessary muscle groups . . . They seem to have lost control of measure and power of their movements.

Catatonia is rarely seen, especially in our present, tranquilized age, but some of the fear and bewilderment inspired by the insane must have come from these sudden, unpredictable transformations.

Catatonia, parkinsonism, and Tourette's, no less than manic depression, may all be thought of as "bipolar" disorders. All of them, to use the nineteenth-century French term, are disorders *à double forme* — Janus-faced disorders, which can switch, incontinently, from one face, one form, to the other. The possibility of any neutral state, any unpolarized state, any "normality," is so reduced in such disorders that we must envisage a dumbbell- or hourglass-shaped "surface" of disease, with only a thin neck or isthmus of neutrality between the two ends.

It is common in neurology to speak of "deficits" — the knocking out of a physiological (and perhaps psychological) function by a lesion, or area of damage, in the brain. Lesions in the cortex tend to produce "simple" deficits, like loss of color vision or the ability to recognize letters or numbers. In contrast, lesions in the regulatory systems of the subcortex — which control movement, tempo, emotion, appetite, level of consciousness, etc. — undermine control and stability, so that patients lose the normal broad base of resilience, the middle ground, and may then be, like puppets, thrown almost helplessly from one extreme to another.

Doris Lessing once wrote of the situation of my post-encephalitic patients, "It makes you aware of what a knife-edge we live on," yet we do not, in health, live on a knife edge but on a broad and stable saddleback of normality. Physiologically, neural normality reflects a balance between excitatory and inhibitory systems in the brain, a balance which, in the absence of drugs or damage, has a remarkable latitude and resilience.

We, as human beings, have relatively constant and characteristic rates of movement, though some people are a bit faster, some a bit slower, and there may be variations in our levels of energy and engagement throughout the day. We are livelier, we move a little faster, we live faster when we are young; we slow down a little, at least in terms of bodily movement and reaction times, as we age. But the range of all these rates, at least in ordinary people, under normal circumstances, is quite limited. There is not that much difference in reaction times between the old and the young, or between the world's best athletes and the least athletic among us. This seems to be the case with basic mental operations too — the maximum speed at which one can perform serial computations, recognition, visual associations, and so on. The dazzling performances of chess masters, lightning-speed calculators, musical improvisers, and other virtuosos may have less to do with basic neural speed than with the vast range of knowledge, memorized patterns and strategies, and hugely sophisticated skills they can call upon.

And yet there are those who seem to reach almost superhuman speeds of thought. Robert Oppenheimer, famously, when young physicists came to explain their ideas to him, would grasp the gist and implications of their thoughts within seconds and interrupt them, extend their thoughts, almost as soon as they opened their mouths. Virtually everyone who heard Isaiah Berlin improvise in his torrentially rapid speech, piling image upon image, idea upon idea, building enormous mental structures which evolved and dissolved before one's eyes, felt they were privy to an astonishing mental phenomenon. And this is equally so of a comic genius like Robin Williams, whose explosive, incandescent flights of association and wit seem to take off and hurtle along at rocketlike speeds. Yet here, presumably, one is dealing not with the speeds of individual nerve cells and simple circuits but with neural networks of a much higher order, exceeding the complexity of the largest supercomputer.

Nevertheless, we humans, even the fastest among us, are limited in speed by basic neural determinants, by cells with limited rates of firing, and by limited speeds of conduction between different cells and cell groups. And if somehow we could accelerate ourselves a dozen or fifty times, we would find ourselves wholly out of synch with the world around us and in a situation as bizarre as that of the narrator in Wells's story.

But we can make up for the limitations of our bodies, our senses, by using instruments of various kinds. We have unlocked time, as in the seventeenth century we unlocked space, and now have at our disposal what are, in effect, temporal microscopes and temporal telescopes of prodigious power. With these we can achieve a quadrillionfold acceleration or retardation, so that we can watch, at leisure, by laser stroboscopy, the femtosecond-quick formation and dissolution of chemical bonds; or observe, contracted to a few minutes through computer simulation, the thirteen-billion-year history of the universe from the big bang to the present, or (at even higher temporal compression) its projected future to the end of time. Through such instrumentalities we can enhance our perceptions, speed or slow them, in effect, to a degree infinitely beyond what any living process could match. In this way, stuck though we are in our own speed and time, we can, in imagination, enter all speeds, all time.

HUSTON SMITH

The Master-Disciple Relationship

FROM *Sophia*

WHEN I WAS INVITED to give this lecture to honor Victor Danner, I knew that nothing short of physical incapacitation could prevent me from accepting. For long before the 1976–77 academic year in which, together with our wives, Victor and I guided thirty students around the world studying religions on location, I had come to regard him with a blend of affection and esteem that very few academic colleagues have drawn from me: that trip vastly deepened our friendship. And when I was asked for the title for my remarks, that too came easily. It was clear to me that I wanted to address the master-disciple relationship, for two reasons. First, during that round-the-world trip I came to look up to Victor Danner as something like my master — not in the full-blown sense of that word that I will be describing here, but certainly as my mentor in matters far exceeding his expertise as an Islamicist. The other and confirming reason for choosing this title was that it brought to mind an essay concerning religious masters that I had read many years ago. It appeared in a volume of essays by Professor Joachim Wach titled *Essays in the History of Religions,* and it impressed me to the point that I promised myself that when I had time I would return to that essay, this time not just to read it but to study it. We all know, though, what roads paved with good intentions lead to — I never got back to that essay, and I saw this lecture as providing the prod to do that. I found Wach's essay quite different from what I wanted to say; still, I happily credit him with sparking many of the ideas I will be trying to develop.

Let me begin by staking out my trajectory. I will not concern myself with the conceptual content of what spiritual masters teach, which obviously differs from master to master. Instead I shall try to describe the character of the master's vocation, the kind of person that fits this role. Second, I shall not concern myself with whether the masters I shall be mentioning by name perfectly exemplify the type or only approximate it. Disputes over degrees are notoriously indeterminable; as someone remarked, we could argue all night as to whether Julius Caesar was a great man or a very great man. Instead I shall be invoking Max Weber's notion of "ideal types." In the technical sense of that term, which Weber moved into the terminology of sociology, an ideal type resembles a platonic form; whether it is instantiated is secondary, because its primary object is to keep our ideas in order. But regarding instantiation, I will say that the much-publicized recent rash of fallen gurus who betrayed their vocation is no ground for deprecating the vocation as such, which, I believe, is the highest calling life affords. Religious masters have contributed immeasurably to civilizations, if indeed they did not launch every civilization we know about. As channels for the divine, the greatest pace-setting masters did set civilizations in motion, but nothing in what I say here turns on that opinion. To come back to and restate this second methodological point, it is the ideal type of the master that I will be trying to depict.

Third, I will range cross-culturally in my illustrations of the master's vocation. I found Professor Danner's descriptions of Sufi masters so mesmerizing that I started my preparations for this lecture thinking that I would concentrate on them, but as I got into the subject I realized that those waters are too vast to allow for wading, which is all that I, who am not an Islamicist, could manage. Any stab I might make trying to nuance the differences between the Prophet Muhammad, the prototypical Islamic master (may peace be upon him), and the masters who followed him — the first four caliphs and their successors; the imams in the Shiite tradition, and masters who are known as Sufis (of which Jalal al-Din al-Rumi is the best known in the West), to mention only obvious subdivisions — would be unworthy of a lecture mounted by the Department of Near Eastern Languages and Cultures [of Indiana University]. So I will fall back on my professional enclave as a comparativist and draw my examples from a variety of religious traditions, while noting that I will be skipping over China. Lao Tzu is too obviously mythological to be brought to focus, and though the high regard of Confucius's disciples shines through every page of the *Analects,* the aphoristic character of their reports leads me to consider Confucius, as the Chinese themselves do, as their foremost teacher rather than a religious master. Nor will I cite Socrates, though Plato's portrait of him as master is as convincing as any on record. And while I am mentioning exclusions, let me say that I place prophets in a different category from masters, although some prophets were also masters — I have already mentioned Muhammad. In Judaism it is the Hasidic *rebbe,* literally "master," rather than biblical prophets or ordained rabbis (teachers), who comes closest to the master as I am presenting him here.

My fourth and final guideline is of a different sort, for it is really no more than a didactic device. Contrasts help to sharpen the contours of topics, and so I shall profile the master mostly by contrasting him to teachers. It speaks well for the city of Bloomington to learn that there is a large community contingent in the audience this evening, but I assume that most of you who are here are either teachers or students, so I will etch the master-disciple relationship — in Sanskrit the *guru-chela* relationship and in Arabic the *sheik-murid* relationship — by contrasting it with the relationship between teachers and students. To keep from rambling, I will itemize the contrasts, but as there is no logical sequence in the order in which I will be discussing them, I shall not number them but demarcate them by placing a bullet before each point.

Having now announced my trajectory, I am ready to set out.

I

• What brings students to their teachers is a body of knowledge or a skill that the teacher has mastered and to which the student aspires. Feelings, positive and negative, naturally enter, but they are byproducts of this central objective which brings them together. It is not primarily the teacher as a person who is respected, but what he possesses and can deliver to the student. Comparably, it is not who the student is as a complete person that interests the teacher, but his willingness and ability to learn — other sides of his selfhood are beside the point. The entire relationship is born from, and lives by, shared interest in the object of study. This means that both parties in the relationship are replaceable. Students can shop around for teachers and drift from one to another, and teachers will welcome new generations of students.

The situation in the master-disciple relationship is otherwise. Here the personhood of both parties is central. (It would be less precise to say the personalities of both parties, for *personality* tends to suggest the public image that the party in question presents to the world.) The master does not enjoy the disciple's esteem because he conveys something that is useful in any utilitarian respect. Nor is it a distinguishable attribute of his total self that he seeks to transfer to the disciple — to repeat, a specifiable skill or body of knowledge. What is significant for the disciple is the master's total self, whose character and activity are unique and irreplaceable. In this crucial respect it is like love. More accurately, it is love in the purest sense of that word, though it is risky to use that word, which has been rendered almost useless through its preemption by commercialism (hot dogs "made with a little bit of love"), sex ("making love"), sentimentality (racks of Valentine cards), and innumerable other debasing inroads. Like the master-disciple relationship, authentic love is focused on a unique, irreplaceable person. With the exception of Saint Paul in his classic description in First Corinthians, I know of no one who describes authentic love better than Thomas Aquinas, and as his description almost says *in nunce* what I am using this lecture to spell out, I shall summarize it here.

> Love is more unitive than knowledge in seeking the thing, not the thing's reason; its bent is toward a real union. Other effects of love are: a reciprocal abiding of lover and beloved together as one; a transport out of the self to the other; an ardent cherishing of another; a melting so the heart is unfrozen and open to be entered; a longing in absence, heat in pursuit and enjoyment in presence. In delight, too, there is an all-at-once wholeness and timelessness that reflects the total simultaneity of eternity; an edge of sadness; an expansion of spirit; a complete fulfillment of activity without satiety, for "they that drink shall yet thirst."

• Students make up their minds and intend to study, whereas disciples are called to discipleship. One thinks immediately of the tax collector Zachaeus, who, perched in a tree to get a glimpse of Jesus in the passing throng, heard Jesus tell him to come down, and when he obeyed found himself transformed into an entirely different being. Or again, we think of the beautiful story of the flower scavenger Sunita, who became a renowned member of the Buddha's *sangha* when the Buddha, "seeing the marks of *arhatship* shining in his heart like a lamp in a jar," said to him, "Sunita, what to you is this wretched mode of living? Can you endure to leave the world?" Callings such as these bring disciples to their master because in some mysterious, not fully explicable way, they seem to emanate from the master's completeness. Through this completeness, the master enters and becomes an essential part of the disciple's existence.

• Continuing with the contrasts, the teacher and student, united as they are through a bond of work on a common task, form a series of links in which the student in his own proper time will himself become a teacher with talents that might surpass those of his own teacher, but this is unlikely in the case of the disciple. I cannot think of a single case in which a disciple who on becoming a master thought that his bond with his disciples fully equaled the master-disciple cosmos that his own master forged. The teacher heads a school which can gather strength through the work of his successors, whereas the master forms a circle around himself which authentic disciples do not dream of fully replicating. They can radiate some of the charisma they receive from their master, and may attract disciples of their own, becoming thereby masters in their own right. But it will not be the same universe they shared with their own master, and they see it as imitating, not rivaling, the original universe they inhabited.

• In higher education here, teaching typically goes hand in hand with research and publication; teachers can pursue that side of their careers without students, whereas disciples are indispensable for masters to be such. I break in to insert a parenthesis here. To prevent my thesis from suffering death by a thousand qualifications, I am trying to keep the line between master and teacher clear, but obviously there are overlaps — the two do not constitute watertight compartments. Even professors who are chiefly invested in research can find graduate seminars stimulating, and students sometimes cathect to their teachers as if they were masters, as I did in my undergraduate years, when for several years one of my professors served as a father figure and role model for me. But having acknowledged such overlaps, I revert to the difference at issue here, which is that the master-disciple relationship centers in mutuality in principle, where the teacher-student relationship does not. The master only becomes a master in his relationship to his disciples, and only through perceptive and comprehending disciples does he become fully aware of his mastership. We think of Jesus at a turning point in his ministry asking his disciples who people were saying that he was. When they answer, "Some say John the Baptist, but others Elijah, and still others Jeremiah or one of the prophets," Jesus persists and asks, "But who do you say that I am?" Whereupon Simon Peter answers, "You are the Messiah, the Son of the living God." Jesus then says, "Blessed are you, Simon son of Jonah! For flesh and blood has not revealed this to you, but my Father in heaven" (Matt. 16:18). In this sense, it is the disciple who ordains his master to mastership.

We find another example of this in the Bhagavad Gita, which revolves around the dialogue between Krishna and Arjuna on the eve of the battle on the Kurushektra plains that was scheduled to begin the next morning. At the start of their discussion, Arjuna (the prince of the forces of righteousness) is in the superior position, and Krishna is his charioteer. Their standings are reversed, however, when Arjuna, overcome by the thought of killing his kinfolk, is brought to a state of paralyzing existential bewilderment. When he asks Krishna what he should do, he begins his move toward discipleship, questioning being the first duty of discipleship in Hinduism. Given this opening, Krishna seizes the opportunity and immediately takes control of the situation. Not wasting a word, he tells Arjuna that he is a fool. His bewilderment is caused by false premises and phony arguments. Hearing these blunt words, Arjuna very quickly takes on Hinduism's second requirement of discipleship — submission — and acknowledges that he had been careless in regarding Krishna as no more than his friend and kinsman, oblivious of the fact that he was God incarnate. Here again we see the disciple ordaining the master to mastership. The master reads the confirmation of his calling in the eye of his disciple at the same time that the disciple hears destiny calling him through the master.

• Pulling together much of what has been said thus far, we can say that the teacher gives of his knowledge and ability, whereas the master gives — not *of* himself, as we are likely to say, as if his gift could be isolated from the wholeness of his being, but *himself,* pe-

riod. What he is to the disciple he is through the presence of his total selfhood in his every word and deed, right down to what is seemingly trivial. (One thinks of the disciple of the Maggid of Mesritch
who traveled a great distance simply to observe how the *rebbe* tied
his shoelaces.) The master has become who he is through his own
efforts (as inseparably infused with God's grace), and the result, as
I say, is always deployed in its completeness. Disciples never perceive that completeness; to do so would require *being* the master.
Disciples are able to see, moment by moment, only a facet of the to-
tality as vectored by their respective points of view. Nevertheless, at
some level of their being, they sense the presence of the wholeness,
as when Jesus' words are heard as being spoken by "one having authority."

• The teacher as researcher and writer survives in his published
work; it is this that constitutes his visible legacy. The master survives
only in those who have experienced his impact and bear witness to
it. Others can only surmise the full extent of that impact. The disciple testifies to what the master was to him; as he has seen the master, so he paints his portrait to imprint it on his memory and report
it to others. But he alone knows the full force of what produced the
portrait; others can only glean from it what they can. The other disciples do likewise, for the desire to share what they have known
burns in them all and they are eager to tell others of their firsthand
experiences. But, as I have noted, though the master's selfhood is
single, it imprints itself on his disciples in dissimilar ways, thereby
playing out the adage that beauty is (in part) in the eye of the be-
holder. Perhaps the clearest example of the multiplicity of portraits
that result is the four gospel accounts of Jesus, which have recently
been supplemented by apocryphal accounts such as the Gospel of
Thomas — Mark presenting Jesus as wonderworker, John as trans-
parently divine from the start of his mission, Thomas as an Essene,
and so on. Each story becomes a legend, and once in place takes
on a life of its own, which is progressively trimmed to the generic
archetype of the master to make it more easily apprehended. In
reaching out thus to future generations, the stories become traditions that weave their way into the fabric of history.

• Continuing with the point that the two preceding paragraphs
took up, that the incorrigible matrices of space and time require
that the singleness of the masters' selfhood be fractioned by circumstances at hand — Jesus the reconciler is the same Jesus who

drives money changers out of the temple — the master must live in the constant awareness of time's ephemerality. Only this moment, these circumstances, can disclose this aspect of his total self. The Greek word *kairos,* which carries connotations of the fullness of time, is decisive here, for no eternity can bring back what was missed in the moment of transmittal. Only the sacred hour begets the sacred impact, and many hours will be needed to try to piece together retrospectively as much of it as possible.

This makes timing crucial in the work of the master. It does not require that he carefully calculate what he will do or say; in each moment, at his ease, he gives what the moment calls for. All of the sweetness of the moment, with its contextual requirements which are set within horizons that include the apprehension of approaching death, loosen his heart and tongue, and it is as though nothing had been before and nothing will ever be again, and through the frailty of the moment there shines the light of the eternal. A mundane corollary of this is that teachers, when absorbed in their work, tend to resent interruptions, whereas the master's mission consists of nothing but interruptions. It is not hyperbolic to say that dedicated teachers are consumed by projects that they set for themselves, whereas masters consume themselves in simply doing what is at hand, and in so doing they fill the world with light.

• Teachers and students have things in common on which they work together and which unite them. The master and disciple are either directly united or not at all, and they live with each other in this relationship day in and day out. The teacher praises the swift foot, the skilled hand, the sharp eye, and the keen intellect of the student, while in the master's eye there are no such distinctions. Body and soul (to cite but a single example) are not divided, as evinced by the master's demand that the disciple attend to beauty, inasmuch as those who attend to beauty themselves become beautiful, as Plotinus said. One thinks of the apocryphal story in which Jesus, accompanied by several of his disciples, passes a dead dog by the side of the road. His disciples give it wide berth, noting which Jesus remarks, "But are not its teeth like pearls?" (This anecdote also appears as a *hadith* of the Prophet, from which the apocryphal Christian version very likely derived.) With body and soul undivided, the disciple is asked always to live from the core of his being, which too is single, but in a deeper, more hidden, way.

• Being engaged in the same pursuit bonds students to one another. Jealousies, of course, can and do arise — who will get the scholarships? who is teacher's pet? — but typically belonging to the same school and engaging in a common pursuit bonds students to one another. Thank-God-it's-Friday celebration revelries are standard, lifelong friendships are forged, and class reunions are mounted.

Discipleship is different. Being one of a group of disciples is no basis for mutual love, and rivalries flare at the slightest provocation — we think immediately of Jesus' disciples jockeying for who will sit at his right hand in the coming kingdom — for it seems impossible that someone else should have a part in the relationship that ties the disciple to his master, the lifeblood of which is incomparability and uniqueness on both sides. This leaves no path that leads from one disciple to another. The disciple's conviction that he is devoted and open to the master as no other disciple is leads the disciple to expect this singularity to be reciprocated. Such assumptions are foreign to scholarly activity, which (a point I keep returning to) centers on something that exists objectively outside both teacher and student, the knowledge or skill they are united in trying to convey or master, as the case may be. Related here is the issue of betrayal. The impersonality of the bonding subject matter makes the betrayal of a teacher virtually inconceivable, whereas Judas Iscariot stands as an enduring example of the fact that in the master-disciple relationship, that shattering act not only does occur but is understandable. That Rumi's master, Shams of Tabriz, was murdered by disciples who were jealous of his special bond with Rumi is probably not the case (see below), but it is understandable that the rumor arose.

• When students and disciples are deprived of their head, the issue of bonding is almost reversed. Students dispute, often bitterly, over what the teacher was driving at, and rival schools arise. (One thinks of Mencius and Hsun Tzu as rival interpreters of what Confucius taught, which is another reason for classifying Confucius as a teacher rather than a master.) As for disciples, though they were rivals while their master was living, they now find themselves drawn together by the image of their master, which is sacred to them all. Their personal distress, common loneliness, and concern for the future produce a great unity — one thinks of the disciples of Jesus gathering in the Upper Room, where tongues of fire descended on them and the Christian church was born. Such comings-together generate huge spiritual momentums, which time must inevitably erode to some extent. Where some of its original strength is recovered, a new master has arisen, who creates a distinctive order.

• To conclude the differences I have itemized, one can have a succession of teachers but in classic cases only one master. A beautiful poem by Emily Dickinson adapts perfectly to this point.

> The soul selects her own society,
> Then shuts the door;
> On her divine majority
> Obtrude no more.
>
> Unmoved, she notes the chariots pausing
> At her low gate;
> Unmoved, an emperor is kneeling
> Upon her mat.
>
> I've known her from an ample nation
> Choose one;
> Then close the valves of her attention
> Like stone.

II

As far as I can see, the traits that I have been ascribing to masters apply generically to them all, but of course each master is also unique — I know of no master other than Muhammad who had an angel, Gabriel, for his master. In between these logical extremes of sameness and difference there are groupings into which masters fall; the genus contains, admits of species, we might say. Jesus and Krishna were incarnations, while Moses and Muhammad were prophets, a category that is itself complex, for by Islamic reckoning, Moses and Muhammad were prophets, *nabi* (pl. *anbaya'*), who were also messengers, *rusul,* by virtue of launching new religions, which not all prophets do. Again, not all prophets prophesy the future, but Muhammad prophesied about the end of the world. Some masters possess supernatural powers, as did Ramakrishna, who complied with Vivekananda's request for a direct experience of God simply by touching his forehead, but Buddha and Muhammad forswore miracles. Such categories and their subdivisions could be multiplied indefinitely — but rather than let this lecture degenerate into a catalogue, I will devote my remaining space to a single difference that I find most rewarding.

It turns on the issue of tragedy, which figures importantly in the mission of some masters but not all — the missions of Jesus and the Buddha have tragic aspects, but those of Krishna and Muhammad show no trace of it. I will have to enter a gloss on Krishna before I am through, but the paradigmatic portrait of him in the Gita supports the conclusion of students of comparative literature, who tell us that it is the Greeks and Shakespeare who dealt consummately with tragedy, while in India it scarcely appears — perhaps because Brahman's creations are *lila*, his divine play. As for the Prophet Muhammad, if being orphaned and losing one's only son (to say nothing of wives and daughters) is not tragic, the word has no meaning, but those tragedies do not seem to have played an integral part in his mission, as they did in the missions of Jesus and the Buddha. It goes without saying that the category of masters in whose mission tragedy does figure is not exhausted by those two figures, but they are the ones I will focus on.

Tragedy enters first in this class of masters in the requirement that they renounce the world and the best things in it for the sake of what that renunciation will bring to the world. We see this most clearly in the Buddha's realization at an early age that to fulfill his mission he had to abandon his wife and their newborn son, the tenderest ties worldly life affords; but we find it also in Jesus' renunciation, not only of the kingdoms of the earth in his temptation scene, but (as in the Buddha's case) all prospects of having a family and home of his own. "Foxes have holes and birds of the air have nests, but the Son of Man has nowhere to lay his head" (Matt. 8:20, Luke 9:58).

Second, there is the tragedy that these masters realize that what they have to impart is so profoundly contrary to conventional wisdom that even their disciples will be able to comprehend it only partially. This comes out explicitly in Mara's final temptation to the Buddha, that he slip directly from his enlightenment into nirvana because what he discovered under a tree on that holy night was too profound for the world, steeped in *advidya*, ignorance, to grasp. (It wasn't necessary for Mara to go into explanations, but as I tried to show above, the deepest reason for the failure would be that to understand him fully would require that his hearers *become* him, an

He then offered to show me his living quarters. Exiting through the back door of the small living room where we were seated, he introduced me in passing to Iksan, the tiny old woman "who takes care of my physical needs" and was preparing his evening meal. Then he led me into his bedroom where, beside his padded sleeping quilt on the floor, there was set an armchair that faced a television screen. "This is where I watch sumo wrestling in the evenings," he said. "Do you watch sumo wrestling?" When I answered in the negative, he said, "Too bad. It's wonderful." He then ushered me out of the back door, where a half-dozen crates of empty beer bottles were arranged along the wall. "These are the remains of the beer I drink while watching sumo wrestling." And that was it; the cook's tour was completed. We returned to his living room, where, after a few more words, we bade each other goodbye.

As I made my way through the narrow lanes to where I was staying that last night, it became apparent to me that the purpose of this final exercise was to dismantle the pedestal onto which I had placed my *roshi* in the course of the summer. Its elevation had encouraged me to pour everything I had into my summer's training, but the time had come to go my own way.

Anecdote completed, I come back to the main point of this second half of my lecture, which is to bring out category differences in the master's vocation. Having described the parting that figures importantly in the vocation of some masters, I will now turn to their opposite numbers, focusing on a single example in India.

Most aspects of the *guru-chela* relationship in Hinduism fit comfortably into the paradigm I presented in the first half of this lecture, as does the concept of the *archarya,* the perfected guru who teaches by example. Here, though, I am looking at differences, and Krishna is a master who does not leave his disciples. *Dvaitic,* dualistic, Hindus come down hard on this point, looking to *archaryas* like Ramanuja and Chaitanya, founders, respectively, of the Sri Vaishnava school and the Hari Krishna movement, which continues in full force today. Arguing that their rivals — the *advaitic,* nondual, Shaivites, whose chief spokesman is Sankara — were influenced by the Buddha's renunciation of a personal god, the dualists are passionately theistic and try to develop as personal a relationship with their personal deities as they can. Relationship being the lifeblood in theism, the gods of India's theist always come in couples — Radha-Krishna, Sita-Ram, Lakshmi-Narayan — with the goddess always named first, before the god. (In reporting this difference, I seem to be violating one of the guidelines I set for myself at the start of this lecture, where I said I would not be going into differences in what masters teach. I would stick to profiling their role, but I am allowing myself this one exception because in this instance a doctrinal difference leads directly to a difference in masters' understandings of their roles.) In the theistic lineage, disciples cannot conceive of their gurus ever working themselves out of their job and leaving them. They will keep reincarnating themselves for as long as it takes for their disciples to become enlightened, and even after their disciples have dropped the body permanently, their guru will be with them forever in paradise, for (as I say) there is no happiness for theists outside of relationship. (Pure Land Buddhism sides with the Vaishnavites here.) In this mode, gurus, as the ads for diamonds have it, "are forever."

As I come to the close of this lecture, I want to say something that doubles back on everything I have said in it. Scientists have discovered that the deeper they probe into nature's foundations, the more they find that the divisions that carried them toward those foundations turn out to be provisional only, not final; and in much the same way I find that the divisions that I set out to explore and that have structured this lecture — differences between masters and teachers and between kinds of masters — likewise prove to be provisional. The division between gurus who take leave of their *chelas* and those who do not, which I just presented as clear-cut, turns out not to be clear-cut at all. Sri Krishna *does* take leave of his disciples. He abandons them, not (to be sure) in the Gita's story but as the *Puranas* fill in his biography.

Krishna's geographical locale was Vrindavan, but after he has won the hearts of the cowgirls and throngs of others, he abruptly disappears. Whether it was to kill evil kings or to tend to his aging parents some distance away or for some other reason, we are not told, but the fact remains: summarily he leaves Vrindavan, leaving his disciples guruless for the remainder of their days. We can only begin to imagine the sense of abandonment that they had to live with for the rest of their lives.

This does not upset the fact that theistic Hindus never doubt that the cosmic Krishna is forever at their side, but introducing the Puranic account of his life does blur the image of him as a non-leave-taking master with which I began, and it prompts me to look back over my shoulder and take a second look at what I said about no leave-taking in Islam. Muhammad was separated from his followers only by his death at a mature age, but in Shiite Islam, his rightful successor, Ali, was murdered, along with his two sons, and this has placed abandonment at the very heart of this branch of Islam. In the *majlis* in Tehran that I was allowed to attend, as the night deepened, the *fuqara'* worked themselves into a frenzy, bewailing the slaughter of Ali and his sons. In other contexts this turns many Shiites into *penitentes* as they lash their backs with ropes and even swords to maximize their identification with the injustice done to Ali. The parallel with Christian *penitentes* who mutilate themselves to identify with Christ's crucifixion is so close to this as to require no comment. This raises the deep question of the role such suffering plays in a relationship. I can only venture that grief in abandonment may bond disciples to their masters more completely than any other emotion, which might be the truth in the adage that absence makes the heart grow fonder. Sham's abandonment of Rumi — the rumor that he was murdered by jealous disciples "arrives late, circulates in oral context, and is almost certainly groundless" (Franklin D. Lewis, *Rumi: Past and Present, East and West*, p. 193) — drew from Rumi some of his ecstatically griefstricken poems. If this is on the right track, disciples in this camp actively cultivate the sorrow in separation to engender what they consider the highest and purest form of love. We might find them asking if the love between Jesus and his disciples was ever greater than in the poignant pathos of the Last Supper.

Have these last paragraphs deconstructed my entire lecture by admitting that the distinctions that I have used to format it are only provisional? I do not think so, for distinctions have their uses and are indispensable in dealing with life in this world — we continue to work with Newtonian physics, even though we know that its laws are violated in the deeper level of nature. So I do not think that Victor Danner would reject on principle my modest effort to honor him with this lecture. On the contrary: I think he would welcome the fact that the distinctions I have worked with collapse in the end in *tawhid,* affirmation of the Divine Unity. And I am confident that he would deal gently with the infirmities that have preceded that affirmation in the course of this hour.

GARY SNYDER

No Shadow

FROM *The New Yorker*

MY FRIEND DEANE took me into the Yuba Goldfields. That's at the lower Yuba river outflow where it enters the Sacramento valley flatlands, a mile-wide stretch between grass and blue oak meadows. It goes on for ten miles. Here's where the mining tailings got dropped off by the wandering riverbed of the 1870s — forty miles downstream from where the giant hoses washed them off Sierra slopes.

We were walking on blue lupine-covered rounded hundred-foot gravel hills til we stood over the springtime rush of water. Watched a female osprey hunting along the main river channel. Her flight shot up, down, all sides, suddenly fell feet first into the river and emerged with a fish. Maybe fooling the fish by zigzagging, so — no hawk shadow. Carole said later, that's like trying to do zazen without your self entering into it.

> Standing on a gravel hill by the lower Yuba
> can see down west a giant airforce cargo plane from Beale
> hang-gliding down to land
> strangely slow over the tumbled dredged-out goldfields
> — practice run
> shadow of a cargo jet — soon gone
>
> no-shadow of an osprey
>
> still here

DANA TIERNEY

Coveting Luke's Faith

FROM *The New York Times Magazine*

WHEN I WAS A CHILD in Sunday school, I would ask searching questions like "Angels can fly up in heaven, but how do clouds hold up pianos?" and get the same puzzling response about how that was not important, what was important was that Jesus died for our sins and if we accepted him as our savior, when we died, we would go to heaven, where we'd get everything we wanted. Some children in my class wondered why anyone would hang on a cross with nails stuck through his hands to help anyone else; I wondered how Santa Claus knew what I wanted for Christmas, even though I never wrote him a letter. Maybe he had a tape recorder hidden in every chimney in the world.

This literal-mindedness has stuck with me; one result of it is that I am unable to believe in God. Most of the other atheists I know seem to feel freed or proud of their unbelief, as if they've cleverly refused to be sold snake oil. But over the years, I've come to feel I'm missing out. My friends and relatives who rely on God — the real believers, not just the churchgoers — have an expansiveness of spirit. When they walk along a stream, they don't just see water falling over rocks; the sight fills them with ecstasy. They see a realm of hope beyond this world. I just see a babbling brook. I don't get the message. My husband, who was reared in a devout Catholic family and served as an altar boy, is also firmly grounded on this earth. He doesn't even have the *desire* to believe. So other than baptizing our son to reassure our families, we've skated over the issue of faith.

I assumed we had stranded our four-year-old son, Luke, in the same spiritually arid place we'd found ourselves in. When my husband went to Iraq for several months, I thought Luke and I were in it together, a suddenly single mom and a nervous boy whose daddy was in a war zone. I was numb with anxiety when I talked to my husband on his satellite phone, yet Luke was chatty and calm. He missed his daddy, but he wasn't scared. He wanted to see pictures of Dad holding an AK-47. I thought he was just too young to understand.

Then one night Luke and I were watching television, and a story flashed on about a soldier home on leave for his wedding. I tried to switch the channel, but Luke wanted to see, so I let him, thinking, *It's a wedding; it's fine.* But the soldier started talking about how afraid he was of going back, how dangerous it was in Iraq. Out of the corner of my eye, I saw Luke steeple his fingers and bow his head for a split second. Surprised, I said, "Sweetheart, what are you doing?" He wouldn't tell me, but a few minutes later he did it again. I said, "You don't have to tell me, but if you want to, I'm listening." Finally he confessed, "I was saying a little prayer for Daddy."

"That's wonderful, Luke," I murmured, abashed that we, or our modern world, somehow made him embarrassed to pray for his father in his own home. It was as if that mustard seed of faith had found its way into our son and now he was revealing that he could move mountains. Not in a church or as we gazed at the stars, but while we channel-surfed. I was envious of him. Luke wasn't rattled, because he believed that God would bring his father home safely. I was the only one stranded.

Some people believe faith is a gift; for others, it's a choice, a matter of spiritual discipline. I have a friend who was reared to believe, and he does. But his faith has wavered. He has struggled to hang on to it and to pass it along to his children. Another friend of mine never goes to church because she's a single mother who doesn't have the gas money. But she once told me about a day when she was washing oranges as the sun streamed onto them. As she peeled one, the smell rose to her face, and she felt she received the Holy Spirit. "He sank into my bones," she recounted. "I lifted my palms upward, feeling filled with love."

Being no theologian, and not even a believer, I am not in a position to offer up theories, but mine is this: people who receive faith directly, as a spontaneous combustion of the soul, have fewer questions. They have been sparked with a faith that is more unshakable than that of those who have been taught.

After I saw Luke praying for his father in Iraq, I asked him when he first began to believe in God. "I don't know," he said. "I've always known he exists." My husband did return from Iraq safely, but if something had happened to his father, Luke would have known Dad was in heaven, waiting for us. He doesn't suffer from a void like the anguished father in Mark 9:23–24: "Jesus said unto him, If thou canst believe, all things are possible to him that believeth. / And straightway the father of the child cried out, and said with tears, Lord, I believe; help thou mine unbelief." For Luke, all things are possible. At the end of his life, he will be reunited in heaven with his heroes and loved ones, Mom and Dad and George Washington, his grandparents and Buzz Lightyear. Luke's prayers can stretch to infinity and beyond, but I am limited to one: Help thou mine unbelief.

Two Short Essays

FROM *The Sun*

Those Dark Trees

Driving across America the August before I stopped drinking, I found myself in Tennessee, taking note of that big look that trees get in the East at the end of summer: a line of them at the far end of a field, like blooms of dark green ink dropped into water. When you see a group of trees like that, it's easy to think that you could drop everything and just head off into them, the way Robert Frost is always talking about doing in his poems, marching and marching until you arrive at the secret heart of the world. Of course, when Frost talked longingly about disappearing into the lovely woods, he was really talking about death. But what kind? Death in the sense of simple annihilation, of darkness and the merciful extinguishing of consciousness? Or death as goal, as finish line, as the fantastic adulthood for which the life we know is merely a kind of preparatory adolescence? All trees say, *Vanish into us.* But they say it in different ways. Take the kind of trees — ragged, sinister, fringed with litter — that one sees near service stations, or in the background on the evening news. "It was here, in this wooded area less than a mile from where they were last seen alive . . ." Walk into a stand of trees like that, and you risk ending up scratched and sweaty, having traveled for miles in the wrong direction, and not an inch closer to the secret heart of anything than you were when you set out.

Not to dwell on the drinking, but that's what happened with it as well: you started with a simple, clean desire to go and go, but at some point a wrong turn was always taken, and you woke up dead and dull and about as far from the true center as it was possible to get.

Tennessee is a big state. That summer, I was still in it hours after I figured I would have left it behind.

Sometimes in the Shower

Sometimes, when you're taking a shower in a house where the plumbing doesn't work so well, there will be a clank behind the walls, and the water will go cold for a moment. Amid the steam and the white towels, the old truths will suddenly return: life ends badly; comfort and security are cruel illusions; this self of mine that feels so solid and eternal is doomed to sputter and sink, like a would-be nineteenth-century aviator in a grainy photograph, drifting back to earth in his flapping, failed machine.

Then, just as these thoughts are really taking hold, the hot water comes back on, and all is well again. The old truths turn out to be simple fictions created in the darkness and discomfort of other times and other places. It's different now; it really is. The great transit can be made, the impossible operation performed, the football thrown from the far end of the field and caught and carried triumphantly into the end zone. I reach past the shower curtain, turn off the light, and sit down on the floor of the tub. Down here, the water feels like warm rain falling in a distant jungle. And I am a stone statue, brooding in darkness, waiting for the explorers to arrive.

KENNETH L. WOODWARD

The Passion's *Passionate Despisers*

FROM *First Things*

WHAT ARE WE TO MAKE of *l'affaire Gibson* now that his film has turned out to be a huge box office success? Those who, like me, were deeply moved by *The Passion of the Christ* and judged it to be not anti-Semitic have no reason to gloat. The cultural clashes over the film opened wounds we thought had healed, and they exposed currents of hostility toward Christianity that one would have hoped had disappeared. The freewheeling commentary in the general media, with a few notable exceptions, was pitched at too low a level to call this a teaching moment. But it certainly was a moment to listen and learn — and, at times, to laugh.

Last summer, it should be recalled, Gibson's project was on very shaky legs. He had not as yet found a distributor for a film in which he had invested $25 million of his own money. After reading a "received" copy of the script, a self-selected group of six scholars, most of them veterans of Jewish-Christian dialogue, complained of unbiblical and anti-Semitic stereotypes. One of the group, Paula Fredriksen of Boston University, wrote a long and fearful essay, "Mad Mel," in the *New Republic,* predicting that "violence" would break out upon the film's release. Immediately, Abraham Foxman, national director of the Anti-Defamation League, orchestrated a campaign to label the film anti-Semitic. That really got Mel mad, and he responded by showing nearly finished versions of the movie to selected audiences, most of which consisted of politically conservative pundits and evangelical Christians. None of them seemed to find the film anti-Semitic — but then, few of them were Jews. To columnists such as Frank Rich of the *New York Times,* Gibson's screening strategy was part of a "political-cultural war" pitting Jews against Christians, including the Bush White House and the whole conservative wing of the chattering classes.

Thus began an *opéra bouffe* that eventually involved a huge cast, including, on the pro-Gibson side, the pope (apparently) and Billy Graham and his son Franklin (certainly), and featuring Gibson-denouncing appearances by Andrew Greeley and Elaine Pagels, among many others. It also featured Foxman and his competitor in Jewish defense, Rabbi Marvin Heir, director of the Simon Weisenthal Center in Los Angeles, surreptitiously slipping into prerelease screenings. Gibson's publicity people countered their reports with stories of miracles and conversion experiences on Gibson's set in Italy. The Catholic League came to Gibson's defense, while a Jewish Web site, Messiah Truth, called on Attorney General John Ashcroft to investigate Gibson for hate crimes. As prophylactics against a possible outbreak of anti-Semitism, the Catholic bishops and the National Council of Churches published guidelines for watching the film. Appealing to higher authority, Foxman flew to Rome to ask the Vatican to tell all bishops that Gibson's movie is not "the gospel truth."

Hollywood, predictably, backed away from Gibson, thinking him toxic. But once he found a distributor, the effort to render the film financially dead on arrival turned into a boon. Richard Land, the president of the Southern Baptist Ethics and Religious Liberty Commission, scrutinized the film for signs of "creeping excessive Catholicism" and found none, thus clearing a path to the theater door for ten million Southern Baptists. Other evangelicals also rallied to Gibson and his film, not because they lack Jesus films of their own but because they saw the clash over his film as part of a battle between Christianity and secularism. It is likely that those who tried to paint Gibson and his work as anti-Semitic guaranteed, ironically, his unexpected box office success. With enemies like these, who needs friends?

In any case, long before his film opened, Gibson's every comment was closely examined for signs of anti-Semitism. He was denounced by Rich of the *Times* and others as a "Holocaust denier" because he noted in one interview that Jews were not the only people victimized by the Nazis. "Gotcha, Mel!" was the collective response. Gibson's disposition as a traditionalist Catholic who loves the Latin mass and is critical of liberal trends since the Second Vatican Council was routinely interpreted as meaning that he therefore rejects the Church's formal repudiation (in *Nostra Aetate,* 1965) of the charge of deicide against the Jews. Gibson was repeatedly visited with the sins of his father, the aged, addled, and frankly anti-Semitic Hutton Gibson. Admirably, Gibson did not allow Diane Sawyer to provoke him into denouncing his father during his hour-long interview on CBS, and with great patience entertained Ms. Sawyer's headline-seeking question, "Are you anti-Semitic?"

So what is to be learned from all of this? First, Christians and Jews alike can rejoice over the dog that did not bark. Except for one unsettled Pentecostal pastor in Colorado, there have been no reported incidents of anti-Semitism related to Gibson's film. That is remarkable, considering how many millions of Americans have seen the film, and more so because the media have been primed to report any such incidents. Indeed, it was a golden opportunity for any crank looking for headlines to make his voice heard. The lesson, though, is not that in "tolerant" America Jews and Christians now understand each other. As their widely different reactions to the film suggest, there's a lot of misunderstanding yet to confront.

No question, Christians and Jews saw two different films. As John Leo astutely observed in his syndicated column, they walked into the film with different emotions and different preconceptions — and walked out with them intact. Christians know the plotline, and most assume as fact that Jesus died for their sins. No wonder so many wept — for Jesus the suffering servant and for themselves as sinners "washed in the blood of the lamb." Jews who have seen the film (including professional film critics) arrived wary, alert for evidence of anti-Semitism and armed with some knowledge of passion plays past. The story Gibson filmed is not, as one Orthodox rabbi rightly wrote on his Web site, "our story." *New Yorker* critic David Denby, who identifies himself as a secular Jew, bemoaned in his acerbic review the absence of "the electric charge of hope and redemption Jesus Christ brought into the world." But had this been "his" story, Denby might have realized that that Jesus was right before his eyes, in every frame. Gibson's Christ is not the parable-telling, *halacha*-defying rabbi that Reform Judaism at its origins more than a century ago promoted as a figure closer to its own tradition than to Christianity. Rather, he is in this passion — as in the gospel passion narratives — the obedient son of the Father. As I pointed out in an op-ed piece in the *New York Times* on Ash Wednesday, the death of Jesus is the one aspect of the gospels that no other religion can accept. But without *that* Jesus there would be no resurrected Christ, and without *that* Christ there would be no Jesus available to make a film about — whether by DeMille, by Pasolini, by Scorsese, or by Gibson.

In sum, in the months leading up to the release of *The Passion of the Christ,* the only issue that seemed to matter in the media was whether the director was guilty of anti-Semitism. In attenuated form, anti-Semitism was also the subject of the February 16 cover story in *Newsweek,* which had won the heated competition among the three newsweeklies for the exclusive right to screen the film early (I was among those admitted) and to feature it on its cover. The question in its cover line, "Who Really Killed Jesus?" introduced writer Jon Meacham's earnest and careful exploration of whether Gibson had been faithful to the gospels and whether the gospels themselves were trustworthy as history. On the first point, it was obvious that Gibson had gone beyond the scriptures at several points, as film directors, and all artistic interpreters, are wont to do. To address the second point, however, is to scamper down a hole that no prudent rabbit would dare enter, given the long and complex history of biblical scholarship itself.

The consensus of New Testament scholars is that from Mark to Matthew and Luke, the gospel writers shifted the burden of responsibility for the death of Jesus from the Romans to the Jews. But as the late Raymond Brown demonstrated in detail in his magisterial two volumes, *The Death of the Messiah,* "the theory that the Gospels exculpate the Romans by creating a totally fictional, sympathetic Pilate has been overdone." In particular, Brown shows that the assessments of Pilate in the writings of Tacitus and especially Philo of Alexandria are not to be taken at face value — as Meacham takes them — because both writers had political axes to grind. In short, while Gibson surely overdraws the role of Caiaphas, Meacham underestimates the political vulnerability of Pilate, who stands vilified in Christian tradition as a weak magistrate who condemned a just man to death.

None of this would matter if the *Newsweek* story, published two weeks before the film's Ash Wednesday opening, had not become received wisdom to the scripture-lacking and symbol-impaired commentators who followed in Meacham's wake. Bowing to Meacham, Denby in *The New Yorker* charged Gibson with "serious mischief" in assigning responsibility for the death of Jesus, failing to recognize any of the scenes that place responsibility for Jesus' death on all sinful human beings. In an equally clueless review in the *Washington Post,* Ann Hornaday asserted the film's "startling lack of historical context" and declared, "That Jesus and his followers were themselves Jewish is a fact either elided or ignored" by the director. Was she looking for identification tags? Christ — need anyone be reminded? — was not a Christian.

The word *medieval* occurred quite frequently in reviews as a pejorative. In a discussion of the film with this writer on National Public Radio, Denby complained of Gibson's "odd medieval touches, like Satan hanging around among all the Jews through the scourging and all through the crucifixion, which is not in the gospels. That's an anti-Semitic medieval hangover that I found very disturbing." One should not have to remind a man who makes his living reviewing movies that Gibson's Satan — a figure out of an Ingmar Bergman film, as *Newsweek*'s film reviewer, David Anson, aptly noted — functions throughout this film as the visual and constant reminder of the temptation to terminal despair that tortures Jesus even more than his physical punishment. Note to Mr. Denby: Satan is not a medieval invention; he figures prominently as the Adversary in the gospels. Similarly, those reviewers who thought they saw cinematic translations of paintings by Caravaggio (Denby) and Jackson Pollock (Gary Anderson in the *Washington Times*) missed in the long scene with Pilate Gibson's most obvious visual borrowing: the now classic suffering savior painted by Georges Rouault.

The day the film opened, Rabbi Eric H. Yoffie was in the audience in a sold-out theater in Times Square watching *The Passion of the Christ* unfold. Yoffie was deeply offended by what he saw as Jewish stereotypes. "The Jews in this film are evildoers," he later wrote to his colleagues on Reform Judaism's Web site. But he also noticed the woman next to him sobbing throughout the film, and gradually came to the conclusion that such Christians are responding out of deep belief and "really do not understand the charge of anti-Semitism and what Jews are talking about."

Yoffie's modest exercise in what literary types call "reader-

response theory" is a useful way to survey the reactions of the nation's celebrity pundits. In *Vanity Fair,* everybody's favorite urban
atheist, Christopher Hitchens, called Gibson a fascist and the
movie an "exercise in lurid masochism." In the *New Republic,* Leon
Wieseltier let loose with another of his contemptuous screeds
against Christianity in general, medieval Catholicism more generically, and Gibson's "wretched hero" in particular. "A sacred snuff
film" was his most inelegant shot. From the other side of the political aisle, columnists William Safire (*New York Times*) and Charles
Krauthammer (*Washington Post*) found the movie sadistic as well
as anti-Semitic. Indeed, *sadistic, masochistic, pornographic,* and their
variants were the most common adjectives in the lava-laden commentaries published in the *Boston Globe, USA Today,* and *Slate.* Then
there were the efforts to trivialize: A. O. Scott in the *New York Times*
led his review with a Mel Gibson appearance on *The Simpsons,* eventually getting around to comparing *The Passion* to "a slasher film,"
and Garry Wills in the *New York Review of Books* reported that he and
his wife had to "keep from laughing" while watching the movie.

There were also many warnings from the critics that children
watching the film would be traumatized. Never mind the fact that
the movie is R-rated; adolescents who do make it into the theater
will discover an "adult" film whose violence might actually be good
for them. For sure, Gibson's film is brutal, as he promised it would
be. Every biblical film is necessarily a new translation, and Gibson's
visual vernacular is violence. On this score he risks much in his effort to do through violence what other directors have done by
other, sometimes ideological means — to jolt the viewer into a
fresh understanding of an all too familiar story. Not all of his risks
pay off. Critics are right to complain that the central scene of
Christ's scourging goes on far too long, straining belief that any
human being could survive such a brutal whipping and overwhelming the viewer's ability to empathize. Worse, the flashbacks
to pre-passion moments in the life of Jesus fail to provide sufficient
context for understanding why the Jewish religious establishment
wanted to see Jesus put out of the way — a nearly fatal flaw in Gibson's conception.

Above all, Gibson misled both critics and supporters of his film
by proclaiming his fidelity to scripture. As Beliefnet.com demonstrated in its very alert analysis, for almost all of his excessive — and

artistically unnecessary — additions to the biblical materials, Gibson relied slavishly on one book dear to traditionalist Catholics: *The Dolorous Passion of Our Lord Jesus Christ,* written by Clemens Brentano in the early nineteenth century and purporting to be the mystical visions of an illiterate nun and stigmatic, Anne Catherine Emmerich. As Paula Fredriksen and others pointed out, many of the utterances attributed to Emmerich are indeed anti-Semitic, though none of these find their way into Gibson's film. What no one mentioned is that the Vatican halted Emmerich's canonization process in 1928 over concern that Brentano probably embellished her visions considerably. In other words, Gibson drew from a book that the Church considers dubious enough to exclude from material it will consider in her cause for sainthood.

Finally, what can one say about the dark warnings from Frank Rich and others that *The Passion* will surely inflame anti-Semitic violence in the Middle East once it reaches theaters there? Well, there aren't many theaters left in Iraq, but knockoff DVDs of the film have been on sale there for more than a month at this writing, and so far there has been no disturbance. Nor in Egypt, Syria, Lebanon, Jordan, Bahrain, Qatar, or the United Arab Emirates, where the film was released uncensored, according to a report from Cairo by Charles Levinson in the *San Francisco Chronicle,* April 1.

It would be nice, but too much to expect, if Jews and Muslims as well as Christians could see *The Passion of the Christ* and recognize a larger theme: that like Jeremiah and Muhammad, prophets are rarely welcomed among religious establishments. Were I a Jew, I admit, this is one film I would skip. But as the nonviolent responses to *The Passion* so far demonstrate, this is a film that Jews should realize is not about them. It is about Jesus. As a creative interpretation of sacred texts rather than a straightforward reading of a scriptural story, it deserves to be treated with the respect we normally show to all sincere attempts to search out the fullness of God's intention. Sadly, such respect was shown by few critics of Gibson's *Passion.*

CHARLES WRIGHT

Wrong Notes

FROM *Virginia Quarterly Review*

To bring the night sky to life,
                                    strike a wrong note from time to time.
Half for the listening ear, half for the watching eye.
Up here, just north of the Cabinet Mountains,
                                    the Great Bear
Seems closer to me than the equinox, or rinsed glints
In the creek hurrying elsewhere into evening's undergrowth.

The same way with the landscape.
                                    Our meadow, for instance,
Has two creeks that cross it;
                    they join and become one about halfway down.
And that runs under my west window.
These are the flash and lapped scales
That trouble the late sunlight,
                    and spark the moon fires and moon dregs.

At other times, it seems invisible, or they do,
Moving slowly in dark slides
                                    from beaver break to beaver break.
Muscling down from spruce shadow through willow shadow.
Above its margins the deer graze,
                                    two coyotes skulk and jump,
And clouds start to herd together like wounded cattle.

And what does this matter?
                    Not much, unless you're one of those,

As I am, who hears a music in such things, who thinks,
When the sun goes down, or the stars do,
That the tune they're doing is his song,
That the instruments of the given world

                              play only for him.

FRANZ WRIGHT

Prescience

FROM *The New Yorker*

We speak of Heaven who have not yet accomplished
even this, the holiness of things
precisely as they are, and never will!

Before death was I saw the shining wind.
To disappear, today's as good a time as any.
To surrender at last

to the vast current —
And look, even now there's still time.
Time for the glacial, cloud-paced

soundless music to unfold once more.
Time, inexhaustible wound, for
your unwitnessed and destitute coronation.

Contributors
Notable Spiritual Writing of 2004

Contributors

Christopher Bamford is the author of *The Endless Trace: The Passionate Pursuit of Wisdom in the West* and *The Voice of the Eagle*. He is editor in chief of Anthroposophic Press (Steiner Books) and Lindisfarne Books.

Brian Blanchfield is the author of *Not Even Then,* a book of poems. He teaches creative writing and literature at Pratt Institute of Art in Brooklyn, New York.

Scott Cairns is the author of five collections of poetry: *The Theology of Doubt, The Translation of Babel, Figures for the Ghost, Recovered Body,* and, most recently, *Philokalia: New & Selected Poems.* His work has appeared in the *Atlantic Monthly, Paris Review, New Republic, Poetry, Image: A Journal of the Arts and Religion, Spiritus, Western Humanities Review,* and many other journals. He is currently a professor of English at the University of Missouri.

Richard Chess has published two books of poetry, *Tekiah* and *Chair in the Desert.* His poems are included in *Telling and Remembering: A Century of American Jewish Poetry* as well as other anthologies. He directs the Center for Jewish Studies at the University of North Carolina at Asheville, where he is also a professor of literature and language.

Robert Cording teaches English and creative writing at Holy Cross College, where he is a professor of English and holds the Barrett Chair of Creative Writing. He has published four collections of poems: *Life-list,* which won the Ohio State University Press/Journal award, in 1987; *What Binds Us to This World; Heavy Grace;* and *Against Consolation.* His new book, *Common Life,* will be published in 2006. His poems have appeared in *The Nation, Image, Georgia Review, Kenyon Review, New England Review, Poetry, DoubleTake, Orion, Paris Review, The New Yorker,* and many other magazines. He lives in Woodstock, Connecticut, with his wife and three children.

Harvey Cox is the Hollis Professor of Divinity at Harvard Divinity School and the author of many books, including *When Jesus Came to Harvard: Making Moral Choices Today; Common Prayers: Faith, Family, and a Christian's Journey Through the Jewish Year;* and *Fire from Heaven: The Rise of Pentecostal Spirituality and the Reshaping of Religion in the Twenty-first Century.*

Andy Crouch is a columnist for *Christianity Today* and a member of the editorial board of *Books & Culture.* For many years he was a campus minister at Harvard University and the editor of the magazine *re:generation quarterly.* His book on Christian cultural responsibility, *Culture Makers,* will be published in 2006. He lives with his family in Swarthmore, Pennsylvania.

Brian Doyle is the editor of *Portland* at the University of Portland in Oregon. He is the author of five collections of essays, most recently *Spirited Men,* about writers and musicians, and *The Wet Engine,* a book about the "magic and muddle and miracle and music and wrangle and wrassle and wonder of hearts."

David James Duncan is a novelist, essayist, and self-styled "compassion activist." He lives, fly-fishes, and prays in his closet in western Montana.

Jean Bethke Elshtain is the Laura Spelman Rockefeller Professor of Social and Political Ethics at the University of Chicago and cochair of the Pew Forum on Religion and American Public Life. She is the author of many books, including *Jane Addams and the Dream of American Democracy, Democracy on Trial,* and *Augustine and the Limits of Politics.*

Margaret Erhart is the author of *Crossing Bully Creek* and other novels. She lives and catches bugs in northern Arizona.

Helen Garner is the author of many books of fiction, journalism, and essays, among them the novels *Monkey Grip* and *The Children's Bach* and the essay collections *True Stories* and *The Feel of Steel.* Her most recent book is the Australian bestseller *Joe Cinque's Consolation.* She lives in Melbourne.

Todd Gitlin, who teaches journalism and sociology at Columbia University, is the author of two novels as well as many books on contemporary history, politics, and media.

Natalie Goldberg is the author, most recently, of *The Great Failure: A Bartender, A Monk, and My Unlikely Path to Truth.* She has written nine other books, including *Writing Down the Bones, Wild Mind, Thunder and Lightning,* and *Top of My Lungs.* She teaches writing workshops and retreats at the Mabel Dodge Luhan House in Taos, New Mexico.

Mary Gordon is the author of eight works of fiction and four works of nonfiction, including a biography of Joan of Arc. Her latest novel is *Pearl.* She has won a Lila Acheson Wallace Reader's Digest Award, a Guggenheim fellowship, and an O. Henry Award for best short story. She teaches at Barnard College and lives in New York.

Patricia Hampl is the author of numerous books, including the memoirs *A Romantic Education* and *Virgin Time,* the essay collection *I Could Tell You Stories: Sojourns in the Land of Memory,* and the forthcoming *Silken Chamber.*

Brooks Haxton has written seven books of poetry, the most recent being *Uproar: Antiphonies to Psalms.* Many of his translations from the Greek, French, and German also explore spiritual questions. He teaches at Syracuse University.

Edward Hirsch's most recent book of poems is *Lay Back the Darkness.* His most recent prose book is *The Demon and the Angel: Searching for the Source of Artistic Inspiration.*

Charles Johnson, a 1998 MacArthur Fellow, received the National Book Award for his novel *Middle Passage* in 1990. He has published three other novels, including *Dreamer, Oxherding Tale,* and *Faith and the Good Thing,* as well as three story collections, *The Sorcerer's Apprentice, Soulcatcher and Other Stories,* and *Dr. King's Refrigerator and Other Bedtime Stories.* He is the S. Wilson and Grace M. Pollock Endowed Professor of English at the University of Washington in Seattle.

Maria Poggi Johnson teaches theology at the University of Scranton in northeastern Pennsylvania. She is the editor of a volume of sermons by John Keble and is working on a book about her experiences of living among Orthodox Jews. She is married with four children.

Heather King is a commentator for NPR's *All Things Considered* and the author of the memoir *Parched.* She lives in Los Angeles.

Philip Levine's many books include *Breath; So Ask: Essays, Conversations, and Interviews; The Bread of Time; Toward an Autobiography; The Mercy; The Simple Truth* (Pulitzer Prize for poetry, 1995); and *What Work Is* (National Book Award for poetry, 1991).

Barry Lopez is the author of *Arctic Dreams,* the illustrated fable *Crow and Weasel,* and several essay and short story collections, including *About This Life* and *Resistance.* He is a recipient of the National Book Award and other honors.

Thomas Lynch is an essayist, poet, and funeral director. His books include *The Undertaking, Still Life in Milford,* and *Bodies in Motion and at Rest.*

Bill McKibben is the author of many books, including *Wandering Home: A Long Walk Across America's Most Hopeful Landscape: Vermont's Champlain Valley and New York's Adirondacks; Enough: Staying Human in an Engineered Age,* and *The End of Nature.*

W. S. Merwin's books include *The Pupil, The River Sound,* and *The Folding Cliffs.* He was awarded the Pulitzer Prize for poetry in 1971.

Richard John Neuhaus is the editor in chief of *First Things* and the author of numerous books, including *As I Lay Dying: Meditations upon Returning; Death on a Friday Afternoon: Meditations on the Last Words of Jesus from the Cross;* and *The Naked Public Square: Religion and Democracy in America.*

Oliver Sacks is the author of many books, including *Oaxaca Journal, Uncle Tungsten, An Anthropologist on Mars, The Island of the Colorblind,* and *The Man Who Mistook His Wife for a Hat.*

Huston Smith's many books include *Why Religion Matters: The Fate of the Human Spirit in an Age of Disbelief, Beyond the Post-Modern Mind,* and *The World's Religions.*

Gary Snyder is the author of *Danger on Peaks, Mountains and Rivers Without End,* and many other books. He was awarded the Pulitzer Prize in 1975 for *Turtle Island.*

Dana Tierney is a writer living in Washington, D.C., with her husband, John, and son, Luke. She has written for the *New York Times,* the *Washington Post,* and the *New York Times Magazine,* among others. She is finishing a novel about artwork by slaves that was discovered in the cellar of a colonial Virginia mansion.

Ptolemy Tompkins is the author of *This Tree Grows Out of Hell, Paradise Fever,* and *The Beaten Path* and is a senior editor at *Guideposts* and *Angels on Earth* in New York.

Kenneth L. Woodward, the author of three books, is a contributing editor at *Newsweek,* where he was religion editor for thirty-eight years.

Charles Wright's many books include *Buffalo Yoga, A Short History of the Shadow, Negative Blue,* and *Black Zodiac,* which won the Pulitzer Prize for poetry in 1998.

Franz Wright's *Walking to Martha's Vineyard* received the 2004 Pulitzer Prize for poetry. Earlier volumes include *The Beforelife* and *Ill Lit: Selected & New Poems.* Wright teaches occasionally and is a volunteer facilitator at the Center for Grieving Children in Arlington, Massachusetts. His new collection, *God's Silence,* will appear early in 2006.

Philip Zaleski is the editor of the *Best American Spiritual Writing* series. His most recent book, written with his wife, Carol Zaleski, is *Prayer: A History.* He is a senior editor at *Parabola* and a research associate in religion at Smith College.

Notable Spiritual Writing of 2004

SELECTED BY PHILIP ZALESKI

ANNE E. CAMPISI
"The Language for Light," *Mars Hill Review*, no. 22
SCOTT DARNELL
"Meeting Myself in the Cell House," *Turning Wheel*, Fall
EAMON DUFFY
"The Mass Bells of Maremma," *Commonweal*, November 5
ANTHONY ESOLEN
"A Geography of Kind," *Touchstone*, May
ISABEL HILTON
"The Buddha's Daughter," *The New Yorker*, March 29
EDWARD HOAGLAND
"Small Silences," *Harper's Magazine*, July
DAVID HOLLANDER
"Tender Prey," *New York Times Magazine*, August 1
THOMAS HOWARD
"The Quirkiness of Charles Williams," *Touchstone*, December
PICO IYER
"Move Over and the View Changes," *Shambhala Sun*, July
JON KOESSLER
"Why I Return to the Pews," *Christianity Today*, December
MARTIN E. MARTY
"Which Luther?" *Christian Century*, February 10
CHERYL MERRILL
"A Creature of Many Parts," *Fourth Genre*, Fall
MIA NUSSBAUM
"A Portrait of Dorothy Day," *Notre Dame Magazine*, Autumn
LINDSEY O'CONNOR
"While I Was Sleeping," *Christianity Today*, February
NOELLE OXENHANDLER
"Cold Hard Cash and the Middle Way," *Tricycle*, Summer

STEPHEN G. POST
  "Alzheimer's & Grace," *First Things,* April
MICHAEL J. SANDEL
  "The Case Against Perfection," *Atlantic Monthly,* April
VALERIE SAYERS
  "The Word Cure," *Image,* Winter
ELIEZER SHORE
  "Standing Under the Mountain," *Parabola,* Spring
JOHN TALLMADE
  "The Wild Within," *Orion,* August

THE B·E·S·T AMERICAN SERIES®

THE BEST AMERICAN SHORT STORIES® 2005

Michael Chabon, guest editor, Katrina Kenison, series editor. "Story for story, readers can't beat the *Best American Short Stories* series" (*Chicago Tribune*). This year's most beloved short fiction anthology is edited by the Pulitzer Prize–winning novelist Michael Chabon and features stories by Tom Perrotta, Alice Munro, Edward P. Jones, Joyce Carol Oates, and Thomas McGuane, among others.

0-618-42705-8 PA $14.00 / 0-618-42349-4 CL $27.50

THE BEST AMERICAN ESSAYS® 2005

Susan Orlean, guest editor, Robert Atwan, series editor. Since 1986, *The Best American Essays* has gathered the best nonfiction writing of the year and established itself as the premier anthology of its kind. Edited by the best-selling writer Susan Orlean, this year's volume features writing by Roger Angell, Jonathan Franzen, David Sedaris, Andrea Barrett, and others.

0-618-35713-0 PA $14.00 / 0-618-35712-2 CL $27.50

THE BEST AMERICAN MYSTERY STORIES™ 2005

Joyce Carol Oates, guest editor, Otto Penzler, series editor. This perennially popular anthology is sure to appeal to crime fiction fans of every variety. This year's volume is edited by the National Book Award winner Joyce Carol Oates and offers stories by Scott Turow, Dennis Lehane, Louise Erdrich, George V. Higgins, and others.

0-618-51745-6 PA $14.00 / 0-618-51744-8 CL $27.50

THE BEST AMERICAN SPORTS WRITING™ 2005

Mike Lupica, guest editor, Glenn Stout, series editor. "An ongoing centerpiece for all sports collections" (*Booklist*), this series has garnered wide acclaim for its extraordinary sports writing and topnotch editors. Mike Lupica, the *New York Daily News* columnist and best-selling author, continues that tradition with pieces by Michael Lewis, Gary Smith, Bill Plaschke, Pat Jordan, L. Jon Wertheim, and others.

0-618-47020-4 PA $14.00 / 0-618-47019-0 CL $27.50

THE BEST AMERICAN TRAVEL WRITING 2005

Jamaica Kincaid, guest editor, Jason Wilson, series editor. Edited by the renowned novelist and travel writer Jamaica Kincaid, *The Best American Travel Writing 2005* captures the traveler's wandering spirit and ever-present quest for adventure. Giving new life to armchair journeys this year are Tom Bissell, Ian Frazier, Simon Winchester, John McPhee, and many others.

0-618-36952-X PA $14.00 / 0-618-36951-1 CL $27.50

THE B·E·S·T AMERICAN SERIES®

THE BEST AMERICAN SCIENCE AND NATURE WRITING 2005

Jonathan Weiner, guest editor, Tim Folger, series editor. This year's edition presents another "eclectic, provocative collection" (*Entertainment Weekly*). Edited by Jonathan Weiner, the author of *The Beak of the Finch* and *Time, Love, Memory*, it features work by Oliver Sacks, Natalie Angier, Malcolm Gladwell, Sherwin B. Nuland, and others.

0-618-27343-3 PA $14.00 / 0-618-27341-7 CL $27.50

THE BEST AMERICAN RECIPES 2005–2006

Edited by Fran McCullough and Molly Stevens. "Give this book to any cook who is looking for the newest, latest recipes and the stories behind them" (*Chicago Tribune*). Offering the very best of what America is cooking, as well as the latest trends, time-saving tips, and techniques, this year's edition includes a foreword by celebrated chef Mario Batali.

0-618-57478-6 CL $26.00

THE BEST AMERICAN NONREQUIRED READING 2005

Edited by Dave Eggers, Introduction by Beck. In this genre-busting volume, best-selling author Dave Eggers draws the finest, most interesting, and least expected fiction, nonfiction, humor, alternative comics, and more from publications large, small, and on-line. With an introduction by the Grammy Award–winning musician Beck, this year's volume features writing by Jhumpa Lahiri, George Saunders, Aimee Bender, Stephen Elliott, and others.

0-618-57048-9 PA $14.00 / 0-618-57047-0 CL $27.50

THE BEST AMERICAN SPIRITUAL WRITING 2005

Edited by Philip Zaleski, Introduction by Barry Lopez. Featuring an introduction by the National Book Award winner Barry Lopez, *The Best American Spiritual Writing 2005* brings the year's finest writing about faith and spirituality to all readers. This year's volume gathers pieces from diverse faiths and denominations and includes writing by Natalie Goldberg, Harvey Cox, W. S. Merwin, Patricia Hampl, and others.

0-618-58643-1 PA $14.00 / 0-618-58642-3 CL $27.50

HOUGHTON MIFFLIN COMPANY www.houghtonmifflinbooks.com